At a time when an increasing number of Americans are seeing the pursuit of happiness as nothing more than a pipe dream, we need to rethink how our government goes about the people's work. Kate McGovern's book makes a compelling and timely case for taking what the business world has learned from applying Lean principles to how we address our most complex social problems.

John M. Bernard, Author, *Government That Works, The Results Revolution in the States*

With real-life examples and drawing on her experience, Kate McGovern demonstrates how Lean can transform government. She shows us what's possible and offers proven roadmaps to success. This is a must-read for any government entity that wants to improve how it serves the public.

Tony Rodriquez, President, Daniel Penn Associates LLC

A Public Sector Journey to Operational Excellence

Lean management can lead to operational excellence, but toward what end? This book examines the power of linking Lean government operations with purposeful public policy. When Lean process improvement principles and techniques entered the public sector after decades of proven effectiveness in private industry, they brought the same transformative potential. These programs can improve public services, boost employee morale, and free up previously underutilized capacity. The freed capacity can then be applied to accomplish important societal objectives. This book has four parts:

Part 1: The Foundation of Continuous Improvement (CI)—The reader is introduced to the field of CI and to Lean principles and techniques as applied to public sector organizations. CI initiatives can improve services, boost employee morale, and free up previously underutilized capacity. This part includes an overview of best practices and strategies for overcoming common challenges.

Part 2: Lean Public Policy—Discussion of both purpose and function. Lean practitioners are systems thinkers. Viewing disparate processes as components of a whole, we seek to integrate functions across silos to maximize value, quality, and efficiency. It would be great if public programs could be designed for optimal functionality. If that were the case, then Lean practitioners would simply apply the Plan-Do-Study-Act/Adjust (PDSA) cycle for ongoing improvement. In the real world, policy making tends to be ad-hoc and reactive. This part explores impediments to leaning existing programs and considers what Lean public policy would look like. Government regulatory functions and health care policy are used as examples.

Part 3: Operational Excellence—Pulling policy and administration together by introducing John M. Bernard's concept of three levels of maturity in government.

Part 4: Putting it together—"What to do, how to do it, and who can get it done." A summary and overview of CI methodology and the prerequisites for the implementation of policies that will lead to progress on societal goals. Drawing lessons from practitioners striving for Level 3 maturity in government, the book closes with a series of recommendations.

A Public Sector Journey to Operational Excellence

Applying Lean Principles to Public Policy

Kate McGovern, MPA, PhD

Routledge
Taylor & Francis Group

A PRODUCTIVITY PRESS BOOK

First published 2024
by Routledge
605 Third Avenue, New York, NY 10158

and by Routledge
4 Park Square, Milton Park, Abingdon, Oxon, OX14 4RN

Routledge is an imprint of the Taylor & Francis Group, an informa business

ISBN: 978-1-032-44545-8 (hbk)
ISBN: 978-1-032-44544-1 (pbk)
ISBN: 978-1-003-37269-1 (ebk)

DOI: 10.4324/9781003372691

Typeset in Garamond
by Apex CoVantage, LLC

Dedication

For Sam McKeeman who introduced me to Lean and Professor Milton Lopes who introduced me to the work of his friend and colleague, Larry D. Terry.

With grateful acknowledgement to John M. Bernard, Mike Rother, and Jason Schulist for sharing their work.

With sincere appreciation to the dedicated CI practitioners who spoke to me about their steadfast commitment to operational excellence.

Many thanks to my sister Patty Scott, who helped me prepare this manuscript along with my husband, Michael Dumond, with whom I share five daughters Amy, Emily, Michelle, Christina, and Katie, and eight grandchildren.

Contents

About the Author

 **Kate McGovern, MPA, PhD** is a Lean trainer and practitioner in the public sector. In addition to facilitating *kaizen* projects for state, municipal, and non-profit organizations, Kate taught Lean Belt programs and public management classes for New Hampshire's Bureau of Education and Training. She has worked as a Lean trainer for the states of Vermont, Rhode Island, South Dakota, and Massachusetts through Daniel Penn Associates. Having previously taught at Springfield College, School of Human Services, Kate is presently an instructional faculty member at College Unbound in Providence, Rhode Island. She is a contributor to the *PA Times* and the author of *Challenges in Pension Governance: A Case Study of the New Hampshire Retirement System*, and *A Public Sector Journey to Lean: Fighting Muda in Times of Muri*.

Introduction

Lean process improvement principles and techniques entered the public sector after decades of proven effectiveness in private industry with the same transformative potential. A robust lean program can improve services, boost employee morale, and free up previously underutilized capacity. The powerful combination of Lean and Toyota Kata in a culture of continuous improvement can enable operational excellence throughout our public sector. A sustained results-driven administration then becomes the platform from which great things can be accomplished.

The Next Frontier for Practitioners: Lean for Social Good

The connection between excellent public service and the accomplishment of strategic goals is far from a straight line. This book will examine the power of linking lean government operations and purposeful public policy.

Consider the following:

> W. Edwards Deming: "The wealth of a nation depends on its people, management, and government more than its natural resources."[1]

Lean is not value-neutral. As the Lean Enterprise Institute explains, "Lean thinking has a moral compass: respect for the humanity of customers, employees, suppliers, investors, and our communities with the belief that all can and will be better off through lean practices."[2]

There are multiple levels of benefits.

A rudimentary understanding of lean methodology using a narrow, technocratic approach can result in efficiency gains. Consistent use of lean

DOI: 10.4324/9781003372691-1

management can transform organizations. Broad application in the public, private, and nonprofit sectors can lead to gains in the overall economy by reducing waste and reallocating resources. The next horizon is to envision the untapped potential for social good. This book will explore how to make it happen. But first, back to the beginning.

My lean journey began while I was an associate professor with New Hampshire's Bureau of Education and Training (BET) and had the opportunity to attend a five-day workshop led by guest trainer Sam McKeeman. I was sold as soon as I saw the potential of using collaborative teams to redesign ridiculous bureaucratic processes. I was all about the mission. As a daughter of a teacher, I was a public service idealist. BET was just the place to spread the word about quality service. During classes in the Certified Public Manager program, BET director Dennis Martino often used the classic example of JFK's visit to NASA. Among the many versions: "During his visit to the NASA space center, as the story goes, President John F. Kennedy noticed a janitor carrying a broom. He interrupted his tour, walked over to the man and asked: 'What are you doing?' 'Well, Mr. President,' the janitor responded, 'I'm helping to put a man on the moon.' "[3]

I felt that Lean was the perfect way to fight all the negative stereotypes of state employees that claimed we didn't care about our customers. I knew that the people who worked in these processes were just as frustrated as the citizens they served. Being on a *kaizen* team was liberating. Employees who had been disheartened by doing things the "way it had always been done" were now working collaboratively to identify improvements. I joined with a like-minded group of early adopters to form the Lean Network, a community of practice that spanned multiple agencies. In my role at BET, I used Sam McKeeman's model to offer lean training. It was fun to see trainees return to the second day of the Yellow Belt class reporting that they had started to apply the principles to household tasks or reorganizing their garages. They were eager to complete their process maps and redesign the workflows. You know the concepts are taking hold when you hear a colleague point to a process and say, "that's unlean." Which raises the issue of terminology.

The Word "Lean"

It is not an acronym, so it is not LEAN. The L may be capitalized or not. As I continue to work with it, I am more inclined to follow the Lean Enterprise Institute's practice of not capitalizing it in most instances. An article in the

Journal of Operations Management suggested capitalizing it when it is used in "the phenomenological sense."[4,5] Since the study of lean is a growing field, the terminology is in flux, capitalization in this book may appear inconsistent. Frankly, I also find it useful as an adjective, describing a process or organization as lean or unlean, or a verb: "let's lean this process."

What's in This Book

The overlay of continuous improvement (CI) work with the administrative and public policy functions of government requires a multidisciplinary approach. It will cross the academic fields of public administration and political science, intersecting with business management, engineering, and performance management.

Case Studies and Profiles of Practitioners

How is CI doing in the public sector? Where is it done well? Readers were introduced to several fledging state Lean programs in *A Public Sector Journey to Lean*, and here, we revisit those initiatives, along with several others. What can be learned from the multi-faceted approach by the Colorado Department of Transportation's Innovation, Improvement, and Engagement Hub? Is there value in housing a Center for Operational Excellence within a state's department of administration, as is the case in Nebraska and Ohio? What are optimal conditions and prerequisites for a sustainable continuous improvement program?

Overview of Lean and Toyota Kata

To make this book accessible to those new to the field, several of the chapters include background, definitions of terms, and examples of applications of CI methodology. These sections are intended to provide readers with an overview, not as a substitute for in-depth study and practice. Appendix E lists some of the many excellent resources available for aspiring practitioners.

Tour of the Four Sections

Part 1 begins with an introduction to the history and application of the principles of continuous improvement (CI). Readers are introduced to the concepts and methodology. The second chapter describes John M. Bernard's categorization of three stages of maturity in government, making it clear how much lean is needed in that sector. Guidance is then provided on how to launch a lean initiative in the public sector, leading to a discussion of public administration in theory and practice in Chapter 5.

Part 2 examines the application of CI to governmental operations. Chapters 6 and 7 illustrate the need to lean bureaucratic and regulatory processes, using specific examples. Chapters 8 and 9 offer case studies of state CI programs, closing with suggestions for an optimal model.

Part 3 acknowledges that among the responsibilities of government, the public policy function is the most difficult to lean. It discusses the complexities inherent in government because public policy is both a political and an administrative function. Chapter 12 contains an overview of CI concepts and methodology including Toyota Kata, providing various examples. Chapter 13 breaks down the challenges of applying CI to policy development.

Part 4 links the promise of CI to make government more effective to its potential to solve complex problems. To facilitate the trajectory of reaction-driven to results-driven maturity in government, Chapter 14 proposes strategies to overcome the threats and sustain the gains in CI initiatives. Chapter 15 explores how results-driven government can become a platform from which social-good-driven government can be built. Wrapping in a broad summary of recommendations, Chapter 16 poses a series of challenges, closing with a reflection on the purpose of government. The charge, as stated in the preamble to the Constitution, is exceptionally broad and ambitious. Beneath the theories, principles, and techniques is an overarching challenge. The quest to accomplish the purposes stated in the preamble to the Constitution:

> **We the People** of the United States, in Order to form a more perfect Union, establish Justice, insure domestic Tranquility, provide for the common defence, promote the general Welfare, and secure the Blessings of Liberty to ourselves and our Posterity, do ordain and establish this Constitution for the United States of America.

To accomplish the bold purposes for which it was established, our government must be well run *and* effective. This book suggests a path to do both.

Notes

1 W. Edwards Deming, *Out of the Crisis* (MIT Center for Advanced Educational Services, Cambridge, MA, 1982–1986), p. 6.
2 Lean Enterprise Institute, *What is Lean?* www.lean.org/explore-lean/what-is-lean/
3 Jitske M. C. Both-Nwabuwe, Maria T. M. Dijkstra, and Bianca Beersma, "Sweeping the Floor or Putting a Man on the Moon: How to Define and Measure Meaningful Work." (Online edition) *Frontiers in Psychology,* September 29, 2017.
4 Tyson R. Browning and Suzanne de Treville, "A Lean View of Lean." *Journal of Operations Management* 67 (2021): 636. DOI: 10.1002/joom.1153
5 According to Dictionary.com: phenomenological: of, relating to, or based on observed or observable facts: "The researchers opted for a phenomenological investigation rather than a purely theoretical study."

THE FOUNDATION OF CONTINUOUS IMPROVEMENT AND OPERATIONAL MATURITY

I

Part I begins with the origin of lean in manufacturing and how its principles are broadly applicable to other sectors. Next, readers are introduced to John M. Bernard's categorization of three stages of maturity in government, making it clear that lean is needed in that sector. Guidance is then provided on how to launch a lean initiative in the public sector, leading to a discussion of public administration in theory and practice.

Chapter 1: Introduction to Lean and Continuous Improvement. A history of quality management, major contributors to the field, and derivation of the term "lean."

Chapter 2: The Three Stages of Maturity in State Government: 1) Reaction-driven; 2) Results-driven; 3) Social-good-driven.

Chapter 3: The *Kaizen* Concept. The most common path for practitioners to begin their journey.

Chapter 4: Lean Management. A discussion of how lean is a management trifecta for the public sector. While counterintuitive to traditional managers, it is essential to building a culture of continuous improvement. The chapter closes with profiles of lean practitioners

DOI: 10.4324/9781003372691-2

in New Hampshire's Department of Health and Human Services and the University System of New Hampshire.

Chapter 5: Theory and Practice. An introduction to the theory of administrative conservatorship, and its connection to the mission-driven responsibilities of public administrators.

Chapter 1

Introduction to Lean and Continuous Improvement

Scholars can go back centuries identifying innovations in production capacity. Advances made in the 1700s to improve craft production continued throughout the 1800s.[1] Early in the 20th century, the Ford assembly line ushered in an era of mass production. The methodology of smooth flow and standard work brought consumer products to an expanding market. However, the new methods were not without problems. There was an apparent trade-off of quality to achieve volume. Rather than accept the trade-off as necessary, statisticians and industrial engineers developed theories of quality management and designed strategies to address these challenges.[2]

Pioneers of continuous improvement management theory and practice in the early to mid-twentieth century include: Walter A. Shewhart (1891–1967), W. Edwards Deming (1900–1993), Joseph M. Juran (1904–2008), Shigeo Shingo (1909–1990), Taiichi Ohno (1912–1990), Kaoru Ishikawa (1915–1989)

Tracing the Roots of Quality Management

As mass production capacity grew in the 1930s, Bell Telephone Laboratories' statistician Walter A. Shewhart proposed a cycle of continuous improvement, Plan-Do-Check-Act (PDCA). W. Edwards Deming further developed (or refined)

DOI: 10.4324/9781003372691-3

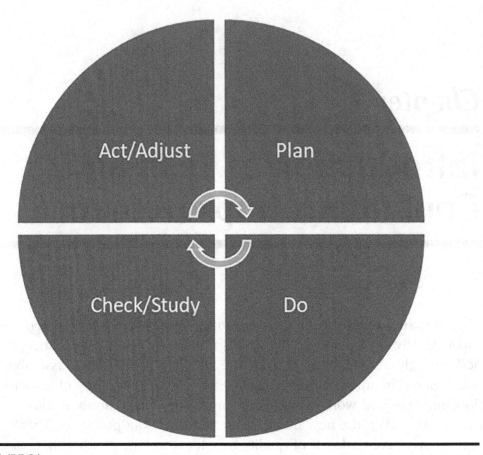

PDCA/PDSA.

principles of quality management with a Plan-Do-Study-Act (PDSA) model, stressing the need to compare the results with the initial predictions.[3]

Much of Deming's work went unheeded by managers in the U.S. After World War II, Deming and Dr. Joseph Juran were invited to Japan to consult with the Union of Japanese Science and Engineering (JUSE) in the rebuilding of that country's industrial base.[4] Eigi Toyodo and Taiichi Ohno applied these concepts for Toyota.[5] Years later, a team of researchers at the Massachusetts Institute of Technology (MIT) were tasked with helping U.S. manufacturers to revisit the lessons.

By Any Other Name

In the mid-1980s, a team of researchers in MIT's International Motor Vehicle Program (IMVP) were studying the success of the Japanese auto industry.

The term "lean" was coined by IMVP researcher John Krafcik to describe the Toyota Production System's (TPS) ability to generate quality products using fewer resources. Krafcik's IMVP colleagues James Womack, Daniel Jones, and Daniel Roos described TPS' story of lean production in *The Machine that Changed the World.*[6] Womack later founded the Lean Enterprise Institute with a mission to advance lean thinking around the world.[7]

As Womack, John Shook, and others developed the concepts, it became clear that lean is more than a set of tools to eliminate waste and improve value. It is a perspective, a way of thinking. And it is a management system. As noted in the introduction, Lean is not an acronym, so it is not LEAN. It may be capitalized or not. As I continue to work with it, I am more inclined to follow LEI's practice of not capitalizing it. I also find it useful as an adjective, describing a process as lean or unlean, or a verb: "let's lean this process."

An internet search will generate many definitions and descriptions. The most comprehensive definitions express the multidimensional aspects:

> Lean is an organizational performance management system characterized by a collaborative approach between employees and managers to identify and minimize or eliminate activities that do not create value for the customers of a business process, or stakeholders.[8]
>
> Lean is a way of thinking about creating needed value with fewer resources and less waste. And lean is a practice consisting of continuous experimentation to achieve perfect value with zero waste. Lean thinking and practice occur together.[9]

Many practitioners refer to this work generically as "continuous improvement" or "quality management" for several reasons. The matter of terminology goes beyond semantics. It is a reminder that the foundational work predates the use of the term "lean," and significant contributions continue to be made advancing the field of quality management without ever mentioning "lean."

From a practical standpoint, the generic language allows a change initiative to be more inclusive and accessible by avoiding the need to learn lean terminology, which includes many Japanese terms.

There is also concern that the term "lean" connotes a reduction of personnel or resources. Without context for the intent of the program, a poor choice of language can undermine efforts. For example, one organization unfortunately referred to a campaign as "lean staffing," which was a major setback for their program. In another case, a group of employees disparaged the initiative by claiming that lean was an acronym for "less employees are needed."

The connotation can be frustrating because lean practitioners know that the threat of layoffs is incompatible with innovation. As Deming said, "Drive out fear, so that everyone may work effectively for the company."[10] Workers who fear retribution are likely to hide mistakes; those who fear layoff may withhold suggestions that could improve operations. Such an approach creates a workplace culture counter to quality management.

With an incomplete understanding of the principles, managers view workers as costs rather than assets, mere extensions of assembly-line machines rather than co-responsible for product quality. Womack, Jones, and Roos, like Deming before them, challenged the prevailing corporate models. Their work is about far more than how to build cars. The fundamental principles and core values can be applied to a broad range of processes, including current challenges across all sectors.

The broad applicability was confirmed and expanded upon when researcher Mike Rother and his colleagues conducted an in-depth study of Toyota from 2004 to 2009, leading to the publication of *Toyota Kata*. The study was driven by two research questions:[11]

1. What are the unseen managerial routines and thinking that lie behind Toyota's success with continuous improvement and adaptation?
2. How can other companies develop similar routines and thinking in their organizations?

Rother found that the tools and practices characterized as "lean" were the visible aspect of the TPS. The use of lean methodologies was effective due to an underlying systematic, scientific way of thinking. The scientific thinking routines were learned, practiced, and reinforced through coaching by managers.[12]

Revisiting Deming's Lessons. After W. Edwards Deming's work was applied to assist in Japan's recovery in the post-war period, he continued to try to reach American managers. In his 1982 book *Out of Crisis*, Deming called for a transformation in American management. His wide-ranging critique of U.S. practices juxtaposed a bold vision of quality management with specific examples. He asserted that the success in Japan did not need to be an isolated example and that the principles are broadly applicable.

Throughout the book, Deming explained in detail why corporate practices in the U.S., such as mergers, acquisitions, and the focus on quarterly profit-seeking, are contrary to long-term success. He observed, "The problem is where to find good management. It would be a mistake to export American management to a friendly country."[13]

To apply Deming's work to current socio-economic challenges, it is useful to begin with his theories on the role of business in society. Notably, he saw no conflict between the goals of profitability and job creation, with businesses having a responsibility to do both. The first point of his 14 Points for Management underscored his holistic view of corporate responsibility: "Create constancy of purpose toward improvement of product and service, with the aim to be competitive and to stay in business and to provide jobs."[14] This was not merely a benevolent or paternalistic view of labor. Quality production requires rank and file employees to have "the right to pride of workmanship."[15] This was in stark contrast to the American factory system, where a rigid, hierarchical structure regarded frontline workers as extensions of the machines.

Changing how people work can be both empowering and stressful, as explained in *The Machine That Changed the World*. Henry Ford's assembly line created continuous flow and standardization, but "the workers on the shop floor were simply interchangeable parts."[16] Each station in the line was expected to maintain the pace of production, and errors were caught only further down the line. When quality inspectors found problems, rework was required, which indicates *muda* (waste).

Deming's advice was counterintuitive to American managers: "Cease dependence on inspection to achieve quality. Eliminate the need for inspection on a mass basis by building quality into the product in the first place."[17] Shared responsibility changes the role of workers, supervisors, and managers.

Upcoming chapters will explore how responsibility is shifted and distributed and how it alters the role of managers to become coaches and change agents. It is easier said than done. Many of the concepts remain elusive for Americans in management roles in public, private, and non-profit sectors alike. The path to learn the fundamental techniques, and to understand and apply principles of lean management and Toyota Kata, is far from a straight line. Applying these concepts to government, and maintaining the organizational focus to sustain those practices is even more challenging.

Notes

1 John Bicheno and Matthias Holweb, *The Lean Toolbox*, 5th edition (PICSIE Books, Buckingham, UK, 2016), p. 322.

2 An annotated bibliography in Appendix E references a rich body of literature on this topic.

3 Anthony Manos and Chad Vincent, editors. *The Lean Handbook* (ASQ Quality Press, Milwaukee, WI, 2012), p. 137.

4 W. Edwards Deming, *Out of the Crisis* (MIT Center for Advanced Educational Services, Cambridge, MA, 1982–1986), p. 489.

5 James P. Womack, Daniel T. Jones, and Daniel Roos, *The Machine That Changed the World* (Free Press, A Division of Simon & Schuster, Inc., New York, NY, 1990–2007), p. 9.

6 James P. Womack, Daniel T. Jones, and Daniel Roos, *The Machine That Changed the World* (Free Press, A Division of Simon & Schuster, Inc., New York, NY, 1990–2007).

7 *The Lean Enterprise Institute*. www.Lean.org

8 Shayne Kavanagh and David Krings, "The Eight Sources of Waste and How to Eliminate Them," *Government Finance Review*, December 2011, p. 19.

9 Lean Enterprise Institute, *What is Lean?* www.lean.org

10 W. Edwards Deming, *Out of the Crisis* (MIT Center for Advanced Educational Services, Cambridge, MA, 1982–1986), p. 23.

11 Mike Rother, *The Toyota Kata Practice Guide* (McGraw-Hill Education, New York, NY, 2015), p. 5.

12 Sylvain Landry, PhD, *Bringing Scientific Thinking to Life: An Introduction to Toyota Kata for the Next Generation of Business Leaders (and those who would like to be)* (Les Éditions JFD Montréal, Montréal, 2022), p. 19.

13 W. Edwards Deming, *Out of the Crisis* (MIT Center for Advanced Educational Services, Cambridge, MA, 1982–1986), p. 6.

14 Deming's 14 Points for Management are in Appendix A.

15 W. Edwards Deming, *Out of the Crisis* (MIT Center for Advanced Educational Services, Cambridge, MA, 1982–1986), p. x.

16 James P. Womack, Daniel T. Jones, and Daniel Roos, *The Machine That Changed the World* (Free Press, A Division of Simon & Schuster, Inc., New York, NY, 1990–2007), p. 40.

17 W. Edwards Deming, *Out of the Crisis* (MIT Center for Advanced Educational Services, Cambridge, MA, 1982–1986), p. 23.

Chapter 2

The Three Stages of Maturity in State Government

The field of continuous improvement (CI) has incredible transformative potential for government, yet many initiatives fail to reach that level. Can such arrested development be prevented if administrators understand the transformation as a progression? John M. Bernard, the author of *Government That Works*, took on this challenge in a White Paper, "Level Three Government," presenting a three-tier model.

Maturity Level One: Reaction-Driven

The reaction-driven stage is probably the most familiar. It is activated by stimulus-response. Something happens; elected leaders and administrators scramble. Managers hasten to correct the symptoms, without addressing the root cause. Priorities are set by crises, news cycles, or anecdotes.

Lean initiatives can ameliorate bureaucratic frustrations common in Level One. However, progress may be uneven as each new governor brings new priorities along with new senior staff and administrators.

For example, New Hampshire's early program made significant gains at the Department of Motor Vehicles (DMV). With support from then-Governor John Lynch and the commissioners of the five largest agencies, energized lean practitioners collaborated to redesign processes in other agencies. They formed a Lean Executive Committee (LEC) to coordinate efforts among agencies and hosted a Lean Summit in 2012. Lean work has continued

DOI: 10.4324/9781003372691-4

John M. Bernard.

during subsequent administrations. However, the recommendation of the Commission on Innovation, Efficiency, and Transparency (2015) calling for a comprehensive CI program was not implemented.

Similarly, in Rhode Island, it is unclear if the Executive Order (2015) by former Governor Gina Raimondo requiring the use of lean in all agencies will be renewed following a transition in the Governor's office. The EO was effective, though, allowing the state to make inroads in several agencies, with more than 100 lean projects.

Level One Reaction-Driven	
Purpose	Short-term problems
Results	Perception of action
Focus	Blame, making it go away

What drives action	Heat: Events, problems, discoveries, screwups, power plays, requests for information, news stories
Who drives action	Special interests, legislators, media, watchdogs, whistle-blowers

Maturity Level Two: Results-Driven

States reach the second level of maturity when they establish best practices to achieve measurable outcomes. In this results-driven stage, managers are working toward established goals and engaging employees in meeting customer needs while driving out process waste. Targets are set for core processes. This purposeful combination of improvement techniques with strategic focus on achieving specific goals drives the operation.

Managers engaging in Level Two understand the distinction between measuring outputs (e.g., the total number of permits issued) vs. outcomes (e.g., the timeliness for issuing permits to qualified applicants). For example, Rhode Island's Department of Business Regulation improved the timeliness for issuing professional licenses from 125 days to 73 days.

Notably, leadership is a critical factor in engaging employees in a culture of continuous improvement. Loss of management focus can cause a regression to Level One. Or it can build a foundation for further improvement. Such was the case in Washington when Governor Christine Gregoire's commitment to lean laid the groundwork for her successor Jay Inslee's robust *Results Washington* initiative. Vermont is also among the states striving to reach past Level Two. Governor Phil Scott's 2017 Executive Order called for lean and other CI methods to be used to drive strategic goals, building on the 2014 "Outcomes Bill" that was passed under the previous administration.

Level Two Results-Driven	
Purpose	Achieve measurable results
Results	More efficient and effective government
Focus	Improving customer experience, removing waste in processes, accountability, and transparency
What drives action	Events, problems, discoveries, screwups, power plays, requests for information, news stories
Who drives action	Governor's office and appointed department leader

Support for Results-Driven Work

Starting in 2010, the Pew Charitable Trusts and the John D. and Catherine T. MacArthur Foundation began a Results First initiative to enable the use of evidence-based practices by state and county governments.[1] The five components included budget development, implementation oversight, targeted evaluation, and program assessment.

While assisting 27 states and 10 counties in assessing the value and effectiveness of programs, the project developed the online Results First Clearinghouse Database. In 2021, the database was transferred to the Social Science Research Center at Penn State University. Compiling the work of nine national clearinghouses, the database provides information on the effectiveness of social policy programs. It uses a color-coded rating system, indicating where each program falls on a spectrum from negative impact to positive impact. As of December 2022, the database contained information on 3,235 programs.[2]

For municipalities, What Works Cities is both a resource and a pathway to results-driven management of data and evidence. It offers a certification program that assesses cities on their data-driven decision-making practices. The intent is to "enable Certified Cities to be more resilient, respond in crisis situations, increase economic mobility, protect public health, and increase resident satisfaction."[3]

Governments at the results-driven level of maturity identify significant outcomes to measure, such as poverty rates, job growth, and air quality. Performance is measured regularly to indicate progress or regression, and results are published or made available publicly on dashboards and scorecards. Ideally, measurement tools and reporting software are standard across agencies, pulling the data to enable a statewide view capturing all key indicators. However, the ability to use technology to gather, synthesize, and analyze data is not uniformly available in state and local governments. The more common experience is that each of the departmental silos has a separate system that does not speak to the other systems.

In *Smarter Government*, former Maryland Governor Martin O'Malley described the impact of well-intended reforms that broke agency components into specialized divisions. While intended to focus the efforts, the action subsequently resulted in the legislature creating another layer of bureaucracy for coordination. For example, O'Malley described how the Maryland legislature created a new executive office—the Governor's Office for Children, Youth, and Families—to coordinate the state's three agencies responsible for different aspects of child health and welfare. "Creating coordinating offices can make us feel better, but they don't necessarily make things work better," O'Malley said. He recommended the creation of common platforms for collaborative action: an intelligent enterprise.[4]

O'Malley credited guidance from the GIS mapping software company, Esri, for encouraging the development of a common map rather than trying to translate different data collection methods among the departmental silos. O'Malley reflected, "People born in the early 1990s might think these technologies have been around forever . . . but this technology is all still very new for governments of, by and for the people."[5] John Bernard described the system used in Maryland as a "closed-loop, fact-centric management process using heatmaps and all forms of data to better get at root causes."

There are several challenges highlighted here. First, not every governmental unit has the knowledge to assess and select an optimal system, or the resources to purchase, install, and utilize it. Millions may be wasted on systems in futile attempts to create operational connections among siloed agencies. Even if successful, the governmental unit becomes reliant on an external vendor for ongoing functionality.

We Don't Know What We Don't Know

Some of us went to college when the computer was behind a wall, and we communicated with it using punch cards. How do we keep up with technology and its relationship to productivity? How can governments keep up with the technological expertise necessary to move forward with advanced data management? How can this expertise be shared? It would be unlean for each of the thousands of governmental units to figure this out on its own. What is the most efficient and cost-effective way to assure that governments have technological capabilities essential for effective results-driven operations?

Consider the increasingly rapid advancements in artificial intelligence (AI). In a column for *Governing*, Donald F. Kettl generated the following text using the chatbot ChatGPT:

> The rise of artificial intelligence (AI) technology has significant implications for state and local governments. One of the main implications is the potential for AI to improve the efficiency and effectiveness of government services. For example, AI-powered chatbots can provide 24/7 customer service for citizens, while machine learning algorithms can analyze large amounts of data

to identify patterns and insights that can inform decision-making. Additionally, AI can be used to automate routine tasks, such as processing paperwork and data entry, freeing up government employees to focus on more complex and value-added tasks. However, there are also concerns about the impact of AI on jobs and privacy, and governments will need to consider these issues as they implement AI-based solutions.[6]

Optimal Components for Results-Driven Government

Among the preconditions for a results-driven government is a unit housed within the office of administration, or the governor's office. A common element of successful efforts is the creation of or existence of the position of Chief Operating Officer (COO) or Chief Performance Officer (CPO) with operational responsibility for the executive branch. The COO/CPO works with the governor's office and agency heads to implement policies and report progress. The work of operations requires a different mindset than political work, and the commitment to make progress in operational sophistication demands a top executive's full-time attention. These capabilities, combined with mission-focused lean management, can bring the state solidly into Level Two and has the potential to bring a state toward Level Three maturity.

Maturity Level Three: Social-Good-Driven—Helping People Thrive

Once proficient at results-driven operations, states can advance to the third stage, which is Social-Good-Driven and entails tackling complex social problems. By utilizing the skill of process thinking, analytics can be applied to examine root causes of social problems. As Bernard explained, "The foundation of Level Three is applying what has been learned in Level Two to social challenges."

Maximizing governmental capacity to help people thrive is a multidisciplinary challenge. It will require states adopting CI management systems that allow them to stop reacting to symptoms and achieve operational maturity. Drawing from the work of scholars and practitioners of public policy, with resources like those provided by Penn State's Social Science Resource Center, elected officials and administrators can use CI methodology to trace root causes of social problems, establish countermeasures, set targets, and track progress.

There is much room for innovation. Chapter 12 will discuss several applications of CI principles, including the use of Toyota Kata (TK) by practitioners and nonprofits to solve community problems, applying scientific thinking to social goals. None of this is a "set it and forget it" endeavor: the CI concept of Plan-Do-Study-Act/Adjust will be the path to Level Three. A combination of knowledge, skill, and purpose, funded by the previously wasted resources, has transformational potential.

Level Three Social-Good-Driven	
Purpose	Transform people's lives
Results	Better quality of life for more people; lower longer-term social cost
Focus	Using facts to identify root causes and evidence of efficacy for solution selection; solving real societal problems; facts about performance; evidence-based solutions
What drives action	Events, problems, discoveries, screwups, power plays, requests for information, news stories
Who drives action	Governor, department, and program leadership; frontline expert

Bernard points out that the largest departments in most states are the departments of human services and corrections. He sees a potential trajectory: moving from reaction-driven human services with overlapping programs, to results-driven effective human-service delivery, to social-good-driven polices that will address the root causes of social problems.

To achieve this, Bernard asserts that lean is the most viable strategy to transform government. The next chapter details how to launch a lean initiative.

Notes

1 Pew Charitable Trusts, *Project: Results First Initiative.* www.pewtrusts.org/en/projects/results-first-initiative/about
2 Penn State Social Science Research Institute, *Evidence-to-Impact Collaborative. Results First Clearinghouse Database.* https://evidence2impact.psu.edu/what-we-do/research-translation-platform/results-first-resources/clearing-house-database/

3 What Works Cities, "Build a Government Residents Can Count on." *Bloomberg Philanthropies.* https://whatworkscities.bloomberg.org/

4 Martin O'Malley, *Smarter Government: How to Govern for Results in the Information Age* (Esri Press, Redlands, CA, 2019), p. 272.

5 Martin O'Malley, *Smarter Government: How to Govern for Results in the Information Age* (Esri Press, Redlands, CA, 2019), p. 4.

6 Donald F. Kettl, "AI Is Here. How Will Government Use It—and Regulate It?" *Governing*, January 20, 2023. www.governing.com/next/ai-is-here-how-will-government-use-it-and-regulate-it

Chapter 3

The *Kaizen* Concept

The move from reaction-driven to results-driven government can begin with a lean initiative. For a solid launch, the best go-to tool is a structured improvement project, known as a *kaizen*. The term *kaizen*, like the term lean, is multi-faceted. Its essential meaning is "change for the better," which is the guiding principle for CI work. Practitioners also use the term operationally, saying they are conducting "a *kaizen*" or "a *kaizen* project." This can be a rapid improvement activity or a structured event over several days.

A successful *kaizen* can demonstrate proof of concept and quantifiable gains. In a typical *kaizen*, employees engage in collaborative problem-solving by redesigning a particularly troublesome process. They learn how to use process mapping to expose redundancy, rework, and bottlenecks. The technique is eagerly embraced by public servants frustrated by routine business functions laden with complexity and wasteful activity. As Ken Miller noted in *Extreme Government Makeover*, "The work of government is noble. The people in government are amazing. The systems of government are a mess."[1] Lean can be used to fix our broken and inefficient systems.

Fixing the processes is not a one-time event. It is a continuum based on the Plan-Do-Check-Act/Adjust (PDCA) cycle. Each new version of a process is an experiment to be confirmed. Practitioners assess processes by collecting data and posing questions. How does it work for the customers? Does it produce reliable results? Do errors require rework? Do all the steps add value? Adjustments will be made as needed, continuously enhancing quality and efficiency.

DOI: 10.4324/9781003372691-5

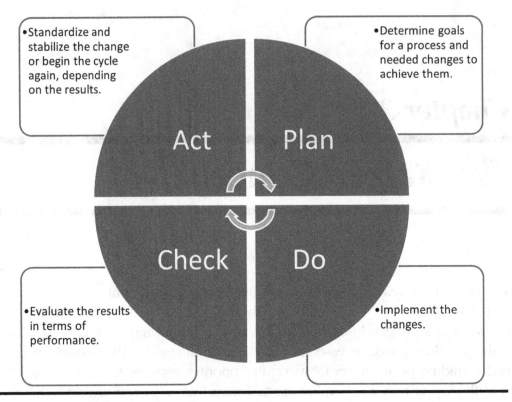

PDCA.

Launching a Lean Initiative with a *Kaizen*

For a strong launch, top leadership must champion the effort and require the management team to participate. A member of the management team is identified to be the sponsor of the first *kaizen* project.

To prepare for the project, the sponsor selects a particularly troublesome or archaic process and appoints a *kaizen* team composed of the employees who do the work throughout the process. The team may include an employee from another division who can bring fresh eyes to the project. A lean facilitator is identified to work with the sponsor and the team. Together, they develop a charter outlining the goals for the project.

Chartering

The charter is a document that defines and authorizes the event. It identifies the team members, the end-user customer, and the project goals and scope. The charter also determines the bookends: the first and last steps in the process to be leaned. During the project, a team might recommend narrowing or expanding the bookends, but the charter establishes the initial scope. Team composition, time allocated for the event, and proper project scope are all core components.

Each charter has a problem statement. The team needs a clear understanding of the problem, and they need to agree on what they are trying to solve. Lean practitioners differ on the format and the level of specificity. The team may phrase the problem statement as a question starting with "how."

Example: Residents complain about the permitting process. Problem statement: How can the permitting process be streamlined so that all qualified applicants receive their permit within 10 business days?

The charter sets measurable goals for the team, based on the data about current production and service delivery levels. Examples:

Reduce the number of applications returned for rework from _____ to _____.
Decrease the amount of time to issue a routine permit from _____ to _____.

The charter also identifies the customer(s) and stakeholders. The customer for the process is the end user at the final step of the process boundary established for this project. There are also internal customers at each step of the process, as the work is passed forward. There may be others who benefit from this process, such as the public at large; they are stakeholders.

Sample charter from a Yellow Belt training program

Charter for out-of-state travel authorization process	
Opportunity statement: Process description and business case for the project	The governor has asked for a 10% reduction in the time the agency spends on paperwork, and in addition, she says she will no longer be reviewing requests for out-of-state travel. The DHHS Commissioner agrees to sponsor a *kaizen* event to reduce internal paperwork.
Problem statement: In the form of a question starting with "How."	How do we reduce paperwork for the out-of-state travel process, while assuring that the travel is professionally appropriate and costs are covered by the current budget?
Project scope and boundaries: The first and last steps in the process	From the time the employee makes the request to the point travel is approved.

Key performance indicators: time, money, quality	Time: Reduction of time by 10%. Cost: Expenses must not exceed allocated budgets. Quality: Send the appropriate staff to professionally relevant trainings and conferences.
End-user customer	Employee seeking travel authorization.
Anticipated barriers	Risk-averse administrators, complaints by elected officials, administrators unfamiliar with the travel budgets.
Resources available	Time of the team and facilitator.
Facilitator(s)	One or two lean practitioners to guide the team. Optional: the project may use facilitator(s) from a different agency.
Team leader/project manager	A team member responsible for event logistics and coordination with the sponsor and facilitator.
Data manager	A team member responsible for project documentation.
Team members	Employees at various ranks throughout different divisions within the agency, including at least one member from the finance department.
Fresh eyes	An employee from another agency who is unaffiliated with the process.
Stakeholder (optional)	Ex) A local town official whose community benefits from DHHS expertise gained through professional conferences that is disseminated locally.
Sponsor: DHHS Commissioner	Signature and date.

During the *kaizen* event, the facilitator guides the team to map the current state (exactly as the process is conducted), review the workflow, and assess the value and purpose of each step. They also calculate the intervals between the steps to measure the impact of hand-offs, loopbacks, and rework. The information may be included directly on sticky notes in a process map, or on separate forms. These metrics matter. Documenting the time to conduct the work establishes a baseline for measuring improvements once the process change is implemented.

Assessment of Value

Once the current-state workflow is established, each step is assessed for the value it adds to the customer. The team considers which of the non-value-added steps are necessary to keep, and why, and which can be eliminated. Steps required by regulation that add no value to the customer may add value to stakeholders such as the public at large. These conversations are important to clarify why each step should remain or be removed from the process.

Then, the facilitator guides the team in preparing a future-state map showing the new workflow. Below is a sample data sheet and a summary table for comparing the findings from the current state and the expected timeline for the future state. Some practitioners use different terminology, with "work time" referred to as "process time" and "cycle time" called "lead time."

STEP NAME:
A. **Work time:** the actual work time to complete the task. Work time for this step = _____
B. **Cycle time:** The time it takes to complete the step: from the end of the previous step to the end of this step—including wait times, setup time, routing time, actual work time, and any delays. Cycle time for this step = _____

Note: Color-coded assessments of value. Green = value added; Red = non-valued added (*muda*); Yellow = non-value added to the customer, but necessary to operate the business. Optional: Orange = value added to stakeholders.

Summary Table

	Current State	*Future State*	*% Change*
Total Work Time			
Total Cycle Time			
Total # Steps			
#Value added to the customer			
#Non-valued added			
#Non-value added—necessary			

After designing the future state, the team presents its work to the sponsor for approval. This phase may also include discussion of a proposed interim state. Next, the sponsor and team must manage the implementation, adjust as needed, quantify, and celebrate the gains. Once the new workflow is underway, new metrics are needed to confirm that the improvements work as expected. The check and adjust phases of the PDCA cycle allow for corrections of any unintended negative consequences while keeping the waste from returning.

Successful implementation can produce dramatic results. One of the early *kaizens* in New Hampshire enabled the Department of Employment Security to go from processing 6% of its appeals within 30 days to 86%. In 2012, then-Governor John Lynch convened a Lean Summit where he awarded a proclamation to the team that had moved New Hampshire from 50th to 16th in the country in case aging.

Expertise: Imported or Home Grown

Building a solid foundation requires initial expertise. Some states have positions such as Chief Improvement Officer who are authorized by the governor to initiate and sustain the program across state government. Large agencies may also have a comparable position reporting to the commissioner.

Lacking an internal resource, a consulting firm may be hired to jump-start the project. In this instance, it is essential to have a plan for a smooth transition to internal resources. There are several critical components to this model. First, the contract should acknowledge and support a transition to internal training staff, and it should stipulate that all training materials used in the program will become public property. Secondly, the organization must commit to continue the internal program, so the initiative does not wither away when the external resource is no longer available.

For organizations using a consultant, advanced planning is key. Tony Rodriguez, president of the consulting firm Daniel Penn Associates (DPA), recommends that clients adopt a roadmap to ensure a smooth transition. It begins with the organization identifying its goals, so the program is aligned to meet the long-term objectives. Once the program is underway, visible achievements are shared, building confidence in the initiative, and training develops internal capacity. At this point, the consultant is still providing guidance and coaching to assure that the initial projects are implemented successfully. To prepare for the transition, leadership must appoint a coordinator and create proper infrastructure to manage the ongoing effort. At this stage, consistent leadership commitment is essential, or the initiative will fizzle out after conducting a few projects. In order to stay on the roadmap for achieving strategic objectives, Rodriguez emphasizes the critical role of leadership engagement "that keeps the candle burning" for sustainable continuous improvement.

Whether assisted by a consultant or internal from the start, a successful initiative requires a champion with vision and commitment who has the authority to require administrators and managers to fulfill their responsibilities to assure the program's success. Managers play a critical role in identifying the organization's primary value streams and core processes to be targeted for improvement. As project sponsors, they work with lean coordinators to set goals and assign teams. And they must allocate sufficient resources for a training program that is open to all sectors of the organization.

Funding Stream Barriers

Even if lean training is offered as part of the curriculum of a state training program, it is not necessarily available to all employees. Such remains the case in New Hampshire. State employees who work for agencies with training budgets may be able to attend if their agencies agree to pay the tuition. The process itself is unlean. Invoices are sent and accountants move the money from one state agency to another. Aside from the administrative inefficiency, the lack of access to training impedes workforce development. Dennis Martino, former State Training Officer characterized the circumstances as "haves and have nots." He explained:

> In the public sector, agencies have numerous funding streams. Some are based on fees for services. Others on general income taxes or property taxes or federal funding. This crazy quilt of a funding plan creates an inequity for advancement of staff and creates some havoc for elected officials to do effective long-term planning. As a former Training Officer for the State of NH, I witnessed a great disparity in training funds for staff.
>
> There is an adage. "A rising tide lifts all boats." Here is where cooperative efforts across agencies can create the high tide. States have benefit plans for health, disability, and retirement that cross over from agency to agency. If the state could view training as a benefit (to all), it could pool money to allow any employee from any agency to participate in sponsored training such as Lean, Conflict Resolution, Project Management and Strategic Planning.

Agencies and employees would all prosper. And yes, the biggest beneficiaries would be the citizens.[2]

Integrating IT

How often are specifications for new IT systems prepared without leaning the workflow first? In the most wasteful scenario, a vendor is required to customize the new system to replicate an existing antiquated process. Lean practitioners understand that, as Bill Gates put it: "The first rule of any technology used in a business process is that automation applied to an efficient process will magnify the efficiency. The second is that automation applied to an inefficient operation will magnify the inefficiency."[3] Public sector organizations are often unable to include an IT representative on *kaizen* teams. Subject to chronic short-staffing, IT personnel are stretched thin with urgent projects. And, with IT staff organized in separate silos, typical sponsors of lean events lack the authority to assign IT members to project teams. It takes a sponsor with a significant span of control to charter a project with both IT and program staff. When a high-level sponsor does authorize such a *kaizen* event, implementation may falter as the employees return to their silos.

Organizations that automatically include IT representation on lean projects maximize the effort. The IT specialist can help to reduce the nonessential quirks that drive up the cost and complexity of any system. As the team examines the purpose of each requirement, they can determine which should be maintained, modified, or eliminated. The IT member's expertise assesses the optimal amount of automation for the new workflow and helps the team to formulate an implementation plan. IT specialists proficient in Agile can update the business requirements to adjust to progressive improvements in the workflow. However, even if a team member has the technical expertise to automate a process, there may be other barriers. For example, a "wet" signature with a notary seal may be required by law or rule. If such archaic provisions are subject to administrative discretion of the sponsor, they can be removed immediately. Changes requiring action of governing bodies or other administrative entities must come later in the PDCA continuum.

Learning Other CI Tools

While process maps are an excellent introductory tool, there are many more for practitioners to learn. Commonly used tools include Pareto charts, the

5 Whys, fishbone diagrams, A3s spaghetti diagrams, and Suppliers-Inputs-Process-Outputs-Customer diagrams (SIPOCs).[4] They are not mutually exclusive with process mapping; several of the techniques are helpful during *kaizen* projects to facilitate brainstorming and seek root causes.

Many CI tools predate the term "lean." Pareto charts, for example, are based on work by economist and sociologist Vilfredo Pareto (1848–1923), who found that around 80% of the wealth was held by about 20% of the people. Dr. Joseph Juran subsequently applied the 80/20 rule to management. The Pareto principle states that roughly 80% of the effects come from 20% of the causes. Pareto charts combine a bar chart with a line graph to identify the "vital few"—the roughly 20% of factors which cause 80% of the problems. Absent this analysis, *kaizen* teams may focus on anecdotal perceptions of the problem, failing to adopt appropriate countermeasures for the most significant factors.

There are many resources to guide users through the early stages of a lean initiative. The *Lean in Government Starter Kit*, produced by the Environmental Protection Agency (EPA) is an excellent reference. It offers sample documents, definitions of key terms, and descriptions of tools, and it is available online.[5]

Proficiency with CI tools can occur in training programs or be modeled by practitioners in the workplace. With deliberative practice, proficient use of tools will become a natural part of the PDCA cycle. The culture of continuous improvement requires activities at all levels of the organization, from "just do it" to formally chartered *kaizens* to complex projects.

Training to Build Capacity

Lean is not trademarked, and it is open to interpretation. As LEI notes, "lean is not dogmatic. It is not a rigid, unchanging set of beliefs and methods."[6] Practitioners may differ in approach, emphasis, and terminology. Training programs may offer progressive levels of "belt" proficiency. The range is typically from white to yellow to green to black and master black belt. Some programs combine the disciplines to offer Lean-Six Sigma belts.

It's not surprising that the growing community of practitioners has different styles and approaches. As the use of lean continues to expand beyond manufacturing, the tools and techniques are constantly evolving.

The lack of standardization may seem somewhat paradoxical since standard work is one of the core tenets of lean. As Deming said, "variation is the enemy of quality." The principle of continuous improvement coexists with standard work, as the improved product replaces the previous product. As Taiichi Ohno explained, "Without standards there can be no *kaizen*."[7]

Regardless of the terminology, the optimal training program incorporates theory and practice—teaching the principles and applying techniques. Trainees learn to conduct real projects, creating a cadre of rookie practitioners who can be paired with more experienced facilitators for *kaizen* projects. Mentorships further reinforce the skills.

Sample training programs

Programs	Description
White Belt	An overview of lean concepts and techniques preparing participants to identify opportunities for improvement projects in their organizations. Available online for all employees.
Yellow Belt	A hands-on introduction to the philosophy and methodology of lean process improvement. Participants apply *kaizen* process-mapping techniques to an actual work process and construct an implementation plan to enact the improvements. Tools learned: the 5 Whys, fishbone, and spaghetti diagram.
Green Belt	Facilitation and change management. Classroom session on how to guide a group through a *kaizen* event and the challenges of organizational change, followed by a required practicum. Tools practiced: Pareto charts, SIPOC, Improvement Kata. *Pre-requisite: Yellow Belt.*
Black Belt	Combination of classroom study, mentorship, and practical application. Study Shingo, Toyota Kata, and Hoshin Kanri. Conduct a capstone project to apply skills and understand lean from an operational and strategic perspective. *Prerequisites: Yellow and Green Belts; application with personal statement and A3 report of Green Belt practicum required.*
Lean for Leaders	A one-hour workshop that prepares directors and administrators for their role in lean initiatives and lean management. Available for agency management teams.
Maintaining Green and Black Belt active status	• Learning: Have a mentor and mentor others. Share lean articles and insights. Participate in networking events. Practice Toyota Kata. • Application: Facilitate cross-agency *kaizen* projects and prepare A3 reports. Use other tools and seek opportunities to apply them. • Verification: Share your A3 reports with your mentor and your agency's CI coordinator.

Public sector organizations need trained lean facilitators within their ranks. With management commitment, the skilled practitioners can be shared among agencies. A facilitator from another agency arrives without preconceived notions about existing processes, biases about potential solutions, or perceived alliances within the work group.

Organizations with mature lean programs have a network of experienced practitioners. These networks are nurtured to evolve from a community of practice to a community of excellence.

The optimal working model has a role for everyone in the organization:

■ The Governor articulates unambiguous support for the initiative and requires each department head to schedule a Lean for Leaders workshop for their management teams.
■ The Commissioner of each agency appoints a coordinator and sets the expectation that everyone in the agency will participate.
■ Equal access to training is available, regardless of funding source. Supervisors assist by modifying schedules and plans for coverage, so staff can attend training.
■ Agency managers identify strategic priorities and key performance indicators (KPIs), the foundation of project charters.
■ Lean coordinators work with managers to track the progress and report the metrics. They work with sponsors to construct charters, schedule projects, and identify facilitators.
■ Division directors and bureau chiefs sponsor projects, approve the changes, and assure implementation. If a project requires personnel from multiple bureaus, the sponsor should be someone with authority over those bureaus.
■ *Kaizen* teams document current workflow, identify improvements, redesign the process flow, create an implementation plan with a timeline, and present it to the sponsor. Each team has a project manager to track the progress of the implementation plan and update the team members and the sponsor. If necessary, the sponsor seeks assistance from upper management to assure follow-through on implementation.
■ Everyone: celebrate the wins and build lean culture.

Setting a Foundation

A solid launch will energize early adopters and win over skeptics by demonstrating proof of concept with quantifiable successes. However, lean is much more than a series of kaizens. It is a perspective based on value. Consistent application of the principles at all levels of government can transform business operations and outmoded accountability systems.

As projects continue and work processes are steadily improved, those who participate as team members acquire a deeper understanding of *kaizen*. With a robust training and mentoring program, all staff learn to use a range of lean tools, integrating their use throughout the workplace. Gradually, the newly acquired skills and techniques become habits. Practices that increase value and decrease inefficiency are baked in, without structured *kaizen* events.

And that's just getting started—there's much more to lean management that will be described in the next chapter.

Notes

1 Ken Miller, *Extreme Government Makeover: Increasing our Capacity to Do More Good* (Governing Books, Washington, DC, 2011), p. 206.
2 Martino, Dennis. *Interview via email*, 2023.
3 Bill Gates, as quoted by 2013 Lean Systems Summit. The Lean Collaborative, Portland Maine.
4 Several of these tools will be discussed in Chapter 12.
5 Environmental Protection Agency, *Lean in Government Starter Kit 4.0*, 2017. www.epa.gov/sites/default/files/2017-11/documents/lean-starter-kit-version-4.pdf
6 Lean Enterprise Institute, *What is Lean?* www.lean.org
7 James P. Womack, Daniel T. Jones, and Daniel Roos, *The Machine That Changed the World* (Free Press, A Division of Simon & Schuster, Inc., New York, NY, 1990–2007), p. 290.

Chapter 4

Lean Management

The contrast between hierarchical control and shared responsibility is core to understanding lean management. While the Ford assembly line was an innovation in mass production by using smooth flow and standard work, Toyota added the component of customer value by designing an innovative management system. Unlike the hierarchical management structure in the U.S., where frontline workers were treated as extensions of the machines, Toyota engaged the entire workforce in principles of continuous improvement.

The appropriate alignment of authority and responsibility is exemplified by Toyota's use of the Andon cord. When the cord is pulled, the assembly line stops. Workers have the responsibility to stop the line when an error is noticed, so that it can be addressed immediately. In contrast, workers under traditional management would need to ask permission to stop the line. Even if a supervisor could be contacted in time, the line might need to keep moving to maintain production volume. Traditional manufacturing relies upon the quality checks at the end of the line.

Lean principles empower workers with the expectation that they know their jobs and they share responsibility for quality. The lean mantra of "accept no defective product, make no defective product, pass along no defective product" is operationalized by the fact that any worker is expected to stop the line if something is not right. In lean management, all workers are responsible for product excellence. The principle is broadly applicable across industries and sectors. Quality is enhanced when the people who do the work are engaged in continuous improvement, rather than delegating the role to supervisors or quality control units.

DOI: 10.4324/9781003372691-6

Traditional management can impede the organization's ability to generate customer value. Jim Womack's *Gemba Walks* makes a distinction between traditional ("modern") management compared to lean management with respect to process flow.[1] The hierarchical management structure focuses on vertical functions and departments in the organization as mechanisms of optimization and control. Most enterprises are organized vertically, with each department functioning as its own silo as it interacts with other departments.

Lean management focuses on horizontal flow of value across many organizations, from raw materials to the end-use customer. Value flows across the silos to the customer, moving horizontally across the organization.[2] Lean tools are needed to cross the silos to maximize the quality and flow of the product or service to the customer.

The transition to lean is not intuitive to those who have always worked in a system of hierarchical management. The shift is equally challenging for those at the top who think they are required to have all the answers, as it is for frontline workers who believe that they are powerless over inefficient systems. Students in Yellow Belt classes often say that they know how things could be done better, but "they" won't let us make changes. In a lean system, "they" becomes "we" as quality becomes everyone's responsibility; workers have ownership, and management has trust.

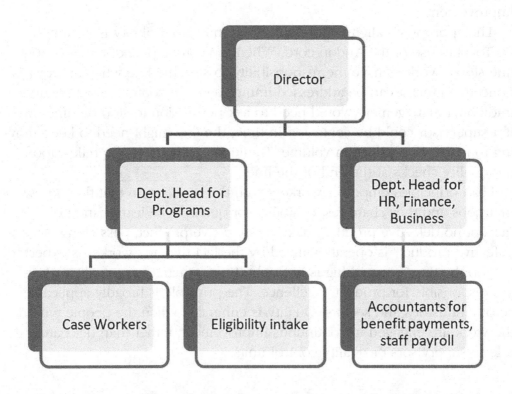

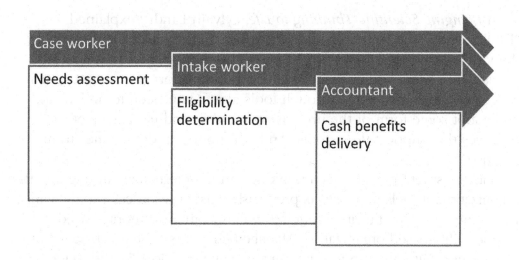

A Management Trifecta for the Public Sector

With the top managers all-in, delivering better, faster public services is just the start. Lean attains its full power when it becomes a way of doing business, not just a set of techniques. The trifecta of improved services, increased employee morale, and redeployment of previously wasted capacity creates a surge toward operational excellence. However, the progression is not automatic, nor is it easily sustained.

Government Is Different. And It's Not

Lean principles and techniques have the same transformative potential for the public sector as in private industry, though it is naïve to suggest that implementation is easy. Both public and private sector programs face the same core threat: the loss of commitment by leadership.

Initiatives falter when leaders lose focus and fail to invest the time and resources necessary to achieve meaningful long-term results. Corporate leaders may be more concerned with the next quarterly stock valuation. Political leaders may be more concerned with the next election. In either case, short-term gains are sought at the expense of systemic change.

Lean management is both a top-down and a bottom-up system that relies on frontline managers to play a key role. Top leadership articulates the mission and identifies the priorities. Responsibility is placed at the lowest possible level, where work is taking place at the *gemba*—the place value is made. There, frontline managers play a key role in teaching and coaching.

In *Bringing Scientific Thinking to Life*, Sylvain Landry explained, "Until recently, the lean community focused on the tip of the iceberg: the visible lean tools. Tools can be viewed as important best practices, yet as we've seen, you can't achieve or sustain performance improvement and competitive advantage through tools alone: you need to understand and adopt some form of the underlying mindset and management practices that support these tools. And that understanding comes from practice."[3]

With persistent practice, lean thinking can be internalized throughout the organization. It fuels purpose, as previously wasted resources expand capacity for mission. The transition requires a shift from an authority-based to a responsibility-based organization. Management shifts from a debate about who owns what and who has the right to make decisions (authority) to a dialog about the right thing to do (responsibility).

Top leadership's responsibility includes articulating unequivocal support for the effort and appointing a statewide coordinator to lead the initiative across the departmental silos. Administrators, managers, and supervisors need to be trained in the principles of lean management and in the role of managers as sponsors of *kaizen* projects and as coaches.

Each division should have practitioners who can help to organize projects, demonstrate tools, and spread lean culture in the workplace. They join a community of practice, further enhancing their skills, mentoring others, and modeling a commitment to continuous improvement.

As Bert Teeuwen advised in *Lean for the Public Sector*, "Choose for the role of embedded lean practitioners people who are good or can be good at enthusing others. They possess the skills to notice signs of resistance, overcome these, and to get the most from the teams. These are competencies other than making a good value stream map."

Achieving a Culture of Continuous Improvement

The current state of the continuous improvement programs is uneven— capacity and focus vary widely across the country. While some state Lean programs have faltered due to turnover of key staff and shifting priorities of elected leadership, other states have continued their work despite shutdowns during the height of the COVID-19 pandemic. Adaptations such as online training, virtual *kaizens*, and self-service web access to tools and templates have helped sustain many of the improvement programs.

Failure to Launch

Variables of leadership focus, continuity, and commitment exist in government. There are numerous potential points of failure. Lean initiatives are at greatest risk during the transition from the initial *kaizens* to a broad application of principles. After celebrating early efficiency gains, leaders tend to lose focus. While certain aspects of a CI program may survive, a lack of commitment by leadership prevents the organization from achieving a culture of continuous improvement.

Attrition Poses a Similar Threat

The leaders who initiated the lean program are replaced by those with other priorities. An incoming chief executive officer may see lean as a management fad gone by. Or an emerging crisis can shift the focus. Training is discontinued and coordinator roles remain unfilled. Lean skills and principles are not dispersed widely enough to take hold throughout the organization.

Top elected leadership in the executive and legislative branches can make or break a lean initiative. Dedicated lean practitioners do their best to keep going, but they are swimming upstream. If management has not created a permanent position charged with coordinating a comprehensive program, there is no mechanism for reaching across siloed agencies to tackle processes under the jurisdiction of departments where the effort has languished. The talents of these practitioners are underutilized, while deeply entrenched organizational inefficiencies remain in place. The transformation falls short of its potential.

Arrested Development Is Not All Bad News

These efforts are not in vain. While a truncated program will not achieve broad cultural change, a series of disparate projects can still achieve significant gains. Even without management support, dedicated CI practitioners work within their own scope of authority. In some states, ad hoc peer groups are sustaining communities of practice, prepared to ramp up when called upon to do so.

Across the country, lean efforts are going strong within state agencies. Programs in transportation and environmental protection will be profiled in Chapter 8. Here, we begin with a review of two of the major units of New Hampshire's state government—the Department of Health and Human Services (DHHS) and the University System of New Hampshire (USNH). Here are their stories.

Heather Barto.

Story of a Lean Leader, the Impact of Lean Thinking, and the Culture of Continuous Improvement

Heather Barto's story exemplifies how lean principles can be woven into daily work. Her career, connecting with colleagues who share her commitment to principles of quality customer service, demonstrates the proliferation of lean culture.

Since readers were introduced to Heather Barto in *A Public Sector Journey to Lean*, she has been promoted to manage the Contracts Quality Management unit at New Hampshire's Department of Health & Human Services (DHHS), following her work as Senior Process Improvement Specialist in that agency's Lean office.

Going back to where it began, Barto recalled her introduction to Lean while attending New Hampshire's Certified Public Manager (CPM) program. There she met two practitioners, John MacPhee of the Department of Health and Human Services (DHHS) and Roberta Bourque of the Department of Safety (DOS). A part of lean training, they presented a program known as the "John and Roberta Show" due to their contrasting facilitation styles. MacPhee was low-key and collaborative while Bourque's motto was "proceed until apprehended!" Barto said, "They absolutely were a show as their perspectives and approaches were very broadly different." It carried the lesson that the field was open to practitioners developing their own style for guiding project teams.

Following her training as a Continuous Improvement Practitioner (CIP), Barto reached out to MacPhee for advice on starting a Lean group where she worked at the Division of Public Health Services (DPHS). She became the Lean liaison, coordinating projects at the division level for a number of years, reporting regularly to MacPhee, who served as coordinator for the entire DHHS. As a result, DPHS projects began making their entrance to the department's dashboard for lean work. This was a new concept for the State of New Hampshire, whereby a division lead would coordinate projects with a *kaizen* team, then report to a department lead, and from there the results would get reported up to a commissioner level. The structure worked smoothly, enabling Lean to be used throughout the agency. As Barto explained, "This is what made my relationship so easy and efficient with John over the years; connecting to the larger entity and value."

The partnership was made official in 2017 when then Commissioner Nick Toumpas established the Lean Services Office within DHHS, with MacPhee as Lean Director and Barto as Senior Process Improvement Specialist. They worked on projects for divisions within DHHS including Children, Youth, and Families and Elderly and Adult Services to modernize their processes. In one such project, a paper invoice process was leaned in preparation for conversion to electronic invoicing. Barto recalled the results were "a smooth like butter process saving hours on both the DHHS side and on the vendor side. The repurposed hours provided value back to the department and to the vendor, with financial savings clearly due to Lean." She also noted the value of Gemba walks as essential to the work, recalling "a sense of freedom to run projects in the way that they needed to be run." The experience was a pivotal point in her career, and she credited MacPhee's sound leadership as a key factor in her success.

A few months into the new position, Barto began investing in strategy across the department; building mini teams and champions in every division. She described the impact:

> To see these sizeable changes in how individuals conducted
> their work, approached their program teams, and then changed
> the way they conducted DHHS business, was an immense

honor. To be truthful people trusted us and we had no stop sign in terms of uncovering inefficiencies with the work, negotiating with team members, and many times voting on the top priority improvements that should be presented to leadership. Really quite amazing to see how staff were using Lean in various shapes and sizes.

With fellow Black Belts, Barto convened a Lean Learning Collaborative, a friendly, innovative environment of continuing education and support for the Lean practitioners. Topics included creative problem-solving, demonstration of tool use, interactive case studies, and even neurological components about how the brain functions with the uptake of information. It served multiple benefits, as Heather explained, "We had an atmosphere ripe and hungry for structure, unleashing creative approaches, and plenty of mentoring opportunities." Highlights of Heather's mentees:

■ Black Belt Colin Premo in the Division of Child Support Services modeled Lean thinking and philosophy during staff meetings. He and Heather collaborated on project that entailed traveling around to district offices within the state and learning about their work, with strong support from senior director, Karen Hebert. Karen was thrilled with the onboarding of introduction to Lean concepts, the status report meetings, and the diagrams provided, and she wanted all staff to know about the work. She wrote an article in the unit's newsletter highlighting the team efforts, progress of the work, innovations brought to the unit, and excitement from lean.

■ Black Belt Jill Fournier in the Division of Program Quality and Integrity began training an entire bureau in Lean Yellow Belt with a systematic way of tracking tool introduction and observation of the usage of methods. She often shared the percentage of staff trained, which was nearing 85% pre-pandemic. Jill and Heather collaborated regarding onboarding of tools as she got her bearings for the style and type of format she wanted to roll out. Jill is well known as a solid trainer and fantastic mentoring resource in the department.

■ Following her three projects at New Hampshire Hospital, Barto worked with Black Belts Chuck Bagley and Suzy Easterling-Wood to create curriculum for Lean Yellow Belt credentialing. They recruited two Green Belts to co-teach some of the tools and facilitate training exercises for root-cause reviews and cause-and-effect diagrams.

Barto described the project management aspect of Lean work:

> The project requests were flying in left and right. Leadership appreciated the final reports, often sharing them with vendors and stakeholders, and to gather business requirements for system changes. Initially, projects were tracked in Teamwork, and later the Brightwork project management software. We adopted standard business steps of managing projects as our primary mechanism to communicate with leadership and managers. Additionally, we began using a governance process across our department to assure that all of our projects were in alignment with mission, strategy, value, and priorities. This helped assure that were spending the right amount of time and the right amount of money in the right places. Although most of the Lean projects did not have a dollar amount attached to them, there were costs such as staff time and the commitment to trying a new process. Some projects required IT functionality changes, and alignment was pivotal.
>
> I jumped on board at the opportunity for project governance [and] looked to integrate project management best practices. Using this model, I developed deeper relationships with division heads and agency leadership. This led to additional trust for our project teams' recommendations. Bottom line my motto was always "the program success is my success!"

Among the many innovations Barto and MacPhee used in DHHS was an expansive approach for project chartering to allow for spin-off mini-Lean projects, dubbed "while we are here." This option allowed them to deal with issues that emerged during the core project, rather than closing out and starting a separate project. The impact and achievements were greater, and it saved team members, hard pressed for time, from having to schedule secondary projects. Barto is quick to remind leadership that team members have a regular full-time job and the lean work in addition to that, stating, "we need to make time for improvement work."

She noted, "The only drawback was that there were only two of us, and the more comprehensive projects meant fewer projects during a calendar year. However, it resulted in a higher quality product when we tackled an entire value stream. The business area could use this information for strategy planning and resource allocation. This often paid dividends forward and helped for resource and position planning in the budget process."

As the DHHS lean initiatives continued to gain momentum, Barto was a regular in the training department's change-management courses, highlighting the need for the tools of Lean, such as 5S method, the five whys, and the eight types of waste: all easy ways to begin changing the way the work is conducted and adding value back into the customer. She gave lectures at the New Hampshire Technical Institute's Engineering program on the state government's application. She recalled that "to walk into the college campus and see your face on a poster announcing your talk up in front of the large screen was a whole new feeling of . . . this is real now." Throughout 2017 and 2018, she continued to provide presentations both in state and out of state, including at the regional Lean Summit in Maine and the annual summit at the University of New Hampshire. Then, Barto was tapped for the COVID-19 pandemic response. She recalled:

> Before we moved to 100% remote, I was asked to provide an urgent executive-level evaluation of the initial response being conducted with the public health partners. Based on interviews, data collected, and observations, I quickly provided recommendations to the Incident Commander, Dr. Elizabeth Daly. Although it was not a fully Lean project, I drew on the skills, deep value of relationships, and ability to facilitate quick and pointed discussions to consolidate the requests of the team. Before my very eyes was a team desperate for standardization, process development, consistent work-load balancing, procedures, and more resources! I put together this information for Dr. Daly to paint an accurate picture of the limited and strained resources, and provided recommendations for short-term and long-term improvements for sustainability. . . . During the height of the pandemic response, I continued to apply my skills in a priority role in the Incident Command Team's Planning Branch, completing several projects.

In March 2022, Barto was promoted into a management position to plan and develop a new program in quality management. She explained:

This new unit is tasked with developing standards and practices for quality and performance management in the contract compliance and management processes. This will ultimately provide our department's contract managers with a standardized framework to manage contracts, develop contracts aligning with division strategies, [build] clear performance measures, [add] transparency to our work, and ultimately [add] value for our beneficiaries in the community. My wonderful colleague Denise Krol is lean-trained and a credentialed Project Management Professional through the Project Management Institute. I've hit the jackpot with her background and superior level of organizational skills. Oftentimes we like to say that we're going to whip up a recipe combining lean project management and contract management which will be [a] solution to approach for most of our business challenges. As I hire more people in my unit, they need to be lean-trained and up to speed on current methodologies to supply the best innovations and most efficiency in the way we do our work to support the department.

Looking back over the work to build a culture of continuous improvement, Barto noted:

Over the years I continue to hear about all of the great work that we've done, and where our reports have become invaluable. Often times our reports have been shared with vendors as they are performing the pre-design and planning work for system, development, or functionality changes, or overhaul of a system, or a redesign of a brand new shiny system.

As John and I would often say, it must begin with the people. We spent hours documenting processes with standardized tools and perfecting the formats needed for our leadership as well as front line staff. We spent time documenting detailed processes and got to know every single division, at least two times over, with their complex detail processes. The many hours we spent with frontline staff, middle, and upper management is value added for the department and years to come. I am the lucky one who knows about all the inner workings of the entire department, and I believe that is [a] one-of-a-kind role, for now.[4]

USNH

The University System of New Hampshire (USNH) Enterprise Lean Team, led by Senior Process Engineers Dagmar Vlahos and Tom Lencki, incorporates consulting, training, mentoring, and process-improvement methodology, with the goal of fostering a positive lean culture.[5] Dagmar, now a Master Black Belt, received her Six Sigma Black Belt while at Fidelity Investments. Tom, now a Master Black Belt, got his Lean Black Belt while a Sergeant with the New Hampshire State Police. Drawing from his experience in the military, he has introduced the Challenge Coin as an award of distinction for achievement in lean at USNH.

The Enterprise Lean Team has worked on a series of business transformation projects that have helped the state colleges and universities within the University system of New Hampshire navigate the changing landscape in higher education. This includes transitioning human resources to a shared services model across all campuses, transforming technology services to an Enterprise-wide solution, and incorporating Lean thinking into the University of New Hampshire and Granite State College merger.

Tom Lencki and Dagmar Vlahos.

Adapting to the pandemic closures and opportunities for technical development, lean projects can be conducted online using the Miro collaboration tool. Training is available at the White, Yellow, Green, and Black Belt levels. At the close of 2022, USNH had more than 40 trained facilitators. Among the more than 100 processes improved, some are at the individual departmental level while others span departmental silos and cross campus initiatives.

A Lean Project That Streamlined an Administrative Process

Admissions counselors travel to recruit students and may be away for days or weeks at a time. While on the road, they collect receipts with no way to submit their expense reports. The finance department would consistently reach out to them requesting their travel expense paperwork. It was time-consuming for both finance staff and admission staff, resulting in delayed payments, which were out of compliance with policy for the timeliness of expense reports.

A Lean project was initiated, and a team evaluated the expense report process. The project resulted in an automated process where admission counselors were able to take a picture of their receipt(s) with their phone or laptop while traveling, complete a simplified expense form directly on their phone or laptop, and electronically submit the report, which included electronic routing and approval with on-time submission to finance. So, when they were waiting in a parking lot at a school, sitting at the airport, or in their hotel room, they could take less than five minutes to submit their expense report.

Previously, upon return from travel, an admissions counselor would spend the entire first day back in the office compiling receipts, filling out forms, making copies, and manually submitting their expense report, whereas now they are spending that entire first day following up with schools they visited and connecting with potential future students.

Envisioning an Ideal Future State

The Enterprise Lean Team's ideal future state within higher education is to strive to continue building a positive Lean culture, where ideas are encouraged and welcome at every level, where every employee is a problem-solver and innovator, and where employees do not think of Lean as an additional duty but a natural evolution of their work. Additionally, [they hope to] ensure a stronger leadership engagement in Lean methodology and messaging.

Before continuing to assess the factors common to successful CI programs, it is valuable to dig deeper into the context. While seeking to understand the range of challenges faced by lean practitioners in government, we move next to the field of public administration.

Notes

1 Jim Womack, *Gemba Walks* (The Lean Enterprise Institute, Cambridge, 2011), p. 77.
2 Jim Womack, *Gemba Walks* (The Lean Enterprise Institute, Cambridge, 2011), p. 77.
3 Sylvain Landry, Ph.D., *Bringing Scientific Thinking to Life: An Introduction to Toyota Kata for the Next Generation of Business Leaders (and those who would like to be)* (Les Éditions JFD Montréal, Montréal, 2022), p. 133.
4 Heather Barto currently manages the DHHS Contracts Quality Management unit. She also manages her own business at www.heatherbarto.com and can be found on LinkedIn.
5 University System of New Hampshire, *Enterprise Lean Team. Lean in Higher Education.* www.usnh.edu/lean

Chapter 5

Theory and Practice

Since bureaucratic and political systems tend to resist change, and lean management is counterintuitive for traditional managers, it is useful to begin with an examination of the field of public administration. A successful transition to lean management requires a certain amount of risk taking on the part of administrators.

The Theory of Administrative Conservatorship

One of the important contributions to academic work in the field of public administration is the theory of administrative conservatorship as articulated by Larry D. Terry.[1] He asserts, "public bureaucracies are national treasurers because it is through these institutions that the authoritative allocation of resources is made to sustain the Republic's cohesion and moral balance."[2]

The theory argues that an empowered, invested leadership is the best chance for bureaucracies to stay on mission. The duty to conserve the agency's mission requires managerial and leadership capacity, insight, and integrity.

Terry questions the efficacy of restrictive policies for assuring bureaucratic accountability. He attributes much of the procedural inefficiency to "Americans' deeply rooted fear of bureaucracy,"[3] explaining that well-meaning attempts to control bureaucracies made them rigid and unresponsive. Risk-averse leaders who rely on rigid policies are an impediment to accomplishing the mission and cause employees to become discouraged and disengaged.

DOI: 10.4324/9781003372691-7

Terry also identifies administrative malpractice as a violation of public trust. It can manifest as corruption, or it can be subtle. For example, a leader who wishes to avoid controversy can allow the agency to drift off-mission. As he points out, "administrative officials can violate the spirit of the law without violating the letter of the law."[4]

By labeling administrative malpractice, Terry has called out the self-serving careerism that compromises the integrity of the profession. Arguably, risk-averse bureaucrats commit administrative malpractice through passive acceptance of the status quo. While the failure to act is generally less apparent than overtly unethical acts, its impact is potentially devastating.

The transition to lean management challenges administrators, managers, and supervisors to leave their comfort zones. Risk-aversion, a relatively mild manifestation of administrative malpractice, is a common impediment to successful lean events.

Motive Matters in Risk Avoidance

Sometimes a maze of bottlenecks is established based on a single negative event. Cautious administrators or image conscious politicians vow to make sure it never happens again by insisting on redundant layers of checking. The incident may have been due to individual misconduct or to a lack of training. Rather than deal with the individual or seek the root cause, staff are assigned to review the work of others.

In keeping with Deming's guidance to "cease dependence on inspection to achieve quality" by "building quality into the product in the first place," *kaizen* teams try to reduce the number of times an item is reviewed. However, risk-averse administrators may be hesitant to eliminate redundant layers of checking. The reluctance could be motivated by prudence or intransigence. Or, as a colleague mused, "When is an abundance of caution an abundance of CYA?" When responsibility is diffused, blame can be shifted or avoided.

The classic case is a request by a public employee to travel out of state. It is a good topic for an introductory CI class. Ask the participants how many signatures are required. If it's a laugh line, you know they have some risk-averse administrators. The requirement for multiple authorizations gives them the illusory comfort of control, presuming that the series of signoffs protects the organization. Reinforced by the fear of a bad outcome, such processes are very difficult to dislodge. There is a nagging trepidation that if the process as we know it goes away, there could be a negative consequence for which blame will be assigned. There is hope, though. With a good CI training program, some of these managers can be converted and become sponsors of *kaizen* projects to streamline such processes.

Mission-Driven Public Servants

In any orientation to lean, start by asking the participants to think back to when they started their jobs. Did they ever ask a supervisor or colleague why a process was done in a certain way? The answer will be recited in unison: "Because that's the way it's always been done!" It is the rallying cry to enlist public employees as lean activists.

In a typical scenario, aspiring change agents eagerly join *kaizen* teams seeking workflow improvements. They redesign the process. The project sponsor is expected to approve the changes. What happens next and why?

Consider the possible outcomes if the process is solely at the discretion of the agency's administration:

- Optimal: The sponsor approves the changes, either in full all at once, or to be phased in or tested for a trial period. The team measures the outcome. Consistent with PDCA, adjustments are made as appropriate. The team maintains metrics on the process performance and continues to make improvements.
- Suboptimal: The sponsor lacks authority to approve comprehensive changes. Some changes are made, and the process is marginally improved. The team and sponsor seek a sponsor of higher rank willing to charter a project with a more comprehensive scope.
- Bust: The sponsor refuses to approve any of the changes, or equivocates, offering vague support, without requiring the redesigned process to be used as the new standard.

The Lean in Government Starter Kit has a recommendation to minimize the likelihood of a "bust" scenario. It has a sample Sponsor Contract which sets expectations for behaviors to help ensure the team's success:

- Passionate: Enthusiastic support of the team to ensure team success.
- Strategic: Using the project activity to advance a business objective by improving the performance of the targeted process while being aware of the impact to the total system.

- Committed: Engaged from planning the project through sustainment of implemented process changes.
- Risk Taking: Encourage creative thinking to drive paradigm-breaking results.
- Open Minded: Influence the team to develop the best solution without introducing preconceived ideas.

Sponsors are expected to sign the contract, indicating that they understand their critical role and agree to follow the project-preparation checklist with the team leader.[5]

Another series of possibilities occurs when certain changes are external to the authority of the agency due to a rule or statute:

- The sponsor authorizes changes within the agency and contacts the appropriate regulatory authority or governing body to work for the broader changes. The sponsor and the team present their work and the governing body is persuaded to act.
- The sponsor fails to get permission for the external changes but continues to work with the team to measure the progress of the authorized changes and prepare to make the case again.
- The sponsor says it is unlikely that the governing body will make any changes and never approaches them with the request.

In each of these scenarios, the sponsors acted differently. In managing organizational change, it is valuable to understand why some administrators and managers are more likely to support change initiatives than others. What would cause administrators to be leaders in such campaigns? And, if they are invested in leading a lean initiative, are they prepared to require unit managers to get on board?

Integration of Theory and Practice

Consider a scenario where the lean initiative is going well. Aspiring change agents eagerly join a *kaizen* team seeking workflow improvements. They redesign the process. The manager who is sponsoring the project is expected to approve the changes. The manager can adopt the team's recommendations in whole or in part or opt to test the proposed changes for a trial period. In either case, the team would measure the outcome, and adjustments would be made as appropriate.

Alternatively, a risk-averse manager refuses to reduce redundant layers of checking, even though the team has addressed quality-control concerns. The team is disillusioned, and the initiative is undercut, losing energy and credibility. Other managers stop sponsoring projects and focus on other priorities. Agency administrators are reluctant to expend political capital pressuring long-term bureaucrats comfortable with "the way it's always been done." Wasteful practices remain in place, frustrating the employees and their customers.

The administrators could be facing what has been characterized as "the frozen middle," the most change-resistant component of the bureaucracy. Ideally, if the unit managers had any reservations about the lean program, they would have been addressed prior to launching the initiative. However, it is difficult to anticipate passive resistance. Unit managers may agree to sponsor *kaizens* and simply fail to follow through with recommended changes.

Is it possible the recalcitrant managers believe they are protecting the integrity of valuable programs? Or are they just trying to preserve their own power and privilege? How do administrators assess the circumstances and hold them accountable? The lean initiative is at risk of withering away.

As administrators grapple with managing the frozen middle, it may be useful to reflect on their duty as conservator of the agency's mission. If the organization's top leadership is fully aware of the potential gains and fails to act to reset the initiative, it is arguably an example of administrative malpractice. As Terry noted, administrators "must not be weak or subservient, nor must they be empire builders or public entrepreneurs conceptualized in a pejorative sense. Rather, public administrators must honorably hold up the administrative side of the governance equation."[6]

Administrators, managers, supervisors, program staff, and frontline employees may also benefit by referencing professional codes of ethics for public employees. These tenets reaffirm the idealism of public service.

Professional codes of conduct support the obligation to take risks in the public interest. So, should administrators require managers to implement changes proposed by *kaizen* teams? Is an administrator's failure to authorize changes that would improve public services an example of administrative malpractice or a reasonable difference of approach? To evaluate actions (or lack thereof), it is useful to seek guidance from a professional code of ethics.

Consider the Code of Ethics of the American Society for Public Administration (ASPA).[7] Among the Code's eight tenets are:

- Promote the interests of the public and put service to the public above service to oneself.
- Respect and support government constitutions and laws, while seeking to improve laws and policies to promote the public good.
- Be open, transparent, and responsive, and respect and assist all persons in their dealings with public organizations.

Turning away from an opportunity to improve public services, boost employee morale, and expand the capacity for mission would certainly be an unfortunate choice, if not an unethical one. It is also a scenario likely to keep the organization from developing the capacity to address complex problems.

As Larry Terry reminds us, public administrators play an essential role in our nation. In *The Premonition: A Pandemic Story*, Michael Lewis introduces readers to the bravery of public servants going above and beyond. While careerists cowered out of fear of being fired, the heroes fighting the pandemic risked much more than a paycheck:

> Sara Cody, health officer in Santa Clara County, had issued the country's first stay at home order . . . and now Sara Cody needed round-the-clock police protection. Nicole Quick, the health officer in Orange County, seeing the virus ramping through her community, had issued a mask order only to have the CDC waffle about the need for masks. She'd been run out of her job and, finally for fear of her safety, the state.[8]

In a series of open letters to state employees entitled "We are in Trouble, We Need Your Help," John Bernard wrote, "It's government employees—appointed/hired government employees. Yes, the dreaded term, bureaucrats, also known as administrators, and public or civil servants. Why? Because these people actually implement the programs created by the laws that exist and that are added. How they choose to implement determines how effective and efficient our government is. Our public servants have much more power for good than most Americans know."[9]

Discussion of the role of public administrators in solving society's most challenging problems will resume in chapter 14. The next two chapters will explore how states can lean the design and operations functions—particularly the regulatory responsibilities and benefit programs.

Notes

1 Larry D. Terry, *Leadership of Public Bureaucracies: The Administrator as Conservator* (M.E. Sharpe, New York, NY, 2003).

2 Larry D. Terry, *Leadership of Public Bureaucracies: The Administrator as Conservator* (M.E. Sharpe, New York, NY, 2003), p. xv.

3 Larry D. Terry, *Leadership of Public Bureaucracies: The Administrator as Conservator* (M.E. Sharpe, New York, NY, 2003), p. 4.

4 Larry D. Terry, *Leadership of Public Bureaucracies: The Administrator as Conservator* (M.E. Sharpe, New York, NY, 2003), p. 77.

5 Environmental Protection Agency, *Lean in Government Starter Kit 4.0* (2017), p. 104. https://www.epa.gov/sites/default/files/2017-11/documents/lean-starter-kit-version-4.pdf

6 Larry D. Terry, *Leadership of Public Bureaucracies: The Administrator as Conservator* (M.E. Sharpe, New York, NY, 2003), p. 29.

7 American Society for Public Administration. *Code of Ethics.* www.aspanet.org/ASPA/Code-of-Ethics/ASPA/Code-of-Ethics/Code-of-Ethics.aspx

8 Michael Lewis, *The Premonition: A Pandemic Story* (W.W. Norton & Company, New York, NY, 2021), p. 291.

9 John M. Bernard, *We are in Trouble, We Need Your Help*, January 20, 2022. www.linkedin.com/pulse/we-trouble-need-your-help-john-m-bernard/

LEANING GOVERNMENT OPERATIONS

Lean practitioners assess organizational function by focusing on the production of value. They identify the streams of effort that are required to produce each of the products and services.

There are three streams of work by government mechanisms identified by Jim Womack: (1) enacting policies; (2) designing enforcement and delivery mechanisms; and (3) operating those mechanisms.[1] Part II examines the need and the potential to lean the design and operational functions of government.

Chapters 6: Breaking Bad Bureaucracy. This chapter describes the problem of inefficient delivery mechanisms using examples such as the Veterans Health Administration's hiring process.

Chapter 7: The Goldilocks Standard for Lean Regulation. This chapter discusses the purpose and function of regulations, discussing challenges such as those experienced by the Food and Drug Administration.

Chapter 8: Moving to Results-Based State Government. This chapter describes state CI initiatives in various stages of development. It highlights work in New Hampshire, Vermont, Washington, and Colorado.

Chapter 9: A Model for CI in State Government. This chapter describes the Centers for Operational Excellence (COEs) in Nebraska and Ohio and proposes a checklist of recommended components for a COE.

DOI: 10.4324/9781003372691-8

Chapter 6

Breaking Bad Bureaucracy

Administrative Hazing: Intentional or Not?

Not all unlean processes are caused by overly cautious bureaucrats. Sometimes they seem to be intentionally designed to create barriers. From the customers' perspective, these processes certainly seem like hazing.

For example, college graduates working in nonprofit agencies might assume that the process to request student-loan forgiveness was intentionally constructed to make it unlikely their applications would be approved. Without electronic options, mobile millennials belatedly realized that hard copies of essential documents were mailed to previous addresses. And, as one borrower noted, the requirement to produce proof of nonprofit work should not be necessary because a record of qualifying employment would be readily available from the Internal Revenue Service or the Social Security Administration. Why couldn't that information be shared with the Department of Education? Perhaps it would take an act of Congress.

To state employees requesting permission to travel out of state, the convoluted approval process may appear merely an inefficient way to conserve the budget. Or a passive-aggressive way for managers to avoid saying "no." Or for managers to avoid the task of prioritizing the purposes for which travel would be appropriate.

Similar questions could be asked about human-service and entitlement programs. If an application process is detailed and difficult, fewer people will qualify. The program would not need to budget for all who are eligible, only those able to navigate the application process. Or perhaps the application process is difficult because the designers are opposed to the wide

DOI: 10.4324/9781003372691-9

availability of social programs. It could be a matter of both budget and political philosophy.

Unlean Bureaucracy

Regardless of the intentionality of these processes, it is evident that complex regulations thwart the efficient implementation of many mission-critical programs. Layers of bureaucratic hurdles exist to assure that programs are used solely for the intended purposes. Lean process design would ensure programmatic integrity without barring access to qualified individuals. Too often, though, programs are full of choke points and bottlenecks. Consider several examples:

- Rental assistance intended to help tenants and landlords during the eviction ban at height of the pandemic. Five hundred jurisdictions each set up their own programs. As of August 2021, only 16%[2] of the $46 billion appropriated had been distributed, while millions of tenants still faced eviction, and landlords were not getting paid.[3]
- Student-loan forgiveness program for public service. In October 2021, the news program *60 Minutes* reported that 98% of applicants were deemed ineligible. Of 180,000 veterans with student loans, only 124 had been approved for debt forgiveness.[4]
- Veterans' disability and pension claims. As of June 2022, 187,540 veterans had been waiting more than four months for a decision.[5]
- The Special Immigrant Visa (SIV) program intended to allow Afghans and Iraqis who served with U.S. forces to emigrate to the United States. The process kept tens of thousands of qualified applicants waiting for years. In July 2022, while more than 74,000 Afghans[6] remained in limbo, the Biden administration announced plans to streamline the process so that applicants would need to file only one form, and applications would go through a single government agency.[7]

Quality, accuracy, and pace are important in the each of these processes. In the case of the visa program, it can be a matter of life and death for those left behind in Afghanistan. An accurate and expeditious vetting process would make it possible to honor the commitment to the Afghans who served as allies without allowing Taliban infiltrators into the country. At the end of 2022, veterans' groups were still trying to rescue their Afghan partners, urging Congress to pass the Afghan Adjustment Act to fix the SIV process.

Few programs carry the extraordinarily high stakes of saving the lives and honoring the commitment to those who served without sacrificing national security, yet every government program has an impact. Programs are set up to accomplish a stated purpose. Unworkable administrative processes thwart those purposes. During a crisis, there is a risk for an unlean reaction. Under pressure to act, policy makers tend to create new agencies, programs, and regulations without assessing and fixing what is already in place.

As the winter of 2022 came with hundreds of unhoused people at risk, pressure increased on Rhode Island Governor Dan McKee. *The Providence Journal* reported that the Senate President said, "There's almost $300 million sitting in that [housing] fund. I want to see it go out. . . . I was not pleased during COVID when there was so much money available for rentals to pay landlords for utilities. And our housing groups were not getting that money out. I don't know what they were waiting for but that money did not go out in a timely fashion."[8]

Perhaps the "housing groups" referred to were tangled by regulations from the federal or state level. Perhaps they used an unlean application and distribution processes. Perhaps the responsibility was dispersed among too many organizations. As is often the case, an additional layer of administrative coordination was established. Faced with the criticism, Governor McKee pointed out that the new cabinet level Department of Housing still needed to hire staff.[9] Within weeks, the housing czar had sent a letter of resignation explaining: "Housing and homeless programs are currently being administered and led by several different state agencies as well as multiple non-governmental and quasi-government bodies. . . . This approach has led to limitations on oversight, and to the unintentional creation of inefficient 'silos'—an ineffective practice that the creation of this new centralized agency aims to address."[10] Other complexities involve a 28-member Housing Commission and plans to hire a consultant to write a housing plan.[11]

This bureaucratically complex situation could remind one of Ken Miller's *Extreme Government Makeover.*[12] The title was inspired by the reality television show, *Extreme Makeover Home Edition,* in which a house gets built in seven days. One might wonder how many houses could be built if the *Extreme Makeover* folks had $250 million to use?

Such possibilities aside, consider using a high-level value-stream map to identify the primary functions and appropriate sponsor. The sponsor, a state official of sufficient rank to authorize appropriate changes, would charter a *kaizen*. The task of reducing the bureaucracy without sacrificing the integrity of the program would require a qualified *kaizen* team.

The team would include frontline and supervisory staff from the state and nonprofit agencies doing the work, and several customers (people in need of housing and potential providers such as developers or landlords). The team could also include stakeholders such as an advocate, and a member of the public to bring fresh eyes to the project.

Given the bureaucracy surrounding the problem, it would not be an easy project. In the spirit of continuous improvement, the team may recommend a phased implementation plan to deal with the most urgent human needs first. Throughout the *kaizen*, the principles of quality, efficiency, and standard work would be incorporated into the assessment and redesign of the response to this crisis. The redesigned system would also need to address the requirements for efficient data collection, regulatory processes, and procurement processes.

Crisis and Opportunity

When the pandemic hit, governments suddenly had to conduct essential business remotely. Governors and mayors waived "red tape" requirements, streamlining work processes. Processes were improved at the state, federal, and municipal levels. There were advances in telework, intergovernmental coordination, and procurement processes.

Crisis-driven "just do it" produced remarkable results. Necessity won out over the inertia of "the way it's always been done." Change-agent trainer Brian Elms cited multiple instances. For example, for years, City of Baltimore employees had been advocating a change from requiring "wet" signatures to allowing electronic signatures on contracts. The reform has reduced contracting times by days if not weeks. "We should take this opportunity to permanently transform our services, transactions, and regulatory system," Elms wrote in *Governing*.[13]

There are limits of administrative authority, however. Some reforms made under emergency powers or temporary authorizations may require legislative or regulatory approval to make them permanent. Consider the case of the Veterans Health Administration (VHA) of the Department of Veterans Affairs (VA).

THE VHA: CARING FOR THOSE WHO SERVED

The Veterans Health Administration's (VHA) hiring process is a case in point, judging from a series of reports by the *Federal News Network*. Prior to the pandemic, hiring and onboarding could take up to 90 days.

In May 2020, the agency streamlined the hiring process to meet the emergency staffing needs and was able to bring on 12,000 new staff in eight weeks. Fingerprinting and other vetting previously required upfront were allowed to occur within the first 120 days of employment. Jessica Bonjorni, VHA's chief officer for workforce management, explained, "We were working on making incremental improvements to time-to-hire. . . . But in truth, our private sector counterparts are able to onboard very quickly. This pushed us to get us to a very similar point to our private sector counterparts. It's going to change the way we hire forever."[14]

That was apparently not the case.

In March 2022, the VA was seeking Congressional authorization to make the changes permanent. Bonjorni explained that a team of process improvement engineers is looking at ways to revamp the VA's onboarding process, including allowing the VA to keep temporary flexibilities on background checks in place. However, the request was refused.

There was bipartisan agreement that the changes posed too great a risk. Chair of the House Committee on Veterans Affairs, Mark Takano (D-Calif.), noted that, "It's not difficult to imagine the worst-case scenario." Ranking Member Mike Bost (R-Ill.) also expressed concerns. "The worst thing that could happen is one of our veterans suffer in one way or another by somebody who is either incompetent or has a criminal background. That would be a danger," Bost said.[15]

In May 2022, the average hiring period was 95 days.[16] Bonjorni reported that the VA continued to face a workforce shortage and there were 31,000 candidates in its hiring pipeline. She also said the VA was looking to standardize its human-resources functions across the country.

In October 2022, the agency announced an "all-hands-on-deck" for a "national onboarding surge event" the week of November 14, to get candidates who had already accepted job offers to start work sooner. VA

Undersecretary for Health Shereef Elnahal explained that the Office of Personnel Management granted the VA emergency-hiring authorities at the height of the pandemic that "allowed us to bring on clinicians and then work the rest of the onboarding process on the back end to meet that emergency need." He explained the VA needs to hire about 52,000 people per year just to keep up with attrition and the increasing number of veterans in need of care. Recently passed legislation is expected to give the VA tools to hire faster and more competitively and to improve retention. Elnahal said, "Once the PACT Act is fully implemented, the VA will talk with Congress about areas where we see even more opportunities on expanding our ability to hire better."[17]

Applying lean concepts to the VA hiring process

Lean concept	Application
Lean management aligns authority and responsibility at the lowest possible level.	The VA hiring process should **not** be subject to votes of Congress or emergency orders by the President or the Office of Personnel Management.
Kaizen teams often find that workflow and efficiency can be improved by reordering the sequence of process steps.	The emergency powers allowed the VA to change the sequence of the requirements to reduce onboarding time for new hires.
Standard protocols improve efficiency, minimize errors, reduce rework, and simplify training.	The goal of standardizing the hiring process would improve the system.
Plan-Do-Check-Act/Adjust (PDCA). Decisions to implement changes should be informed by data which may be gathered during a pilot project.	This case is a rare opportunity because the experiment has already taken place and data should be available. Generally, a pilot program takes place after being proposed by a *kaizen* project.
Management sponsors a cross-functional team with process customers to conduct a *kaizen* project.	A VA administrator would sponsor a *kaizen* team composed of people who do the work throughout the hiring and vetting process. The team should also include two customers of the process: a new hire and a veteran who relies on the VA for care, and possibly also a public member as fresh eyes.

The team applies PDCA to check the effectiveness of the proposed changes, consider any unintended negative consequences, and recommend adjustments as appropriate. A lean process would allow for expeditious vetting, minimizing hand-offs and delays while maintaining appropriate quality checks.	Among the questions the team would ask: • During the expedited process, how many new hires did not make it through the final vetting and had to be let go? What were their deficiencies? • Did any substandard care occur because a new hire was not thoroughly vetted? • What is the purpose for each requirement? Are any excessive or irrelevant? • How many veterans wait for care due to short-staffing? What are average wait times by category of service? Have the wait times had a negative health impact on any veterans? • What was the pace of hiring before and after the changes in the process? • Were talented people hired during the more expeditious process who would have taken jobs elsewhere if they had to wait 90 days?
The team designs the optimal process, with an implementation plan and timeline. The administrator who is sponsoring the project works with the team to implement the changes, monitoring and adjusting them as appropriate.	In this case, if the project sponsor lacks the authority to implement the changes, the sponsor will need to make the case to the relevant authority for permission. The team should continue to collect data during this phase.

Applying Lean Thinking to Program Design and Operations

All levels of government needed to adapt during the shutdowns at the height of the COVID-19 pandemic. These adaptations provide a rare juxtaposition of the old and new ways of doing business. Data can be collected on the efficacy of the new processes. Normally risk-averse administrators and legislators may find that their concerns for negative impacts were overblown. Or, if there were some drawbacks to the new way of doing business, adjustments could be made to overcome the problems or to make the process even better.

Arguably, *kaizen* teams are best qualified to evaluate the workflows before and after the emergency procedures and to recommend the optimal approach for providing efficient, high-quality public services without undue risk. Unless this takes place within the context of lean management, authorizing the optimal workflow may still seem like it requires an act of Congress.

The mission-driven purpose of public programs is to serve the common good. In dozens of states, administrators, lean practitioners, and front-line employees collaborate to minimize hand-offs and reduce errors, downtime, and rework.

As improvement initiatives mature into a culture of continuous improvement, they focus on impact. There is an opportunity to view public policy through a lean lens, avoiding the implementation of unlean programs:

■ It is leaner not to set up bureaucratic quagmires in the first place, rather than fixing them later.
■ It is leaner to avoid launching multiple redundant programs than to spend time and effort coordinating them later.

Notes

1 James P. Womack, *Lean Government*, June 26, 2014. www.lean.org/the-lean-post/articles/lean-government/
2 No author, *How Effective Are Pandemic Relief Programs in Housing and Rental Assistance in Reaching Underserved Communities?* www.pandemicoversight.gov/news/events/how-effective-are-pandemic-relief-programs-in-housing-and-rental-assistance-in-reaching-underserved-communities
3 Irina Ivanova, *With Eviction Moratorium Gone, 3.5 Million U.S. Households Could Lose Their Home, Goldman Sachs Estimates*, September 2, 2021. www.cbsnews.com/news/eviction-moratorium-ends-families-risk-losing-homes-analysis/
4 Lesley Stahl, *Military Members Promised Student Debt Relief in Exchange for Ten Years of Public Service Say Promise is Often Broken*, October 3, 2021. www.cbsnews.com/news/student-loan-debt-forgiveness-public-service-60-minutes-2021-10-03/
5 Leo Shane III, *Overdue Veterans Disability Claims Down Almost a Quarter in Last Four Months*, June 21, 2021. www.militarytimes.com/veterans/2022/06/27/overdue-veterans-disability-claims-down-almost-a-quarter-in-last-four-months/

6 D. Parvaz, *Since the Taliban Takeover, Afghans Hoping to Leave Afghanistan Have Few Ways Out*, October 3, 2022. www.npr.org/2022/10/03/1121053865/afghanistan-refugees-visas

7 Barros, Aline, "US to Streamline Application Process for Afghan Special Immigrant Visas." *VOA News.com*, July 18, 2022. www.voanews.com/a/us-to-streamline-application-process-for-afghan-special-immigrant-visas-/6664009.html

8 Patrick Anderson and Katherine Gregg, "RI Legislative Leaders Disagree on Education Funding. Here's What Else is On Their Horizon." *The Providence Journal*, December 21, 2022.

9 Patrick Anderson, and Katherine Gregg, "What are McKee's Priorities for 2023? He'll Start with Tax Cuts." *The Providence Journal*, December 30, 2022.

10 Ian Donnis, "Under Criticism, Saal Resigns as RI's First 'Housing Czar'." *The Public's Radio*, January 11, 2023. https://thepublicsradio.org/article/under-criticism-saal-resigns-as-ris-first-housing-czar

11 Patrick Anderson, "Stefan Pryor picked to lead State Housing Agency." *The Providence Journal*, January 18, 2023.

12 Ken Miller, *Extreme Government Makeover: Increasing our Capacity to Do More Good* (Governing Books, Washington, DC, 2011), p. vii.

13 Brian Elms, *Government's Innovation Surge Shouldn't End with the Pandemic*, April 27, 2020. www.governing.com/next/governments-innovation-surge-shouldnt-end-with-the-pandemic.html

14 Nicole Ogrysko, "VA Says Onboarding Changes Made during the Pandemic Will 'Change the Way We Hire Forever.'" *Federal News Network*, May 19, 2020.

15 Jory Heckman, "VA Seeks Higher Pay Caps for More Health Care Workers to Address High Turnover Rates." *Federal News Network*, March 18, 2022.

16 Jory Heckman, "VA Hired 59,000 Employees This Fiscal Year, But Still Struggles with Workforce Shortages." *Federal News Network*, May 4, 2022.

17 Jory Heckman, "VA Holding 'All Hands On Deck' Event to Onboard Critically Needed Hires More Quickly." *Federal News Network*, October 19, 2022.

Chapter 7

The Goldilocks Standard for Lean Regulation

Lean's origin in manufacturing focused on maximizing value to the customer while eliminating waste in the production processes. Practitioners consider the needs of both internal and external customers. The external customer is the recipient or end user of a product or service. Internal customers are the employees throughout the workflow process. They are customers of those responsible for each preceding step. Discussion of the regulatory function in this chapter focuses on the end-user customer.

Both public and private sector organizations have customers. The buyer is the customer of a manufacturing process. In the public sector, generally the same customer-provider relationship applies. Each of us is a customer when we use public services. There are many reasons to use the services of a government agency that most of us don't think about until we need the service. Customers include people seeking to have a pothole filled on their street, obtain a copy of a public record, borrow a library book, or report an emergency.

The Customer Is Always Right. Or Not

The old adage in business about the customer always being right is not necessarily the case for government. With the dual responsibility for providing services and for enforcing laws and regulations, the government cannot always make customers happy.

DOI: 10.4324/9781003372691-10

There is a dynamic tension in providing good customer service while adhering to regulations. Customers seeking building permits, benefit programs, or driver's licenses may be dissatisfied if they are turned away. There are countervailing pressures to deliver prompt services while assuring compliance.

In addition to providing direct services, the government serves the public at large by enforcing regulations for clean air and water; for safe buildings, bridges, food, and pharmaceuticals; for the judicious use of public funds; and so on. Members of the public rely on regulatory processes for these purposes. We are all stakeholders in the health and safety of our society.

For example, a state environmental agency may issue an administrative order to businesses and individuals to cease activities that are polluting the environment. Improving the efficient dispatch of the order is unlikely to be valued by the person or business receiving that order. However, prompt enforcement of environmental standards benefits the public by keeping our air and water clean and safe. Expeditious action can also deter other potential polluters. It's not about the number of orders issued, it's about the wetlands saved and the aquifers protected.

Assessing the Value of Regulation

An optimal regulatory process accomplishes its intended purpose of public protection with minimal burden on the regulated community (customers). A weak process is laden with unreasonable hurdles and delays commonly known as "red tape." Lean techniques can improve the quality and efficiency of such processes, improving services without sacrificing standards.

Administrators committed to lean management will authorize *kaizen* teams to use PDCA to understand the purpose for the regulations. The project charter should empower the team to recommend reforms that will enhance efficiency, quality, integrity, objectivity, and transparency in the process.

Leaning Permitting Processes

The purpose of a permitting process is to protect the health and safety of the community, not to frustrate the applicants. Responsible developers do not want to be undercut by those using sub-standard materials and shoddy practices, but their level of tolerance for a regulatory process will vary based on the reasonableness of the inspection criteria and the level of inconvenience within the process. The process should allow those who comply with appropriate regulatory standards to receive a timely response.

A *kaizen* project can be used to streamline the process to issue permits expeditiously to qualified customers. The sponsor should be of sufficient rank to be able to authorize the administrative changes recommended by the team. In addition to the staff responsible for the process, the team should include a customer (a permit applicant).

As the project proceeds, the team gathers data for the project, including the most common reasons applicants are rejected or applications are returned for rework. They develop countermeasures such as simplifying forms and allocating staff to assist applicants.

Studying the current-state map of the process, they consider the value of each step. Are some of the regulations archaic or unreasonable? The team may use the "five whys" (a technique to get at the root cause by repeatedly asking "why?") to review the purpose of each of the regulations and recommend revisions if appropriate.

They redesign the process to enhance efficiency, quality, integrity, objectivity, and transparency. Implementation of recommended changes to regulations is dependent on the sponsor's scope of authority. Some changes can be made by an administrator, others require authorization from a governing body. It would be particularly helpful to have the voice of the customer (permit applicant) when the sponsor and team present their recommendations to the governing body.

Leaning Food Inspections

Few of us think about health inspections when we eat at a restaurant. We assume that the food is safe. Restaurant owners and the public can agree that regulation has value. Responsible restaurant owners do not want to be undercut by shoddy operations of competitors, so they appreciate that the regulations help to establish a level playing field. However, their appreciation may wane under a cumbersome regulatory process.

A *kaizen* project team would include staff who work in all sections of the process, as well as a restaurant owner (customer of the process) and a public member (stakeholder in the outcome).

The team would examine the process to understand the purpose of each step and how it serves the public good. Drilling down, they may identify unwarranted impediments such as requirements for notarized documents or redundant reports.

Then, the team would redesign the process to grant prompt approval to qualified applicants while assuring the public is protected. The team may recommend administrative or legislative approval for certain reforms.

As with the permitting process, administrative changes can be made within the sponsor's scope of authority. Again, the customer (restaurant owner) will have an important role when the team and the sponsor present their recommendations to be authorized by the governing body.

Applying the *kaizen* technique to public regulatory processes can find the Goldilocks amount of regulation: not too little, not too much. It can maximize public protection while minimizing red tape. A lean regulatory process can ensure transparent decision-making based on objective criteria.

Goldilocks Regulation for the FDA

Could lean methodology enable the Federal Drug Administration (FDA) to practice Goldilocks regulation? Not too strict, but not too lenient. Not out of touch with emergent conditions, yet uncompromised by political pressure or public opinion. Data driven, without being mired in "paralysis by analysis."

The FDA's mission to protect the public health covers a broad range of responsibilities in addition to the safety of medicines and food supplies. Other regulatory responsibilities are related to medical devices, cosmetics, tobacco, and products that emit radiation.[1] The FDA Commissioner has the authority to grant Emergency Use Authorizations (EUAs) for: "Unapproved medical products or unapproved uses of approved medical products to be used in an emergency to diagnose, treat, or prevent serious or life-threatening diseases or conditions . . . when there are no adequate, approved and available alternatives."[2] The availability of a fast lane for exigent circumstances is crucial when the benefits of a methodical regulatory process are offset by urgent need. No one wants red tape to stand in the way of life-saving medicines or vaccines, nor do we want our loved ones to be harmed by unsafe treatments.

While it is natural to judge actions with the benefit of hindsight, it is important to resist criticizing the outcome of past decisions. Rather, high profile decisions can be used to suggest a standard framework for assessment. CI practitioners would seek to understand the purpose for each of the regulatory standards, as well as the process for approval of tests and treatments.

There has been criticism aplenty in each of the examples below. Consider how lean tools could be applied in each of these circumstances:

Early in the COVID-19 pandemic, the FDA came under criticism for being too restrictive on the approval of diagnostic tests and too lenient with hydroxychloroquine.

- *Too strict about testing for COVID-19?* On January 20, 2020, three weeks after the World Health Organization reported a "cluster of cases of pneumonia of unknown cause" in Wuhan, China, the U.S. had its first confirmed case in Washington State. By early February labs on the west coast were testing to identify cases. At the University of Washington, Dr. Helen Y. Chu was using a flu test that could detect COVID-19; however, the C.D.C. required F.D.A. approval for its use as a screening tool. "But the F.D.A. could not offer the approval because the lab was not certified as a clinical laboratory under regulations established by the Centers for Medicare & Medicaid Services, a process that could take months."[3] Regulations also presented obstacles for the team led by Dr. Benjamin Pinsky at Stanford, which delayed approval of their test until March.[4] On March 1, New York City reported its first case.[5]

- *Too lenient on hydroxychloroquine?* The agency authorized emergency use of hydroxychloroquine on March 28, 2020, "determining that based on the totality of scientific evidence, "it is reasonable to believe that [chloroquine] and [hydroxychloroquine] may be effective in treating COVID-19."[6] Questions arose about apparent political pressure on the agency. Two former FDA scientists expressed concern about the "scant and conflicting supporting evidence." They noted, "When EUA status is sought or granted seemingly under pressure, it may also open a floodgate of efforts to promote unfounded use of other unproven treatments, risking a perception that special interests can influence FDA decisions."[7] "On April 24, the agency issued a drug safety communication warning against the use of these drugs for treatment of COVID-19 outside of the hospital setting or a clinical trial due to risk of heart rhythm problems."[8] The EUA was revoked on June 10, 2020.[9]

The Department of Health and Human Services (HHS) is responsible for the safety of pharmaceuticals. Have industry pressures influenced regulatory policy?

■ *Too strict on importation of drugs from Canada?* Efforts to allow importation of lower- priced Canadian drugs have repeatedly stalled. HHS, the FDA's parent agency, has reiterated[10] safety concerns as a reason to preserve the country's "closed" distribution system.[11] Recent attempts by both the Trump and Biden administrations to override those objections have failed to result in FDA approval of any of the applications by the four states seeking importation permission: Colorado, Florida, New Hampshire, and New Mexico.[12] A lawsuit by the drug industry lobby, the Pharmaceutical Research and Manufacturers of America (PhRMA) may not be the only reason for delays in approval of the states' applications. As Kaiser Health Network reported, HHS Secretary Xavier Becerra said that the Biden administration welcomed applications for drug importation programs from Colorado and other states. But he would not pledge that the FDA would rule on any application in 2023.[13]

■ *Too lenient with OxyContin?* There is evidence connecting the FDA's approval process to the tragic opioid epidemic. Pharmaceutical executive Ed Thompson told *60 Minutes*, "The root cause of this epidemic is the FDA's illegal approval of opioids for the treatment of chronic pain." Thompson explained that OxyContin's initial approval in 1995 was for "short-term" use, but in 2001, FDA expanded the use of OxyContin for just about anyone with chronic ailments. *60 Minutes* reported secret meetings between the FDA and Purdue Pharma, which led to the agency authorizing a change in the label, stating that it could be used, "around the clock . . . for an extended period of time." This change was made without any studies supporting the safety or efficacy of long-term use. Through Freedom of Information Act requests, Dr. Andrew Kolodny learned of the private meetings "where for $35,000 a piece, drug makers paid consultants to, 'sit at a small table with the FDA,' 'hobnobbing with the regulators.'" Among the FDA regulators who went through "the revolving door" to jobs with drug manufacturers were the two who originally approved OxyContin.[14]

Offering a different perspective, Dr. Art Van Zee noted that "[t]he FDA's medical review officer, in evaluating the efficacy of OxyContin in Purdue's

1995 new drug application, concluded that OxyContin had not been shown to have a significant advantage." Arguably, the problem arose later due to the extremely aggressive marketing campaign by Purdue Pharma, which misrepresented the risk of addiction with claims that should have been subject to review. Van Zee explained that the FDA was "limited in its oversight of the marketing and promotion of controlled drugs," concluding that the "public health would be better protected if the FDA reviewed all advertising and promotional materials as well as associated educational materials—for their truthfulness, accuracy, balance, and scientific validity—*before* dissemination."[15]

Does the agency have adequate systems in place for oversight of manufacturing processes?

■ *Too slow to react to a whistleblower concerning baby formula?* In September 2021, a whistleblower notified the FDA of problems at the Abbott Nutrition plant in Michigan, but it was not until February 2022 that the plant was shut down pending safety corrections. An internal review found a "confluence of systemic vulnerabilities."[16] Six of the 15 recommendations mentioned "process." The first finding and recommendation indicate the importance of leaning the processes prior to technology upgrades:

  ■ *Finding*: The FDA maintains multiple systems for the public and other stakeholders to submit product safety and quality complaints, adverse event reports, and product manufacturing concerns across regulated commodity areas. However, the technology that supports some of these systems is outdated, and the lack of coordination between systems makes it difficult for the agency to connect related submissions and rapidly identify emerging safety and quality issues.
  ■ *Recommendation*: The FDA should review its systems and processes for receiving information from external parties, including but not limited to industry, consumers, other federal agencies, and international regulators regarding product safety and quality, adverse events, and manufacturing. The FDA should consider the feasibility, resource requirements, and potential benefits of connecting existing systems or developing a single system to receive, track, and process such information and ensure timely notification of appropriate personnel of potential signals of significant public health threat.[17]

Lean experience in the FDA's Office of Combination Products (OCP). In a case reported in the *Journal of Clinical and Translational Science*, the FDA's Office of Combination Products (OCP) conducted a project to lean the process for product assessment.[18]

The approval process for combination products (those comprised of drug, device, and/or biologic elements) was complex because it required assessment by experts in multiple fields. These products are generally reviewed by the Center for Drug Evaluation and Research (CDER) and the Center for Devices and Radiological Health (CDRH). Both of these Centers had developed lean capacity, including a Lean Management Staff within CDER's Office of Strategic Programs. Taking on the Intercenter Consult Request (ICCR) process as their first cross-agency project, the Lean Management Staff followed the complete PDCA cycle.

The case study summarized the work conducted at each stage of the project. Tools applied included a Strengths/Weaknesses/Opportunities/Threats (SWOT) assessment, process mapping, identification of pain points, root-cause analysis, process redesign, creating and vetting a phased implementation plan, and collecting data on the results. While data were not immediately available for all phases of the product-approval process, the study anticipated that full implementation would "produce efficient, effective review of combination products and offer a model for similar collaboration in medical product development and evaluation . . ., help streamline review, prevent unnecessary delays in product clearance/approval, and make products available to patients sooner."[19]

Discussion

The work by the FDA's in-house lean practitioners to address a process of such complexity bodes well for the continued application of CI tools within a regulatory agency. Below is a summary of the steps in a *kaizen* event to assess a regulatory framework.

- Prepare a charter, identify a lean facilitator, and schedule a *kaizen* event (typically five days).
- Convene a team. As with any lean project, the core team is composed of the staff who do the work in the process (including front-line staff and program/technical staff). Other team members can include practitioners and/or academics (subject-matter experts who can bring a fresh

perspective), customers (those applying for regulatory approval) and members of the public (stakeholders in the outcome).

■ Develop a common understanding of the purpose of the regulations to be leaned.

■ Map the current state of the process, determining the value of each step.

■ Recommend process redesign that would enhance quality, integrity, objectivity, transparency, and efficiency.

■ Prepare, vet, and approve an implementation plan with a timeline.

■ Implement the changes and share the information with the public.

Lean View of Regulation

Deming was not a great fan of regulation, viewing it as a necessary reaction to industry's inability or unwillingness voluntarily to agree to and abide by uniform standards for health and safety.[20] Jim Womack noted, "We in the Lean Community have no standing on whether a government should regulate any activity or provide any service. We can only make the humble suggestion that better decisions can be reached if the debate starts with a clear statement of the actual problem, followed by a structured process to identify and test countermeasures."[21]

A Mission-Based Regulatory Approach. The Environmental Protection Agency's (EPA) "watershed approach" is another example of how a regulatory agency used lean principles to improve the delivery and effectiveness of programs to better serve the agency's mission of protecting human health and the environment. As former Environmental Protection Specialist Patty Scott explained:

> Louise Wise, a manager in EPA's Office of Water, was a big proponent of Total Quality Management (TQM), and in the 1990s, she spearheaded efforts to make the agency and the states adopt a more holistic "watershed approach."
>
> Most water programs operate in very different silos (e.g., stormwater management, wetlands protection, wastewater treatment, estuary and coastal protection, drinking water protection, etc.). Her goal was to make all the offices work in a more coordinated manner. Since there are limited resources, she got the agency and the states to agree to divide the states into watersheds, thereby enabling them to look more broadly at "drainage basins" and focus resources on the most pressing environmental challenges. And rather than looking

simply at chemical water quality, the states were encouraged to use other measurements to assess the overall health of a waterbody, including biological assessments (e.g., macroinvertebrates are better indicators of water quality than chemical tests).

One major emphasis was to assess waters on a rotating basis and then address top impairments within each watershed. Looking at the health of a "watershed" as a whole rather than focusing on, for example, individual facility permits was a huge paradigm shift in the way water protection programs were being implemented.

This was a huge and complex undertaking, but Louise made major inroads. She facilitated frequent and regular meetings with the top managers in all the different water offices. She even succeeded in bringing other media officials like the Office of Air and Radiation to the table. The level of buy-in was incredible.

The managers agreed on a common set of measurable goals and objectives. These changes also had to happen at the state level since the states are the ones that implement many of the on-the-ground programs. EPA developed guidance documents, tools, and other resources to help the states progress towards using a much leaner watershed approach.

As this example demonstrates, the EPA's efforts to lean its operations predated the term lean, and they have continued across administrations. The EPA's *Lean in Government Starter Kit*[22] and other resources were made widely available to state environmental departments, and lean initiatives were encouraged. Discussion of the importance of leaning intergovernmental efforts will continue in Chapter 14.

Notes

1 U.S. Food & Drug Administration (FDA), "FDA Mission." *Webpage Content Current as of March 28*, 2018. www.fda.gov/about-fda/what-we-do#mission

2 U.S. Food & Drug Administration (FDA), "Emergency Use Authorization." *Webpage Content Current as of January 13*, 2023. www.fda.gov/emergency-preparedness-and-response/mcm-legal-regulatory-and-policy-framework/emergency-use-authorization

3 Sheri Fink and Mike Baker, 'It's Just Everywhere Already': How Delays in Testing Set Back the U.S. Coronavirus Response." *New York Times*, March 10, 2020 (updated March 16, 2021).

4 Michael D. Shear, Abby Goodnough, Sheila Kaplan, Sheri Fink, Katie Thomas, and Noah Weiland, "The Lost Month: How a Failure to Test Blinded the U.S. to Covid-19." *The New York Times*, March 28, 2020 (updated October 1, 2021).

5 Taro Kariya, "Rapid Spread of COVID-19 in New York and the Response of the Community." *NIH. National Library of Medicine*, April 30, 2020.

6 Agata Dabrowska and Victoria R. Green, "Treatment of COVID-19: Hydroxychloroquine and Chloroquine." *Congressional Research Service*, May 27, 2020.

7 Jesse L. Goodman and Luciana Borio, "Finding Effective Treatments for COVID-19: Scientific Integrity and Public Confidence in a Time of Crisis." *Journal of the American Medical Association (JAMA) Network*, JAMA 323(19) (2020): 1899–1900. DOI: 10.1001/jama.2020.6434 0

8 Agata Dabrowska and Victoria R. Green, "Treatment of COVID-19: Hydroxychloroquine and Chloroquine." *Congressional Research Service*, May 27, 2020.

9 U.S. Food & Drug Administration, "Coronavirus (COVID-19) Update: FDA Revokes Emergency Use Authorization for Chloroquine and Hydroxychloroquine." *Press Release*, June 10, 2020. www.fda.gov/news-events/press-announcements/coronavirus-covid-19-update-fda-revokes-emergency-use-authorization-chloroquine-and

10 Meredith Freed, Tricia Neuman, and Juliette Cubanski, "10 FAQs on Prescription Drug Importation." *Kaiser Family Foundation*, July 28, 2021. www.kff.org/medicare/issue-brief/10-faqs-on-prescription-drug-importation/

11 U.S. Department of Health and Human Services, *HHS Task Force on Drug Importation*, December, 2004. www.safemedicines.org/wp-content/uploads/2018/03/HHS-Report1220.pdf

12 Phil Galewitz, "States Challenge Biden to Lower Drug Prices by Allowing Imports From Canada." *Kaiser Health Network*, December 14, 2022. https://khn.org/news/article/states-challenge-biden-to-lower-drug-prices-by-allowing-imports-from-canada/

13 Meredith Freed, Tricia Neuman, and Juliette Cubanski, "10 FAQs on Prescription Drug Importation." *Kaiser Family Foundation*, July 28, 2021. www.kff.org/medicare/issue-brief/10-faqs-on-prescription-drug-importation/

14 Bill Whittaker, "Did the FDA Ignite the Opioid Epidemic? 60 Minutes." *CBS News*, February 24, 2019. www.cbsnews.com/news/opioid-epidemic-did-the-fda-ignite-the-crisis-60-minutes/

15 Art Van Zee, "The Promotion and Marketing of OxyContin: Commercial Triumph, Public Health Tragedy." *The American Journal of Public Health* 99(2) (2009): 221–227. DOI: 10.2105/AJPH.2007.131714

16 Courtney Bublé, "The FDA's Internal Review of the Infant Formula Shortage Found Workforce Problems." *Government Executive*, September 21, 2022.

17 Steven M. Solomon, "FDA Evaluation of Infant Formula Response." *U.S. Food & Drug Administration*, September, 2022, p. 5. www.fda.gov/media/161689/download

18 M.J. Rappel, N.L. Hunter, A.I. Alexandrow, K.O. Hair, R.E. Sherman, and R.M. Califf, "Case Study for Lean Management in the Public Sector: Improving Combination Product Review at the Food & Drug Administration." *The Journal of Clinical and Translational Science* 10(3) (2017). DOI: 10.1111/cts.12441

19 M.J. Rappel, N.L. Hunter, A.I. Alexandrow, K.O. Hair, R.E. Sherman, and R.M. Califf, "Case Study for Lean Management in the Public Sector: Improving Combination Product Review at the Food & Drug Administration." *The Journal of Clinical and Translational Science* 10(3) (2017). DOI: 10.1111/cts.12441

20 W. Edwards Deming, *Out of the Crisis* (MIT Center for Advanced Educational Services, Cambridge, MA, 1982–1986), Chapter 10.

21 James (Jim) Womack, PhD, *Lean Government.* www.lean.org/the-lean-post/articles/lean-government/

22 Environmental Protection Agency, *The Lean in Government Starter Kit Version 4.0.* www.epa.gov/sites/default/files/2017-11/documents/lean-starter-kit-version-4.pdf

Chapter 8

Moving to Results-Based State Government

The journey from the reaction-driven to the results-driven level of maturity is not a straight line. Some jurisdictions are further ahead than others. Throwing out the old playbook and adopting lean management is not an easy path. Even if the state's governor understands and embraces the principles, the legislature might refuse to appropriate necessary resources. Many states struggle to meet basic obligations. Employees, supervisors, and managers alike try to keep up with the firefighting. Yet lean activists see signs of hope. While no model is perfect, there is much to be learned from those who have made demonstrable progress.

Mission Matters

The theory of administrative conservatorship, as discussed in Chapter 5, is a reminder of the human variable in public sector work. Dedicated professionals can stand up for their beliefs despite pressures to do otherwise. Those who understand the potential public good to be achieved by lean management are applying it within their own spheres of authority.

In states where the governor is not leading the effort, administrators with separate lines of authority may be able to nurture CI in their own agencies. Although silos remain one of the primary obstacles to lean government, they may provide an opportunity for progressive administrators with the autonomy to lean processes within their agencies.

DOI: 10.4324/9781003372691-11

While not an optimal approach, it is possible that an agency commissioner could start a CI program and reach colleagues laterally. As lean practitioners in that agency gain experience, management could authorize them to train their peers in other agencies. A movement of enthusiastic change agents reaching across the silos, supported by like-minded administrators, might get the governor on board. As Larry Terry noted, "it is time to put leadership back into the administration of public bureaucracies."[1]

The "Night Shift" Persists in New Hampshire

In *A Public Sector Journey to Lean*, readers were introduced to an intrepid band of lean activists in New Hampshire. A high point for the group was when Jim Womack, co-author of *The Machine that Changed the World* and founder of the Lean Enterprise Institute, was the keynote speaker at their 2013 Lean Summit. The initiative was still in the project stage of development when Womack challenged the rookie practitioners to shift their focus from mapping to management. Techniques can improve workflow, but organizational transformation, a much larger task, is the real point, he explained.

When the small group of early adopters had a beer with Jim, he observed, "you're the night shift." It was an aha moment for the aspiring practitioners. They were the night shift because their primary duties (their "day jobs") were not as lean practitioners or coordinators. Regardless of the group's enthusiasm for process improvement, their capacity fluctuated with the demands of regular duties. Yet they bonded together as a community of practice and formed the Lean Executive Committee (LEC), including representatives from each agency with an active lean initiative.

The night-shift impediment played out over the next few years. With rare exceptions, CI was not referenced in state job descriptions. When people left their positions, the "day job" was posted, with the duties of the replacements unrelated to CI. Likewise, when agency administrators who were championing the effort left state government, with them went the potential for broad organizational transformation. As Lean trainer Michael Moranti explained, a sustainable program can't be personality-dependent. It should be able to survive the departure of any individual.

One of the countermeasures to attrition was mentorship, as then-LEC co-chair Heather Barto and others helped to connect trainees with experienced practitioners. Soon, others joined the first wave of early adopters in building a Lean Network. With only a few gaps, LEC continued to convene, with Michael Moranti still teaching Black Belt classes and previous graduates serving as mentors.

Commitment and Resilience at NHDES

While most agencies in New Hampshire either have no participation in lean activities or are reliant on "night shift" practitioners, the Department of Environmental Services (NHDES) has sustained its commitment to CI.

The program, initiated in 2008 by former Commissioner Tom Burack, has continued despite turnover of staff and leadership. Dan Hrobak continued to move the effort forward after taking over from NHDES's first Lean coordinator, Bob Minicucci. Before leaving the agency in 2019, Hrobak had facilitated projects, spread lean culture through "Lunch and Leans," organized a Lean Week with a 5S contest, and collaborated to create an online White Belt program available to all state employees.

The agency renewed its commitment to Lean with the appointment of Linda Magoon as Lean Coordinator and QA Administrator in July 2021. Although staff attrition had taken its toll, Magoon reinvigorated the NHDES Lean Team and continued the 5S contest, adding creative messaging such as "Less Waste Wednesday."

In January 2022, the NHDES senior leadership team officially renewed their commitment by signing an updated charter, which serves as a blanket authorization to charter and conduct Lean events. It affirms the Lean team's mission "to promote and implement continuous process improvement

 Don't Forget to Enter the "5S This Mess" contest!

The Rules:
1. Pick *anything* to 5S – a desk, a drawer, your computer files
2. Take "before" photos
3. 5S the mess
4. Take "after" photos and email to: Linda Magoon, Lean Coordinator
5. Contest Deadline: March 25, 2022
6. Bonus: Mention "Commissioner's Update" in your email and be entered to win a "sweet" prize!

"5S this Mess Contest" at NHDES.

NHDES Lean coordinator Linda Magoon facilitating the WRBP project.

to maximize the department's efficiency and effectiveness to advance the agency's mission to protect, restore, and improve the environment and public health." NHDES Commissioner Robert Scott has been clear in his support, reminding all staff of the requirement to take the White Belt training in their first 90 days on the job.

In addition to a project streamlining the onboarding process for the Winnipesaukee River Basin Program (WRBP), Magoon organizes improvement efforts across divisions within the agency. However, she stresses that it's not all about projects. Her goal is to take Lean beyond the multi-day *kaizen* events with sticky notes on brown paper. She explains, "organizationally, we are in the 'renewal' stage, with the goal of educating folks of various Lean tools, such as 5s, visual management, A-3, that they can use every day both at home and at work, without the angst of brown paper." Toward that end, Magoon is revamping the agency's Lean website, is enrolled in BET's Black Belt program, and serves as co-chair of the statewide Lean Executive Committee. As word spreads throughout the agency that Lean is back, the demand to conduct Lean events is increasing.

NHDES conducts an annual awards ceremony each December. One of the categories eligible for an award is the "Continuous Process Improvement" award. Staff submit nominations and the winner is chosen by senior leadership. The award keeps innovation and improved efficiency in the forefront and recognizes the importance of continuous process improvement.

An Enduring Community of Practice

The New Hampshire case is an encouraging one, where practitioners have kept going despite changes in top leadership. The LEC met online to maintain their community of practice during the pandemic shutdowns. Several of the LEC members credited lean principles for work adaptations within their agencies.

The Department of Revenue (DRA) benefited from previous lean work, explained Black Belt Diane Dawson, whose team won the Governor's award for best project in 2013. The early success prepared the DRA staff to work collaboratively with a vendor to implement technological advances that improved customer service and enabled remote work. Dawson reported, "I would say that we have become more of a lean culture overall. Our staff has been applying lean principles in their daily work without even realizing it or calling it a 'lean event.'"

Although just a couple of agencies officially recognize the role of a Lean coordinator, those coordinators, like Magoon, collaborate with "night shift" practitioners in a handful of other agencies. Each doing what they can whenever the opportunities arise, they have formed a bond of mutual support as change agents. And, while continuing to advocate for a coordinated statewide initiative, they keep using Lean in their daily work. As Black Belt instructor Michael Moranti observed, "We're doing Lean because we like it. No one asked us to do it. That doesn't happen in private industry."

LEC Chair and Lean Black Belt Joe McCue's day-job is as Wellness Coordinator for the Department of Transportation (NHDOT), and he also serves as the agency's Lean coordinator. In the spirit of continuous improvement, McCue has developed innovative approaches both within NHDOT and for LEC.

He models the use of CI tools and has created a series of 30-minute presentations introducing colleagues to Lean, 5S, PDSA, root-cause analysis, and standard work. He has also been offering an in-person White Belt training to augment the online overview. As Magoon noted, "Under Joe's leadership, the LEC continues to be the grassroots, no-budget mechanism to keep Lean/CPI on a statewide level afloat."

With LEC co-chair Linda Magoon, McCue has organized online networking sessions with guest speakers, including Vermont's Chief Performance

Joe McCue, Chair of the Lean Executive Committee and Lean coordinator for NHDOT.

Officer, Justin Kenney. The network sessions resumed in person in 2023.

LEC member and Black Belt Candice Weingartner, working with Magoon, has revamped the Lean New Hampshire website and manages the newly created Lean New Hampshire LinkedIn page. She also continues to be active in lean initiatives in the Department of Information Technology (DoIT).

There is optimism in New Hampshire's CI community. In January 2023, Black Belt instructor Moranti was appointed to the position of Deputy Bank Commissioner, and he is not the only CI practitioner in a similar rank. Black Belt Paul Raymond, who once led a *kaizen* project to improve access to the nutrition program for Women, Infants, and Children (WIC), is now Assistant Commissioner of the Department of Corrections. Other Green and Black Belt practitioners have been promoted into management positions throughout state government.

Deputy Commissioner Moranti explained how lean practice has adapted. He has been using *obeya*, a TPS project-management tool using timely communication and visual management. The *obeya* room depicts milestones and progress to date, as well as countermeasures to ensure project success

Black Belt Candice Weingartner.

and shorten the PDCA cycle.[2] Moranti explained that the shorter cycles are important to demonstrate progress in the age of short attention spans, but at the same time, the long view is essential. You must make sure you're meeting customer needs and accomplishing the mission. "Be patient in execution. Quick cycles and long looks," he advised.

Profiles of Robust State CI Programs

Colorado, Vermont, and Washington are among the states with executive leadership support and legislation on the books calling for results-based government. Colorado's SMART Act and Vermont's Outcomes Bill are examples of how states are striving for Level Two maturity in governmental administration. The following sections detail the legislative and executive actions committing the states to implement best practices in improving processes, setting goals, and monitoring results.

Colorado

Colorado's SMART Act (State Measurement for Accountable, Responsive, and Transparent Government Act) was signed by former Governor John Hickenlooper in 2013 and continued under Governor Jared Polis. The Act called for the use of continuous process improvement to increase government efficiency and for all employees to receive training on operational excellence.[3] It required state government departments to publish annual performance goals and progress reports.[4] Excerpt:

A "continuous improvement system" includes measuring the outcomes of such improvements and may involve some or all of the following strategies:

(a) The development of a process map that describes the procedures by which a department produces goods or serves its customers;

(b) Specific activities to rapidly improve a department's processes that will increase value or decrease staff time, inventory, defects, overproduction, complexity, delays, or excessive movement;

(c) The involvement of department employees at all levels in mapping a department's processes and in making recommendations for improvements, with specific importance placed on the involvement of department employees closest to the customer or end user of the state government product or service;

(d) Providing the means to measure each process in order to demonstrate the effectiveness of each process or process improvement; and

(e) The training of department employees for purposes of mentoring and training other department employees in continuous process improvement methodologies.

The Colorado Department of Transportation (CDOT) is at the forefront of the SMART government concept. CDOT's Office of Process Improvement (OPI) has a robust program structured to engage all employees on improvement projects.

Going into its second decade, OPI has created a self-reinforcing system to support a culture of continuous improvement. As Director Gary Vansuch explains, "It is our responsibility as public servants to be good stewards of taxpayer dollars." The initiative has received national recognition, including designation as a "Bright Idea in Government" from the Innovations

OPI Director Gary Vansuch.

in American Government Awards program, by the Kennedy School of Government.[5]

OPI's methodology overcomes a problem common to many fledging lean programs: enthusiastic *kaizen* teams create ideal future-state maps but are subsequently disappointed by a failure to implement. In a typical scenario, the rookie practitioners assume their process redesigns will go into effect because they were so clearly warranted. The critical project management phase is overlooked. OPI's system addresses that problem and more.

CDOT's Innovation, Improvement, and Engagement Hub

CDOT's Office of Process Improvement (OPI) "works to engage everyone, every day at CDOT in improving safety, products, and services so that we are more effective, efficient, and elegant and to ensure that everyone impacted by change is successful with that change.[6]"

The Hub is a dynamic system of intake, assessment, assignment, and follow-through. The self-reinforcing structure enables a perpetual culture of continuous improvement. Improvements are achieved and documented.

Intake is constantly open, with ideas for small and large changes differentiated by category and scope:

■ The Lean Everyday Idea (LEI) Program encourages ideas for small front-line changes. Improvement idea cards that outline the challenge, innovation, parts needed, and benefit derived are shared, to be replicated as appropriate.
■ The Concept to Project (C2P) Program works to ensure that larger business improvements are successful.
■ The Strategy Service works to design and execute strategic plans that drive CDOT's performance.

Among the ways CDOT reinforces the culture of continuous improvement is with the Innovations Challenge. Employees are invited to submit an "I fixed it" form to be considered for prizes. Criteria for winning include originality, transferability, conservation of resources (time or money), and organizational impact.

CDOT invests in its staff as CI practitioners with ongoing training, mentoring, and networking opportunities. College interns are an integral part of OPI, each contributing to the continuous improvement of the Hub system itself. The Hub also provides a compendium of resources including self-service guides to a range of CI tools and a comprehensive glossary of terms.

Vermont

Several statutory and executive initiatives contributed to the development of continuous improvement in Vermont. In 2014, the Vermont State legislature passed *Act 186* (known as the "Outcomes Bill") in part to collect information on how well the state was doing in achieving desired population-level outcomes for Vermonters, but also in order to determine how to best invest taxpayer dollars. The population-level outcomes (e.g., Vermont has a prosperous economy, Vermonters are healthy, etc.) and indicators (e.g., unemployment rate, percentage of adults who smoke cigarettes) in Act 186 were developed using results-based accountability (RBA), which uses ends-to-means thinking to improve the quality of life for communities and/or the performance of programs. The Outcomes Bill built upon decades of work in this area by the Vermont Agency of Human Services and was a major step towards increased performance accountability and continuous improvement.

Three components of Act 186 pertain to the Chief Performance Office (CPO) in the Vermont Agency of Administration.

1. *3 V.S.A. § 2311.* Annually, the Chief Performance Officer shall submit to the General Assembly the *Annual Outcomes Report* demonstrating the State's progress in reaching the desired population-level outcomes.
2. *3 V.S.A. § 2312.* The Chief Performance Officer shall designate an employee in each agency of State government to be a Performance Accountability Liaison (PAL) to the General Assembly. The liaison is responsible for reviewing with the legislature any population-level outcomes and indicators to which that agency contributes.
3. *3 V.S.A. § 2313.* CPO shall assist agencies, as necessary, in developing performance measures for contracts and grants.

The CPO, in collaboration with the Department of Finance and Management, has also been tasked with developing the annual Programmatic and Performance Measure Budget (PPMB) Report. This report fulfils the requirements in *32 V.S.A. § 307(c)(2)* to report on the programmatic performance measures used to demonstrate the outputs and results of the Governor's budget. Programmatic performance measures are reported using the results-based accountability framework: How much service was provided? How well was service provided? Is anyone better off as a result of our service?

On January 5, 2017, Governor Phil Scott established the Program to Improve Vermont Outcomes Together (PIVOT), as part of his Government Modernization and Efficiency plan, to provide "efficient and effective services and programs that produce results now and into the future."[7] PIVOT combines results-based accountability and Lean process improvement into a unified effort to achieve the Governor's four strategic goals: to grow the economy, protect the most vulnerable, make Vermont more affordable, and modernize state government.

In response to PIVOT, the role of the CPO expanded beyond statutory requirements to the point where now the CPO provides a variety of services to State of Vermont employees, supervisors, managers, and leaders, including:

- Staff development and support
- Process improvement and automation
- Meeting design and facilitation
- Project support and consultation
- Organizational assessment and strategic planning

- Research, data analysis, and reporting
- Office 365 and Power Platform consultation

As Justin Kenney, Chief Performance Officer for the State of Vermont, explains, "Over the years, our approach to continuous improvement at an enterprise scale has changed drastically. We started by offering classroom training for employees and undertaking large projects. After a time, we realized that we weren't quite getting the results we wanted so we shifted tactics. Classroom training for us is now just one of many tools in our tool-box for increasing levels of knowledge, skill, and capability at the employee level, and more often than not the projects we are doing now are smaller in nature and have a higher likelihood of success."

The state is building capacity for operational excellence in accordance with Deming's Points #13 and #14 instructing organizations to "[i]nstitute a vigorous program of education and self-improvement" and "[p]ut everybody in the company to work to accomplish the transformation. The transformation is everybody's job." Therefore, the initiative must assure equal access to training for employees working in all sections of the organization.

Unlike in New Hampshire, where access is limited because agencies are charged a fee to send employees to training, Vermont has a comprehensive

Vermont's Chief Performance Officer, Justin Kenney.

continuous improvement training program. This training program includes skills in scientific thinking, structured problem-solving, performance measurement, change management, facilitation, data analysis, software usages, operational management, and strategic planning.

The Chief Performance Office also provides coaching and mentoring for a professional learning community, including one-on-one consultation. This includes coaching the Advanced Practitioner Network (equivalent to Green Belts in other organizations) and providing peer-to-peer professional development with regular practice in the use of CI tools. Unless eroded by attrition, these Advanced Practitioners are expected to play transformative roles in spreading a culture of continuous improvement. Talent retention is essential, and Vermont's continuous improvement program intends to maximize opportunities for personal and professional growth.

"Training is essential for introducing people to continuous improvement principles and tools, but we see the greatest growth and development when people work directly with our office on a problem relevant to them," says Katie Bockwoldt, Performance Improvement Advisor in the Chief Performance Office. "People often need additional guidance, support, and coaching before they are confident applying continuous improvement tools and concepts on their own. We hope to grow the number of direct assistance and coaching efforts outside classroom trainings in the future."

Performance Improvement Advisor Katie Bockwoldt.

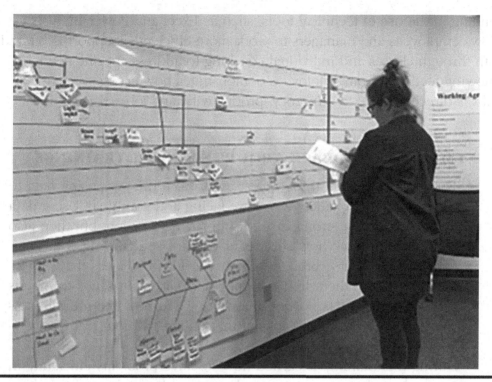

A trainee adds data to a current state process map.

Vermont's Continuous Improvement Training Program

The State of Vermont offers a variety of training opportunities for staff who are interested in learning more about continuous improvement and advancing themselves as professionals in the government sector. The trainings were developed based on the Dreyfus Model of Skill Acquisition and are meant to provide a clear pathway for an individual to grow from a novice to an expert over time. Part of that growth includes in-class training; on-the-job application; long-term coaching, mentoring and support; and opportunities for peer-to-peer learning. As individuals progress through the training series, they gain the ability to:

■ Explain and put into practice basic concepts of continuous improvement;
■ Utilize a variety of tools to identify, understand, analyze, and address problems;
■ Effectively facilitate meetings, events, contentious situations, and teams;
■ Collect, transform, analyze, and visualize data; and
■ Serve as change agents throughout state government.

Training in the use of technical tools, such as Excel and Power BI, also allows employees and managers to work more efficiently. Support is offered both through classes and individual coaching to address specific needs. The following feedback from employees demonstrates how access to technical skills is directly linked to efficiency, productivity, and job satisfaction.

EMPLOYEE FEEDBACK ABOUT TECHNICAL TRAININGS

- The most important thing I took away from this was using data to inform both the challenge you are facing and your goal. Using data not only makes a strong case for improving a system but then also being able to track how successful you are at achieving your goal.
- I felt like the course brought together a bunch of ideas that I knew existed and put them into a framework that made sense to me (as versus random tools floating in space). I see now the great importance of not just saying "let's put that online" without really reviewing the whole process first.
- During this training, I learned how to solve problems efficiently in my work environment. Another thing that I learned is to know how to identify a gap before establishing smart goals to fill out the gap.
- The advanced Excel skills are directly in line with the Governor's efficiency goals. The use of advanced formulas in table format combined with Power Query capabilities in Excel means that data . . . can now be simply added to a single table and updated. In the past, multiple spreadsheets had to be created each month, data cleared from the prior month, manual adjustments made, formulas updated etc. Now, data is simply added and updated. This saves a significant amount of time on routine administrative tasks and allows team members to focus their time working on substantive issues.
- I have improved how I develop Excel workbooks, which [is] a direct result of taking continuous improvement classes. Not only do they show expert use of tools, but they also present smart ways of thinking about problems and finding intelligent solutions.
- [D]aily we are asked to pull data from several areas and systems that do not speak to each other. . . . [T]hese critical trainings . . . improved the integrity of my data and my work in general. . . . [E]ven just learning how to advance my pivots has made a 3-hour task take half that time.

- [I]t is now standardized, and I will be able to pull reports from it. This allows me to track patterns and trends . . . to inform policymakers and the public as well.
- We had been downloading a spreadsheet at the end of each month, analyzing that month, and putting it away. . . . [U]sing Power Query, we were able to link the files in this folder and analyze data for longer time periods and ask more complex questions, which helped our team make more informed decisions!
- Understanding this capability and training more people who can see the big picture, will allow us as a state to manage and evaluate data quickly so that our decisions and work products are much more efficient and effective. This means we hire fewer consultants to do reviews and create reports containing recommendations that we don't use. We can do most of this evaluation of data ourselves, which allows us to make much quicker and much better decisions that we actually own, since we are close to the data. . . . We can plan, based on data, act on it and then check in real time to see if it is working, and adjust the plan.

Washington

The Results Washington initiative remains one of the leaders in state Lean programs. Established by Governor Jay Inslee in 2013 through Executive Order 13–04, it built on the previous Governor Christine Gregoire's Government Management Accountability and Performance (GMAP) program. Results Washington continues the state's commitment to public-sector performance. Its methods were documented in *Government That Works*[8] and in a case study published by the Kennedy School of Government. The study called Results Washington "An Operational Excellence Government Success Story," identifying two components: "performance management and employee-driven process improvement."[9]

Now in its second decade, the non-dogmatic, solutions-orientated approach is still at the core, with Lean Liaisons at each state agency. The work continues to be driven by Governor Inslee's strategic goals: (1) World-Class Education; (2) Prosperous Economy; (3) Sustainable Energy and a Clean Environment; (4) Healthy and Safe Communities; and (5) Effective, Efficient, and Accountable Government.[10]

Results Washington Director, Mandeep Kaundal.

Director Mandeep Kaundal explained the approach:

> Results Washington partners with state agencies to embed Lean
> practices and continuous improvement methodologies/tools to
> increase their efficiency and effectiveness to the public. Some
> of the successes we are experiencing in our state are Results
> Washington's cross-agency projects, which bring agency staff and
> diverse communities and voices to the table to better serve our
> customers. They utilize disaggregated data and ensure that margin-
> alized communities are represented and help to design the out-
> comes. Governor Inslee's Public Performance Reviews bring data
> disaggregation and leverage customers' voices to remedy barriers
> and inequities in state services. Results Washington's Annual Lean
> Conference provides state employees with Lean and continuous
> improvement methodologies/tools to improve processes for their
> customers.

Highlights of Lean Principles

Colorado's Innovation Hub reflects the lean principle linking *kaizen* and standard work. "Kaizen, an expression of the scientific method, requires a baseline of comparison," explained LEI's John Shook:

Standardized work and kaizen are two sides of the same coin—if you try to have one without the other, you will encounter one of two types of serious problems:

- Standardized work without kaizen: Employee motivation is killed, human creativity wasted, problems repeat, unidentified, unsolved, and unabated, employees don't take the initiative, so improvement stops.
- Kaizen without standardized work: Chaotic change, the saw-tooth effect of progress and regress, problems repeat, PDCA not followed, no root cause analysis, progress that is impossible to identify, improvement stops.[11]

CDOT's Hub is both functional and informative—far and away the best to be found. It encourages ideas for improvements, small and large. Yet that is one agency within one state. Among state agency silos, lean programs are most likely to be found in transportation and environmental departments, due to the availability of federal funding and encouragement from their counterparts at the federal level. The Environmental Protection Agency (EPA) was an early leader in promoting lean programs, including tool kits.[12] Among the states without comprehensive lean initiatives, important work continues within these agencies. And CI practitioners within comparable state programs have connected to share best practices and provide support.

Colorado's Vansuch has been a leader in convening communities of practice for those working in transportation departments in other states, and for those in statewide CI programs. It makes sense for CI practitioners to collaborate, because each state has similar responsibilities for managing grants, hiring, and permitting. Vansuch recalled the moment when he realized that teams in Colorado, Maine, and Tennessee were all at different stages of improving their processes for driveway access permits.

Vansuch has set up a network for staff in CI initiatives, which has created many enduring connections. He also helped set up a national network for those in statewide programs, enabling experienced practitioners to collaborate and refer one another for promotional opportunities in other states' programs. There have been setbacks for the network, however, as several robust state programs were discontinued due to a transition of gubernatorial administrations. This and other challenges facing statewide programs will be discussed in upcoming chapters.

Notes

1 Larry D. Terry, *Leadership of Public Bureaucracies: The Administrator as Conservator* (M.E. Sharpe, New York, NY 2003), p. 169.
2 Lean Enterprise Institute, "Obeya." *Lean Lexicon*. www.lean.org/lexicon-terms/obeya/
3 State of Colorado, SMART Act. HB 13–1299. https://operations.colorado.gov/performance-management
4 State of Colorado, *Performance Management*. https://operations/colorado.gov/peformance-management
5 State of Colorado, *Colorado Department of Transportation. Innovation, Improvement & Engagement Hub*. https://sites.google.com/state.co.us/process-improvement/about-opi/contact-us
6 State of Colorado, *Colorado Department of Transportation. Innovation, Improvement & Engagement Hub*. https://sites.google.com/state.co.us/process-improvement/home
7 Governor Phil Scott, *Executive Order 04–17. Program to Improve Vermont Outcomes Together (PIVOT)*. https://governor.vermont.gov/sites/scott/files/documents/eo4pivot%20eo%20final.pdf
8 John M. Bernard, *Government That Works: The Results Revolution in the States* (Results America, Thompson-Shore, Dexter, MI, 2015).
9 Jane Wiseman, "Case Study: Performance Management and Lean Process Improvement—Results Washington, An Operational Excellence Government Success Story." *Harvard Kennedy School*, July, 2017.
10 State of Washington, *Results Washington*. https://results.wa.gov/
11 Lean Enterprise Institute, "How Standardized Work Integrates People with Process." *eBook*, p. 8. https://info.lean.org/en-us/how-standardized-work-integrates-people-with-process
12 Environmental Protection Agency, *Lean and Environment Tool Kit*. www.epa.gov/sustainability/lean-environment-toolkit

Chapter 9

A Model for CI in State Government

Sustainability in State CI Programs

A cursory search of state government websites in early 2023 found roughly 20 states with some form of CI program. Appearance, though, is certainly not determinative of their activity level or effectiveness. Some, like Vermont's, are extremely active without an extensive presence on the public website. Others with a prominent web display have been inactive in recent years.

Regardless of the current level of activity, there is an indication that lean was attempted in nearly half the states in the country. How does it continue in some states and in some agency silos within those states, and not others? What kept it going and what caused it to fade? Consider a preliminary SWOT analysis.

SWOT Lean sustainability in state government

Strengths	Weaknesses	Opportunities	Threats
It works.	Once started, it often withers away.	It can benefit each agency and across all agencies.	Lean practitioners leave their jobs.
It improves services.	It requires continuous learning.	It benefits from continuous learning.	Lean champions leave their positions.

DOI: 10.4324/9781003372691-12

Strengths	Weaknesses	Opportunities	Threats
It boosts morale.	It requires a commitment by elected officials and administrators.	It frees capacity that can be redeployed.	A change in the governorship can discontinue the lean program.
It frees employees' time to conduct higher value tasks.	It requires managerial work to reallocate staff to higher value tasks.	It enhances capacity for mission.	It can be misunderstood as a cost-cutting measure.

A Success Story in Arizona

The Arizona Management System (AMS) has survived a transition in the governorship. While other state lean programs have disappeared with the onset of a new administration, Results Arizona's Government Transformation Office will go on. The Arizona Management System (AMS), initiated by then-Governor Doug Ducey, is being continued by his successor, Governor Katie Hobbs. The results-driven approach is based on the principles of lean management. "AMS is more than a collection of tools and practices; it is also a culture of high performance with a respect for people."[1] The improvement projects focus on priority areas, measuring performance, setting targets, and acting to close gaps. Among the gains reported on the Results.AZ website:[2]

- Community Development and Revitalization staff reduced the review time for Community Development Block Grant (CDBG) applications from 90 days to 30 days by condensing the application, eliminating redundant questions, and enhancing the format to do automatic calculations. This facilitates rural Arizona governments applying for approximately $10 million in federal grants for a wide range of infrastructure, community, and housing needs.
- The Arizona State Approving Agency was not meeting the turnaround goal time for the disposition of applications for educational institutions that can accept GI Bill funds. The staff simplified the application, trained staff to balance the workload, and introduced in-process controls to reduce inspection time. The disposition time was reduced from 14 days to seven days, resulting in more approved applications for schools and training facilities, and enabling more veterans to access education and workforce training.

Essential Components for Results-Driven Government

These threats can be overcome by having unwavering support from the governor, setting clear expectations for agency heads, and creating a unit housed within the office of administration. Such units are headed by a Chief Performance Officer (CPO), like Justin Kenny of Vermont, or a Chief Operating Officer (COO) or Chief Innovation Officer. The titles vary somewhat. In a leaner world, there would be consistency of terminology and structure among states, but the good news is that sustainable programs exist in several states. Potentially replicable innovation is happening—particularly in Nebraska and Ohio.

Ohio

The Office of LeanOhio is within the Department of Administrative Services.[3] It uses Lean and Six Sigma to cut red tape, remove inefficiencies, improve customer service, and achieve measurable results.

Training is conducted by LeanOhio staff and has generated 70 embedded Black Belts, 240 Green Belts, and over 600 Camo Belts. These practitioners are within a network of more than 1,000 state employees who promote Lean, improve processes, and partner with the state to teach Lean tools and strategies.

The network includes Lean Liaisons to each state agency. These liaisons coordinate the initiative throughout state government and within their agencies. This includes identifying improvement opportunities, engaging agency staff in those efforts, and ensuring that changes are implemented and sustained.

From 2011 to 2021, more than 400 projects were facilitated by LeanOhio staff and Lean-trained state employees, within 45 different state agencies, boards, commissions, and elected officials' offices. The improvements will lead to more efficient work and better customer service:

- 64% average reduction in the number of process steps, with more than 13,000 process steps eliminated.
- 55% reduction in handoffs for projects.
- 68% average reduction in start-to-finish process time, for a cumulative reduction of 13,489 days.
- As many as 1,000,000 potential staff hours to be redirected when the new processes are fully in place.

Among the projects featured on LeanOhio's website was the Ohio Nursing Board's Licensing Process, which took place in December 2021. At the time, the Board had a backlog of more than 8,500 applications, with average lead times ranging from three to six months. Using process mapping, the team found 74 points of waste common to administrative approval processes. Upon implementation of identified improvements, it was projected that nurses will be licensed in as little as six weeks. The project metrics: Process steps: 45% reduction, Loopbacks: 80% reduction, Handoffs: 52% reduction, Decision Points: 53% reduction.[4]

Leaning the licensing process was just one of the many projects that showed remarkable results, in keeping with LeanOhio's motto: simpler, faster, better, less costly. The use of internal expertise to make training broadly accessible to the workforce and the deployment of agency Lean Liaisons make the ongoing achievements possible. And the establishment of the network reinforces skills and nurtures a culture of continuous improvement. The model is integrated, effective, and built to be sustainable. It is quite similar to the one used in Nebraska.

Nebraska

Nebraska's Center of Operational Excellence (COE) is a fully integrated model. Under the leadership of Master Black Belt Matthew Singh, the COE is coordinating and leading process improvement projects, training state managers, supervisors, and employees in Lean Six Sigma (LSS) methodology at White, Yellow, Green, and Black Belt levels, and building a community of practice throughout state government. The COE has a *Kaizen* room, located in the State Capitol for training and process improvement projects. Initiated in 2016 by former Governor Pete Ricketts, the program has since conducted more than 900 projects across 18 agencies and saved more than 900,000 hours of time.

The success of Nebraska's COE was highlighted in the report, *How One State Is Excelling at Process Improvement*. The feature in *Route 50* announced, "Every week Nebraska is contacted by other states to learn how it is saving staff time, streamlining projects, and delivering better customer services."[5] Here are some of the key features of Nebraska's program:

> *Practitioners embedded in state agencies.* A community of practice of full-time Process Improvement Coordinators (PICs) with the capacity to tackle a wide range of projects. *Route 50* interviewed Black Belt Shayne

Director of Nebraska's Center of Operational Excellence, Matthew Singh.

Daughenbaugh, who manages projects within and among agencies. Daughenbaugh highlighted the value of having a network with a common language to help break down the silos. He explained, "There's a standard way we do it here. We use the same methodology."[6]

Strategic operational capacity. The Process Improvement Method Guide and Map[7] is designed to select the most appropriate method for addressing particular types of problems. It also indicates the level of practitioner typically assigned to that type of project. Most projects can be conducted by LSS trained teammates or the agency's PIC using a range of LSS tools and *kaizen* events. PICs are also available to assist agencies with communication and change management challenges. Executive Green Belts or Black Belts may lead complex projects using the full Six Sigma methodology, DMAIC (Define, Measure, Analyze, Improve, Control).

Use of metrics to quantify gains. The Highway Safety Grant project, which is highlighted below, is just one of many examples of the COE's ability to measure the improvements in each of the processes, and to identify the resulting gain of staff time for higher value-added responsibilities. Such "soft" savings indicate freed capacity that was reallocated to programmatic goals. Gains in process time, which translate into significant reductions in customer wait times, are also quantified.

Among the hundreds of CI projects, the *Route 50* report highlighted the Highway Safety Grants project. The LSS project was conducted to simplify the process for local law enforcement to access funds for enforcing seat-belt use, promoting sober driving, and other safety initiatives. Even though funding was available for local law enforcement to conduct safety initiatives, the grants program had been underutilized because the application process was lengthy and convoluted.

The project team found that the original process had 126 steps, 32 hand-offs and 96 hours of process time. The team redesigned the process to centralize documentation, delete redundancies, and eliminate handoffs and duplication of work, thus streamlining the process steps. The new process saved an average of 102 hours a month, with a 58% reduction in team-member time.[8]

By enabling a quicker turnaround time from request to approval, the new process ensures funds are readily available to create a safer driving environment for Nebraska motorists. COE's website features a video about the project where team members explain the value gained by the project.[9] In the video, Highway Safety Administrator William Kovarik and former office supervisor Tina Rockenbach explained that the staff time eliminated from routine administrative tasks was redirected to the programmatic goals of the safety initiatives.

Another notable project was conducted by the Department of Motor Vehicles (DMV) to lean the registration process for fleets. The process, which is required for companies owning more than 25 vehicles, was either in-person or through the mail. It required the renewal of each vehicle on the actual month that the registration expires, depending on the county where it was registered. For example, if a company owns 200 vehicles that are registered in five different counties and in three different months, it required 200 individual transactions, with 15 different trips to county treasurer offices or 15 different mailing processes to renew each vehicle by the month the registration expires.[10]

Nebraska's Highway Safety Grants Project.

The redesigned process allowed a single transaction for all vehicles set to expire in the fleet, regardless of the county. The new process was available online starting in 2021, when 20 companies with over 20,000 vehicles were able to e-register their fleets. A team member reported feedback from a company with over 4,000 vehicles: the renewal process that had taken 30 calendar days was reduced to three days.

A Standard Structure for State CI Programs

The success of Nebraska's Center for Operational Excellence (COE) provides valuable guidance for those seeking a sustainable model. The report on the COE in *Route 50* opened by confirming what many frustrated change agents were experiencing: "Over the years, we've seen multiple city, county, and state efforts that focus on achieving higher levels of efficiency and more effective services. Unfortunately, these efforts, which generally go by labels like process improvement or continuous improvement, are often hard to sustain, dependent as they can be on the passions of individual practitioners."[11]

In seeking to understand how Nebraska's program has avoided the fate of so many other initiatives, one can look to a study conducted by Harvard's Technology and Entrepreneurship Center,[12] which describes the COE's evolution and growth.[13] Organizational placement of the COE was strategic, as Governor Ricketts explained: "The Department of Administrative Services is really the linchpin for this. We chose it purposefully because it is the organization that touches all the other agencies. So, we knew that if we wanted to drive this change through every agency we had to have that center of gravity."[14] It would also make COE more likely to continue through the turnover of future gubernatorial administrations.

Initially, consultants were used for the training, with uneven results. Once Master Black Belt Matt Singh was brought on as Director, he built the internal capacity for a robust training program. In addition to requiring the White Belt program for all state employees, the COE trains all supervisors and managers to prepare them for their roles in CI projects. This is significant because program managers, who are the most senior subject-matter experts in their units, are often promoted into managerial roles. Management is a separate skill set, and CI principles and techniques even more so. While courses in Lean or Lean Six Sigma can be found in MBA or engineering programs, they are less common in other academic fields. Comprehensive training at all levels of the workforce is needed to create a broad understanding of CI principles and techniques. This is particularly important for middle managers who have significant responsibilities as project sponsors. (Course descriptions for training programs in Nebraska and Ohio are in Appendix D.)

The program was further strengthened by adding full-time jobs as Process Improvement Coordinators (PICs) embedded within state agencies. These positions had a dual-reporting structure with the agencies in which they were based and the COE. This integrated approach resulted in a team with a standard set of transferable skills across the enterprise. It also allowed the COE to aggregate the data and quantify the gains using standard metrics. And, as Singh explained in the case study, the dual-reporting structure provided "a guidance and support mechanism. . . . If the program goes off track, the COE intervenes to help put it back on track or to support it."[15]

The use of full-time embedded PICs in Nebraska's state agencies created a more cohesive program than that of states in which each agency designs its own program. In the decentralized approach, some agencies have full-time CI positions with various titles and expectations. In other agencies, a motivated change agent may be appointed to act as the Lean coordinator. This is generally someone with regular duties unrelated to CI, so their "day jobs" take priority. While there are great stories of success by these dedicated folks—what Jim Womack referred to as the "night shift"—it is not a sustainable arrangement. The major threat is attrition. If these employees leave, the vacancies are filled using the existing job description, because there was no such position as "lean coordinator."

The COE was also able to deal with another common barrier to successful lean initiatives—the fear that people will lose their jobs. The Ricketts administration made a commitment that the improvements would not result in layoffs. As Deming said, "drive out fear, so everyone may work effectively for the company." Managers sponsoring the LSS projects were able to reallocate assignments because there was plenty of other higher-value work to be done. Going forward, as efficiencies continued, the state would be better positioned to deal with the "silver tsunami" of employee retirements.

To prepare for an enterprise-wide initiative, the Governor set expectations for the agency heads in his cabinet that this was to be a priority of his administration. As an LSS Master Black Belt, Director Singh met with agency heads, eliciting their input and priorities. The program was building from the top down, from the bottom up, and through the middle. All state employees were required to take the White Belt program, and middle managers were expected to receive a Yellow Belt. The COE set a goal to have a PIC for every 250 state employees, with the expectation they would each conduct eight to ten projects per year, each with a 50% reduction in lead time; to meet other metrics of hard and soft savings; and to mentor new practitioners.

As the program evolved, the COE established mechanisms to support the growing community of practice, using cohorts and lunch-and-learns. Throughout the community of practice, there is a strong sense of mission to provide excellent public services and to be good stewards of the tax dollars. The metrics for return on investment (ROI) included tracking both hard and soft savings. Hard savings are calculated on actual dollars saved, such as moving from a name-brand prescription drug to a generic version. Soft savings refers to staff time saved from process improvements, which allows employees' efforts to be reallocated to higher-value duties. As Singh explained for the Harvard study, "Showing quantifiable results with standardized methodology is essential for long-term buy-in and understanding for executives at all levels, including the budget office and the legislature."[16]

Consistent with the principles of continuous improvement and PDCA, Singh visits other states with Lean programs to get ideas and look to the future. While the technical skills were essential, the change management aspect is crucial. Pointing to the importance of exhibiting courage, persistence, and passion, he concluded, "If you have those three things, some of these other decisions are important but those three bullet points can override everything else because ultimately it's about culture change."[17]

To summarize, the COE's nationally recognized success can be attributed to a series of factors:

■ A Director skilled in process improvement and project management who is committed to the development of internal capacity that integrates the training and operational functions.

■ A comprehensive training program that establishes a baseline of understanding of CI principles by requiring the White Belt program for all employees, and wide access to advanced training that produces a growing team of committed change agents.

■ Practitioners at the Green or Black Belt level in full-time jobs in each agency to conduct projects within and among agencies.

■ Training specific to supervisors, managers, and administrators preparing them to identify improvement opportunities, charter projects, support teams, and implement changes.

■ Commitment from the Governor's office for the necessary resources, and the commitment that efficiency gains would not result in layoffs. Also, for setting expectations with agency heads for their active participation and support, including the hiring of full-time Process Improvement Coordinators (PICs) in the agencies.

Checklist for a sustainable CI program with a Center for Operational Excellence

COE structure and function
• Imbed the COE as a division within the state's administrative services or management and budget department.
• Hire a COE director who is a committed CI practitioner.
• Make COE responsible for both training and CI operations.
• Provide an office with workshop space for training and projects.
• Training managed by COE and conducted by internal (state employee) practitioners
• White Belt required for all employees
• Yellow Belt or Lean for Leaders required for all supervisors, managers, and administrators
• Yellow, Green, and Black Belt programs as recommended and designed by COE
• Community of practice and continuing education managed by COE
• Operations managed by COE

Notes

1 State of Arizona, "What is the Arizona Management System?" *Results.AZ.gov.* https://results.az.gov/news-and-events/what-arizona-management-system

2 State of Arizona, "Success Stories." *Results.AZ.gov.* https://results.az.gov/our-results

3 State of Ohio, *Lean Ohio. Webpages.* https://das.ohio.gov/employee-relations/lean-Ohio

4 State of Ohio, *Lean Ohio Kaizen Fact Sheet*, December, 2021. https://das.ohio.gov/static/employee-relations/LeanOhio/Project_Showcase/OBN_Licensing_Fact_Sheet_Dec2021.pdf

5 Katherine Greene, and Richard Barnett, "How One State Is Excelling at Process Improvement." *Route 50*, December 15, 2022. www.route-fifty.com/management/2022/12/nebraska-management-process-improvement/380975/

6 Katherine Greene, and Richard Barnett, "How One State Is Excelling at Process Improvement." *Route 50*, December 15, 2022. www.route-fifty.com/management/2022/12/nebraska-management-process-improvement/380975/

7 State of Nebraska Center for Operational Excellence, *Process Improvement Method Guide*, p. 4. https://das.nebraska.gov/coe/docs/pdf/COE%20Process%20Improvement%20Method%20Guide%20and%20Map.pdf

8 State of Nebraska Center for Operational Excellence, *"State of Nebraska Projects" web page.* https://das.nebraska.gov/coe/projects.html.

9 State of Nebraska Department of Transportation, "Highway Safety Office Grant Approval Process." *YouTube video.* www.youtube.com/watch?v=rBlgrRke-eA

10 State of Nebraska Center for Operational Excellence, *"State of Nebraska Projects" web page.* https://das.nebraska.gov/coe/projects.html

11 Katherine Greene and Richard Barnett, "How One State Is Excelling at Process Improvement." *Route 50*, December 15, 2022. www.route-fifty.com/management/2022/12/nebraska-management-process-improvement/380975/

12 Leadership for a Networked World (LNW) of the Harvard Public Sector Innovation Award Program at the Technology and Entrepreneurship Center and the National Association of State Chief Administrators (NASCA), *Pursuing A Vision: Nebraska's Center of Operational Excellence*, September, 2019. www.lnwprogram.org/content/pursuing-vision-nebraskas-center-operational-excellence-1

13 Leadership for a Networked World (LNW) of the Harvard Public Sector Innovation Award Program at the Technology and Entrepreneurship Center and the National Association of State Chief Administrators (NASCA), *Pursuing A Vision: Nebraska's Center of Operational Excellence*, September, 2019. www.lnwprogram.org/content/pursuing-vision-nebraskas-center-operational-excellence-1

14 Leadership for a Networked World (LNW) of the Harvard Public Sector Innovation Award Program at the Technology and Entrepreneurship Center and the National Association of State Chief Administrators (NASCA), *Pursuing A Vision: Nebraska's Center of Operational Excellence*, September, 2019. p. 5. www.lnwprogram.org/content/pursuing-vision-nebraskas-center-operational-excellence-1

15 Leadership for a Networked World (LNW) of the Harvard Public Sector Innovation Award Program at the Technology and Entrepreneurship Center and the National Association of State Chief Administrators (NASCA), *Pursuing A Vision: Nebraska's Center of Operational Excellence*, September, 2019, p. 9. www.lnwprogram.org/content/pursuing-vision-nebraskas-center-operational-excellence-1

16 Leadership for a Networked World (LNW) of the Harvard Public Sector Innovation Award Program at the Technology and Entrepreneurship Center and the National Association of State Chief Administrators (NASCA), *Pursuing A Vision: Nebraska's Center of Operational Excellence*, September, 2019, p. 12. www.lnwprogram.org/content/pursuing-vision-nebraskas-center-operational-excellence-1

17 Leadership for a Networked World (LNW) of the Harvard Public Sector Innovation Award Program at the Technology and Entrepreneurship Center and the National Association of State Chief Administrators (NASCA), *Pursuing A Vision: Nebraska's Center of Operational Excellence*, September, 2019, p. 15. www.lnwprogram.org/content/pursuing-vision-nebraskas-center-operational-excellence-1

LEANING GOVERNMENT POLICY

Of the three streams of work by governments that were identified by Jim Womack (enacting policies, designing enforcement and delivery mechanisms, and operating those mechanisms) public policy is the most difficult to lean.[1] Part III discusses the complexities inherent in government resulting from the fact that public policy is both a political and an administrative function.

Chapter 10: The three Ps: Politics, Policy Making, and Public Administrators. Public policy as both a political and an administrative function.

Chapter 11: A Case Study in Unlean Public Policy: U.S. Health Care.

Chapter 12: Applying CI to Public Administration. An overview of CI concepts and methodology including Toyota Kata, with examples of how scientific thinking can be applied to solving social problems.

Chapter 13: Lean Policy Development. Breaking down the challenges of applying CI to policy development, using a lean lens to get through the layers of complexity.

DOI: 10.4324/9781003372691-13

Chapter 10

The Three Ps
Politics, Policy Making, and Public Administrators

Among the differences between public and private sector lean programs is the fact that key decision-makers are less likely to be on the same page in the public sector. Conflicts between boards of directors and CEOs appear tame compared to the partisan ideological differences that can thwart the management of the people's business. Yet some parallels can be drawn in the transition to lean management, which, regardless of the sector, focuses on delivering value for the customer.

Both public and private sector organizations can be assessed based on purpose-driven activities. *The Lean Handbook* explains the distinction between companies that focus on making money compared with companies that focus on excellence. Profits are a result, not a purpose.[2] Mike Rother makes the same point in *Toyota Kata*, quoting Alfred P. Sloan, the former president of General Motors: "We are not in the business of making cars, we are in the business of making money."[3] The contrast is evident when Rother notes Toyota's philosophy: "Survive long-term as a company by improving and evolving how we make good products for the customer."[4] Companies with core values of quality production and customer service are the most likely to be successful in the transition to lean management, compared to those whose management and investors are at odds over strategies to maximize profits.

Likewise, elected officials solely interested in the next election may seek across-the-board spending cuts rather than leaning out the waste embedded in the processes. Again, just as in the business world, cost-effective operations are a result, not a purpose.

While egos and power struggles influence decisions in both the corporate and government worlds, the roles in government are more complicated and fluid. If elected officials who set the policy and administrators responsible for carrying it out are not in synch, the misalignment can be wasteful and ineffective. A common result is both too much and not enough. Too little money to fund too many programs. When emergencies arise, additional funds are appropriated to respond to the crisis, without the opportunity to take stock of what is already in place. Such actions are emblematic of the reaction-driven level of maturity.

Cycles of Crisis Response

As the pandemic spread in March 2020, journalist Fareed Zakaria noted, "The United States is on track to have the worst outbreak of COVID-19 among wealthy countries largely because of the ineffectiveness of its government. . . . America is paying the price today for decades of defunding government, politicizing independent agencies, fetishizing local control, and demeaning and disparaging government workers and bureaucrats. This wasn't how it always was. . . . Franklin Delano Roosevelt created the modern federal bureaucracy, which was strikingly lean and efficient. But in recent decades as the scope of government increased, the bureaucracy was starved and made increasingly dysfunctional."[5]

Zakaria cited Paul C. Light's finding that there were seven cabinet departments in 1961 with 17 layers of appointments to fill; by 2017, there were 15 cabinet departments and 71 layers of appointments.[6] When Biden took office in 2021, there were of 83 layers of presidential appointees and 5,000 jobs.[7]

Noting the dichotomy that "[f]ederal agencies are understaffed but overburdened with mountains of regulations and politicized mandates and rules giving officials little power and discretion," Zakaria contrasted the U.S. government's response to the pandemic with those of South Korea, Taiwan, and Germany, among others. The common factor, he observed, was that these governments are "well-funded and efficient and responsive."[8]

Responsiveness is limited by layers of complexity, in what Paul Light characterized as "thickening." He gave examples of the impediments, reporting that, the chain of command becomes even more unwieldy when policy or budget decisions are passed down and back up within each compartment for review and sign-off before moving down to the next relevant compartment. When this complication is factored into the chain of command, veterans' hospital nurses are receiving their policy guidance and budgets through 43 policy and 63 budget signoffs, including regional offices, districts, hospitals, and nurse supervisors.[9]

Leaning the Thickening

"Public managers are often asked to "trim the fat" in times of revenue scarcity. Unfortunately, there is no line item in the budget called fat," noted the Government Finance Officers Association.[10] The fat is not a line item: it exists in layers. And, arguably, CI methodology is the precision instrument that can separate purpose-driven, results-driven functions from waste.

Absent such an approach, elected officials lack the vantage point to know when new policies and programs are appropriate. As John Bernard pointed out, "government has long tried to solve problems by creating new laws, accumulating over the years an enormous pile of unreconciled legislation. For lawmakers, there are few provisions or incentives to clean up that tangle of laws; for agencies that deliver government services, working within the framework of that irrational, illogical tangle of legislation is at best complex and at worst impossible."[11]

Paul Light identified the positions in debates about the size and function of government in four categories: "expanders" (bigger government with some reform); "streamliners" (smaller with some reform); "rebuilders" (bigger with major reform); and "dismantlers" (smaller with major reform). While these different perspectives disagree about policy choices and vary in their definitions of "reform," they share a sense of frustration that government is not accomplishing its stated goals. "Making government work appears to be the key to creating common ground between the dismantlers and rebuilders," Light suggested, adding, "what Americans want from government reform [is] not just a bigger government that delivers more services, but one that converts bold endeavors into lasting achievements and honors the promises it makes."[12]

If Light is correct, the core CI principles could resonate across the political divide. Reducing waste and enacting evidence-based programs could provide a logical, responsible approach. Cautious elected officials could be reassured that efficacy would be validated and adjusted as appropriate, consistent with the PDCA methodology.

With increased awareness and uptake among government leaders, CI could gain momentum as a practical, nonpartisan solution, and the best way to reduce waste and focus on mission. As the baby boomers retire, there is an opportunity to streamline processes without violating the core principle that no one loses their job in a CI initiative. The campaign could gain momentum by going after low-hanging fruit of bureaucratic waste, such as archaic rules requiring multiple check points to confirm the receipt of notarized documents with "wet" signatures.

When such sensible changes are outside their scope of authority, public administrators who are lean managers have a role to play in educating legislators about the consequences of micromanaging. When functioning well, the relationship is symbiotic. Office holders rely on those in the administrative bureaucracy to meet their objectives, and administrators need the legislative approval for appropriate funding levels. However, sometimes administrators must seek permission to do their jobs.

Does It Take an Act of Congress?

Recall the case study of the VA in Chapter 6 when it literally took an act of Congress to allow administrators to reform the hiring process. The elected officials did not want to put any veterans at risk from a bad hire. A lean practitioner would examine the process to identify the optimal method of expeditious vetting and determine the level of risk from the expedited process compared to the risk of veterans unable to access care due to short staffing. Even so, the Congressional committees might still be reluctant to grant permission, not wanting to be responsible if a bad actor got in and harmed a veteran.

As discussed in the VA example, some elected officials are reluctant to part with redundant layers of red tape in the belief that it fosters accountability. In actuality, such policies do the opposite, diffusing responsibility and clogging operations. The multiple layers of checking thicken the bureaucracy and impede efficient operation.

To overcome the micromanaging, administrative leaders need to address the dual concerns of effectiveness and accountability. As stewards of the public funds, administrators must manage lean operations while guarding against misappropriation and embezzlement. Both responsibilities are indicative of Level Two maturity, results-driven government. These responsibilities include:

- Articulating goals with quantifiable deliverables that answer the question, Are we doing better at what we have been asked to do?
- Implementing appropriate internal controls to prevent fraud or theft, without crippling operations.

Accountability, Personal Responsibility, and Trust

Consider the elements of trust, competency, and character. Could those trained in traditional management learn to build an organization where employees have both the permission and the responsibility to stop the assembly line? How about making decisions about hiring staff, attending conferences, or purchasing products? What level of checking is appropriate? Lean trainer Sam McKeeman observed that you can't have someone you don't trust stopping the line at Toyota. He noted that as trust goes up, the cost of doing business goes down, and productivity goes up. You build a trusting culture with people who are competent and of good character: hire good people, train them well, and get out of the way.

Consider how the "5 Whys" might be used to understand legacy systems. Asking "why" five times can drill down toward the root cause of a problem. For example:

> Problem: Vendors are charging late fees on our invoices. Why? We can't pay them in the 30-day period required. Why? The Accounting Department sends payment at the end of each month. Why? The department heads are frequently late in forwarding the invoices to Accounting. Why? The department heads need to check with the frontline supervisors to confirm that the product was received. Why?

This chain of reasoning could lead a manager to charter a *kaizen* project, assigning a team of staff from accounting and other departments to design a new workflow for the accounts payable process. The team could drill down further into the root cause by asking "why" again: Why do department heads sign invoices? The answer could be that a frontline supervisor once bought something unauthorized or inappropriate.

A single mistake or malfeasance by one employee, one time, may have resulted in additional process requirements. The team should consider ways to mistake-proof the process, other than using a "hard stop" on every invoice by requiring a department head's signature. They could propose spot checking or other techniques to screen for errors or dishonesty. What is the optimal design of checks and balances for fiduciary stewardship? How can a process be built for efficiency and integrity?

Reducing Bureaucratic Burdens

In April 2022, the federal Office of Management and Budget (OMB) undertook a renewed effort to reduce bureaucratic burdens in meeting eligibility requirements.

An OMB memo directed agencies to consider the impact of the application process, including rules for scheduling required phone calls or in-person meetings or needing a third party for help navigating the program. The memo noted, "Every step in the process represents a burden that could result in individuals or entities justifiably becoming too discouraged to complete the process and thus not receiving public benefits for which they are legally eligible." Agencies were also asked to consider the adverse impact of needing to navigate multiple agencies, and "consider any statutory discretion they have to reduce duplicative information requests or otherwise improve coordination across federal agencies to facilitate burden reduction."[13]

A robust lean program within and among federal agencies could address improving customer services both in each agency and among agencies. However, dismantling or untangling redundant and overlapping programs would likely need an act of Congress. Toward that end, CI tools used by the administrative agencies of the executive branch could be used to prepare recommendations for appropriate legislative action.

Leaning Hiring

The fact that public-sector hiring is generally a more lengthy process than that of the private sector makes it difficult to attract talent in a tight labor market. As change-agent trainer Brian Elms posted on LinkedIn: "Recruiting tip #1 Public Sector Edition. Stop taking an average of 119 days to hire a new employee."

The Internal Revenue Service (IRS) had a goal of hiring 5,000 employees in 2022. With just 2,880 hired, the agency continued using contractors and a combination of voluntary and mandatory overtime, reducing a backlog of 20.5 million tax returns to 10.5 from June to October.[14]

The inability to lean hiring impedes progress on mission-critical programs, with potentially serious consequences. In 2021, Rhode Island appropriated funds to add 91 workers to protect abused children. Four months later, none had made it through the hiring process. A lean process would allow for expeditious vetting, minimizing hand-offs and delays while maintaining appropriate quality checks.[15]

Leaning the hiring processes is only one component. Hiring more workers into an unlean bureaucracy is an unlean solution. A robust results-driven program can address the causes of backlogs throughout the operation.

Leaning Regulation

Bipartisan cooperation could be instrumental in leaning regulations. This is distinct from deregulation. It would be unlean to go back to the days when meat-packing plants could taint the food supply and industries could dump toxic waste into land and water. While deregulation would be counterproductive, so is leaving layers of archaic requirements. Lean regulation would accomplish its purpose without placing unnecessary burdens on customers or stakeholders.

CI methodology can provide the objectivity lacking in elected officials who view regulation through an ideological lens. The simplistic goal of either cutting or expanding government fails to consider the purpose and effectiveness of each regulation. As discussed in Chapter 4, *kaizen* teams would include the people who do the work, along with customers and stakeholders, in redesigning regulatory processes.

The objectivity of properly structured *kaizen* events might also mitigate the impact of self-interested efforts by industry to weaken regulations. The strategy of "regulatory capture" encompasses a series of tactics, as explained by Senator Sheldon Whitehouse in *The Scheme:* "You try to control who gets appointed to the agency, and stack it with friends of industry. . . . You can also make sure that friendly members get cushy, well-paid, low-effort jobs when they leave the agency (the proverbial revolving door). . . . You can launch lobbyists at Congress to threaten the agency, putting its funding at risk or challenging its powers."[16]

The potential impact of industry lobbying was highlighted when toxic chemicals were released from a massive train derailment in East Palestine, Ohio, in February 2023. Noting that Congress delayed regulations that would have required more trains to be equipped with electronically controlled pneumatic (ECP) brakes, *The Hill* reported, "The four largest U.S. railroads and their trade association together spent over \$480 million on federal lobbying over the last two decades, according to data from nonpartisan research group OpenSecrets."[17]

While CI methodology cannot singlehandedly balance the scales, arguably, a series of well-structured, well-facilitated *kaizen* events could be a win-win. The regulated industries would be relived of undue burdens, while the agencies would improve their operations, becoming more effective in accomplishing the mission to protect the public. When the *kaizen* teams are chartered by an appropriate sponsor who has the authority to approve administrative changes, the processes can be leaned immediately. And the report-outs of these events could be made available to the public.

Leaning the Silos of Government

The executive branch of government seldom functions as a single organization; rather, it is a series of subsystems. John Bernard explained:

> States have their domains of expertise, each with its own accountabilities: Police and fire, public health, health insurance, Medicaid, environmental quality, employment, workplace health and safety, business/banking/insurance regulation, elections, drivers/doctors/therapists/financial advisors/barbers/etc. licensing, agriculture, building standards, human services (child, domestic and elder maltreatment, foster care), child support, universities, education, corrections (adult and youth), economic development, insurance commission, revenue/taxes, highway/roads building, and maintenance, motor vehicles, alcoholic beverages/marijuana, highway safety, emergency management, water safety, administration, planning, forestry/natural resources, management, retirement systems, lottery, parks, fish and wildlife, as well as administering federal programs for community and regional development, transportation, and employment services.[18]

The federal government, as well as state governments, is siloed into agencies, with bureaus and subdivisions within each agency. Variation in statutory regulations diffuses responsibility and authority. With the appropriate allocation of resources and leadership commitment to a comprehensive lean initiative, enhancing effectiveness and removing waste across the enterprise is an elusive but not impossible task. It is also an incredibly important one. Fragmentation of function was addressed as a factor in *The Premonition: A Pandemic Story*:

> Inside the U.S. government were all these little boxes. The boxes had been created to address specific problems as they arose. "How to ensure our food is safe to eat," for instance, or "how to avoid a run on the banks," or "how to prevent another terrorist attack." Each box was given to people with knowledge and talent and expertise useful to its assigned problem. . . . Each box became its own small, frozen world. . . . People who complained about "government waste" usually fixated on ways taxpayer money got spent. But here was the real waste. One box might contain the solution to a problem in another box, or the person who might find that solution, and that second box would never know about it.[19]

CI methodology would map each value stream across the silos prior to developing countermeasures to address the fragmentation. The countermeasures would be guided by focus on mission and value for the customer, and the management has the personnel and technology necessary for efficient operations. The approaches will be discussed in Chapter 12.

Public Administrators as Conservators of Mission

As Larry Terry noted, "the skills and professional expertise of career civil servants are needed more than ever. Political leaders cannot and should not be expected to solve alone all the complex problems facing our Republic. . . . Bureaucratic leaders have much to offer, and political leaders can benefit from their assistance, counsel, and advice."[20]

Richard Hatchett, one of the leaders of the "Wolverines," the informal group of scientists and public health doctors portrayed in *The Premonition* who tried to mount an effective response to the COVID-19 pandemic, reflected, "Government—and the value government provides—isn't just the whim of whoever happens to be elected at the moment. That government provides continuity across administrations and should be the repository of accumulated institutional experience and wisdom."[21]

Public administrators with institutional knowledge and commitment to mission have the proper vantage point to sponsor CI initiatives. A developing culture of continuous improvement enables an increasing capacity to focus on impact. The value, purpose, and function of existing programs can be strengthened and sustained by managing through the PDCA cycle. Viewing public policy through a lean lens, these administrators are well-positioned to guide policy makers to understand:

■ It is leaner not to set up bureaucratic nightmares in the first place, rather than fixing them later.
■ It is leaner to avoid launching multiple redundant programs, rather than spending time, effort, and money to coordinate them later.

Optimally, and with a lot of work, a collaborative relationship between elected and administrative actors could evolve and continuously improve.

"Run Government Like a Business": A Public Policy Parable[22]

Larry started every campaign speech the same way. "We need to run government like a business—my business experience makes me the right choice to represent this district." Well-respected in the community for operating the local market in the center of town, Larry easily won a term in the state legislature.

When he took office, Larry voted against budget proposals for a range of government expenditures. He led the fight to slash line items for equipment purchases, facilities maintenance, and staff training. He supported the continuation of a year-long hiring freeze.

Yet these policies did not yield the expected results. Larry's constituents began calling him to complain about long waits for routine items such as license renewals or building permits. They wanted him to fix it. Falling asleep that night asking himself what else could be done to run government like a business, Larry woke up at his market. A series of odd events took place.

Sally, the long-time manager of the market, announced that she was retiring and moving out of the state, but she had a great candidate in mind to step into the position. Larry and Sally interviewed the candidate and offered him the job on the spot, which he accepted immediately.

Suddenly, a deep, booming voice announced, "NO! You can't violate the hiring freeze!" Larry was startled. He replied, "Please—this is a critical position for my business—can't you make an exception?" The voice answered, "Some limited exceptions are permitted." "Certainly, this would qualify for an exception," Larry pleaded; "I can't run my business without a manager." The voice replied, "Perhaps. The Committee meets on the 15th of each month. To get on the agenda, you must complete a justification request documenting the impact and submit it with the required signatures." "But we're entering the fall foliage tourist season," Larry protested; "we expect three tour buses to stop in our town each weekend—what if the Committee won't give the approval to hire my manager?" "You can appeal and have it reconsidered in a subsequent meeting," replied the voice.

Larry struggled through the start of the tourist season without a manager. Without a replacement for Sally, the stock was not efficiently managed—they ran out of popular items and had a surplus of others. Perishable overstock went to waste. Larry tried to keep track of employees' schedules, but he ended up filling in when unexpected absences occurred. He was exhausted, yet he could see that his customer service continued to decline in quality, along with his profit margin.

Then, with a bus load of tourists about to arrive, one of the three cash registers broke down. Larry called the company and asked for an emergency repair call and rush order replacement. He had done business with this company for years, and the manager immediately agreed to accommodate Larry's schedule.

The voice boomed, "NO! You cannot violate the contracting and purchasing policy!" "What?" Larry cried. "I've done business with this company for years! They always treat me fairly." "Every two years, you must put your equipment maintenance contract out to bid," explained the Voice. "Ok—maybe I can't do the maintenance now—but can I please buy a new cash register?" Larry begged. "I'm sorry," responded the voice; "there is a freeze on equipment purchases."

The wait for service in Larry's market grew longer as customers lined up to check out at the two remaining registers. Lines backed up into the aisles, blocking access to products. Some customers left in frustration.

Then, an early season storm arrived, blanketing the parking lot in three feet of snow. Larry called the company that provided snow removal service and scheduled a time to clear the lot.

The voice returned: "NO! The facilities maintenance budget has been eliminated for the remainder of the calendar year. The Committee did not anticipate significant snowfall prior to January." Larry did not bother asking if he could appeal the Committee's decision. He took his old snow blower out of the storage shed and it took him all morning to clear the parking lot. By that time, his early-bird customers had gone to another store.

The next day, Larry jumped out of bed with a new mission: "Let's run government like a lean business!"

He led the charge to repeal the hiring freeze and restore the funding for equipment and facilities maintenance. He persuaded his colleagues to disband the committees that micromanaged hiring and purchasing, allowing public managers to move budgetary line items based on business needs.

Larry introduced legislation allowing agencies to roll-over 25% of unexpended funds to the following year, tasking agency heads with long-term planning for equipment replacement and facilities maintenance. He recruited a team of the state's leading technology experts to examine the archaic IT systems and make recommendations for appropriate upgrades to be considered in the next budget cycle.

He persuaded the Governor to issue an Executive Order requiring all agencies to use lean management and process improvement techniques. Agency heads were tasked with setting strategic goals according to the programmatic priorities established by the policy makers. The Governor hired an experienced lean practitioner to head a new Office of Operational Excellence. The initiative included basic lean training for all state employees, recruiting lean practitioners, tracking the progress of the process improvements, and measuring the accomplishment of strategic goals.

Notes

1 James P. Womack, *Lean Government*, June 26, 2014. www.lean.org/the-lean-post/articles/lean-government/
2 Anthony Manos and Chad Vincent, editors, *The Lean Handbook* (ASQ Quality Press, Milwaukee, WI, 2012), p. 287.
3 Mike Rother, *Toyota Kata* (McGraw-Hill Education, New York, NY, 2010), p. 62.
4 Mike Rother, *Toyota Kata* (McGraw-Hill Education, New York, NY, 2010), p. 38.

5 Fareed Zakaria, "Trump's Claim Turned Out to be a Cruel Hoax." *Fareed's Take. Global Public Square. Cable News Network (CNN)*, March 20, 2020. www.cnn.com/videos/politics/2020/03/29/trump-claim-coronavirus-fareeds-take-gps-vpx.cnn

6 Paul C. Light, "People On People On People: The Continued Thickening of Government." *The Volker Alliance*, October 4, 2017. www.volckeralliance.org/resources/people-people-people

7 Paul C. Light, "More Americans Want 'Very Major' Government Reform." *Government Executive*, July 19, 2022.

8 Fareed Zakaria, "Trump's Claim Turned Out to be a Cruel Hoax." *Fareed's Take. Global Public Square. Cable News Network (CNN)*, March 20, 2020. www.cnn.com/videos/politics/2020/03/29/trump-claim-coronavirus-fareeds-take-gps-vpx.cnn

9 Paul C. Light, "People On People On People: The Continued Thickening of Government." *The Volker Alliance*, October 4, 2017. www.volckeralliance.org/resources/people-people-people

10 Shayne Kavanagh, "Less Time, Lower Cost, and Greater Quality: Making Government Work Better with Lean Process Improvement." *White Paper. Government Finance Officers Association*, p. 1. www.gfoa.org/sites/default/files/GFOALeanWhitePaper.pdf

11 John M. Bernard, "Our Efficiency-Killing Tangle of Laws." *Governing.com*, June 19, 2012 www.governing.com/blogs/bfc/col-efficiency-tangle-laws-regulations-outcomes.html

12 Paul C. Light, "The Coming Showdown Over Government Reform: How the Dismantlers and Rebuilders will Shape the 2020 Election." *The Brookings Institution*, April 18, 2019. www.brookings.edu/research/the-coming-showdown-over-government-reform/

13 Natalie Alms, "White House Takes Aim at Administrative Burdens." *Government Executive*, April 14, 2022. www.govexec.com/management/2022/04/white-house-takes-aim-administrative-burdens/365657/

14 Jory Heckman, "IRS Ends Year with Record-breaking Reduction in Tax Return Backlog, But Challenges Remain." *Federal News Network*, December 22, 2022. https://federalnewsnetwork.com/agency-oversight/2022/12/irs-to-miss-year-end-goals-for-clearing-pandemic-era-tax-return-backlog/

15 Tom Mooney, "Months after DCYF Got Money to Fill 91 Positions, No One Has Been Hired." *The Providence Journal*, October 18, 2021.

16 Sheldon Whitehouse, *The Scheme: How the Right Wing Used Dark Money to Capture the Supreme Court* (The New Press, New York, NY, 2022), p. 16.

17 Karl Evers-Hillstrom, "Railroad Pushback to Safety Regulations Scrutinized Amid East Palestine Disaster." *The Hill*, February 23, 2023. https://thehill.com/lobbying/3869561-safety-regulations-ohio-train-derailment-criticized/

18 John M. Bernard, "We are in Trouble, We Need Your Help." *LinkedIn*, January 20, 2022. www.linkedin.com/pulse/we-trouble-need-your-help-john-m-bernard/

19 Michael Lewis, *The Premonition: A Pandemic Story* (W.W. Norton & Company, New York, NY, 2021), pp. 78–79.

20 Larry D. Terry, *Leadership of Public Bureaucracies: The Administrator as Conservator* (M.E. Sharpe, New York, NY, 2003), p. 169.

21 Michael Lewis, *The Premonition: A Pandemic Story* (W.W. Norton & Company, New York, NY, 2021), p. 293.

22 The parable first appeared in *A Public Sector Journey to Lean*.

Chapter 11

A Case Study of Unlean Public Policy
U.S. Health Care

The task of applying lean principles to health care is difficult because the United States does not have a health care system. U.S. health care is delivered by a multitude of entities including public, private, and non-profit institutions and individual providers. To assess U.S. health care through a lean lens, it is useful to examine how the pandemic response was hampered by the unlean nature of public health agencies and layers of jurisdictional authorities.

Lean the Virus

What we witnessed during the height of the COVID-19 pandemic was the antithesis of the lean principles of quality, efficiency, and standard work. There were bidding wars between states amidst supply-chain chaos, inconsistent and redundant data collection, and erratic and conflicting public health guidance.

Without ignoring or excusing the failures of the administration in power in 2020, it is essential to examine the impediments to an effective response that predated this crisis. Addressing those impediments requires much more than changing who is in charge.

DOI: 10.4324/9781003372691-15

Within the country ironically known as the United States, each state devised its own strategy to deal with a global pandemic. Policies on masks varied by state and local jurisdictions. States developed a confounding variation of unenforceable interstate travel policies attempting to limit the contagion.[1]

As the pandemic spread across the country in March 2020, economist Robert Reich wrote, "The dirty little secret, which will soon become apparent to all, is that there is no real public health system in the United States." Journalist Fareed Zakaria noted that the country's capacity to fight COVID-19 was impeded by what he characterized as "America's crazy quilt patchwork of authority with thousands of state, local, and tribal public health departments."[2]

As fatalities reached 227,000 in October 2020, Dr. Irwin Redlener of the National Center for Disaster Preparedness at Columbia University said, "The inconsistency of the response is what's been so frustrating. . . . If we had just been disciplined about employing all these public health methods early and aggressively, we would not be in the situation we are in now."[3]

Non-standard data collection made it difficult to get a clear picture of the extent of the contagion. States had different testing strategies, so reported positivity rates were misleading. States with robust surveillance programs continually tested those in high-risk jobs, which was essential to contain the outbreak in healthcare and congregate settings. However, the positivity rate of those tested for the first time revealed more about the level of community spread. Both figures had value, but only in context. Without uniform reporting criteria, state-by-state comparisons were full of noisy data that obfuscated decision making.

The global health initiative Resolve to Save Lives urged policy makers to address the information catastrophe, noting that, "Unlike many other countries such as Germany, Senegal, South Korea, and Uganda, the United States does not have standard, national data on the virus and its control. The United States also lacks standards for state, county, and city level public reporting of this life-and-death information."[4]

The data collection dilemma and other impediments predated 2020. In *The Premonition: A Pandemic Story*, Michael Lewis described the unlikely group of heroes who struggled to break through maddeningly dysfunctional bureaucracies, risk-averse and image-conscious politicians, and the profit-driven medical-industrial complex. Among the lessons in the riveting nonfiction narrative:

There was no system of public health in the United States, just a patchwork of state and local health officers, beholden to a greater or lesser extent to local elected officials. Three thousand five hundred separate entities that had been starved of resources for the past 40 years.[5]

In September 2021, journalist Ed Yong reported, "More Americans have been killed by the new coronavirus than the influenza pandemic of 1918, despite a century of intervening medical advancement."[6] He described a reactive "cycle of panic and neglect." Analyzing crisis-driven responses from cholera in the 1830s to HIV in the 1980s, Yong found that interest lapsed once an immediate threat had abated. He concluded, "progress is always undone; promise, always unfulfilled."

Dr. James McDonald put it plainly: "It's time to reference Humpty Dumpty, because why not, right? But I think this is indicative of where we are as a nation. We spend a lot of money giving all the king's horses and all the king's men trying to put Humpty Dumpty back together again. And that's now just to the hospitals, and hospitals are very important. We're fortunate to have them. But what we really need to do is invest in prevention, like Humpty Dumpty shaped like an egg. Where were the people next to Humpty Dumpty, saying, 'Look, you're shaped like an egg, you shouldn't be sitting on a wall!'"

He explained, "Public Health literally saves your life every day. . . . [I]f you had clean water to drink today, [if] you went to a restaurant and had a healthy meal, if you actually had air to breath that was clean, if you went to a health care provider who was competent. . . . [J]ust a few examples of how public health saved your life today. Public health is invested in keeping you healthy.[7]"

Yet the capacity of state and local health departments varies widely, with many functions dependent upon grants from the Centers for Disease Control (CDC). Dr. David Himmelstein compared the arrangement to having the military apply for grants to fund its ongoing responsibilities.[8]

In an effort to mitigate the dysfunction of the jurisdictional layers within and among the entities responsible for public health, lean practitioners have taught managers and employees in public health departments how to streamline program administration. Waste is reduced, and programmatic quality is improved. Hospitals use lean to improve administrative efficiency and patient care. Yet such incremental measures alone cannot address the need for a cohesive system.

Lack of a System to Face a Global Pandemic

By May 17, 2022, one million Americans had lost their lives to COVID-19. As of February 3, 2023, the Johns Hopkins' Coronavirus Resource Center reported that the U.S. had the 15th highest fatality rate in the world, at 337.17 per 100,000.[9,10]

The lack of a cohesive public health system was only one factor that impeded an effective response. The lack of universal access to health care also had a significant impact. The reliance on employer-provided plans made thousands of people vulnerable to policy disruptions due to unemployment during pandemic shutdowns. The number of preventable deaths related to uninsurance and under-insurance was increased by employment disruptions due to the pandemic. Researchers from the Yale School of Public Health reported that "a single-payer universal healthcare system would have saved about 212,000 lives in 2020 alone." Further, the study calculated that a universal system would have saved "$105.6 billion of medical expenses associated with COVID-19 hospitalization."[11]

Examining the demographics, the Kaiser Family Foundation found that COVID-19 did not impact all Americans equally:

> Black, Hispanic, and AIAN[12] people have experienced higher rates of COVID-19 infection and death compared to White people. . . . The higher rates of infection among people of color likely reflect increased exposure risk due to working, living, and transportation situations, including being more likely to work in jobs that cannot be done remotely, to live in larger households, and to rely on public transportation. Black, Hispanic, and AIAN people have experienced the highest age-adjusted death rates amid each resurgence period, reflecting higher rates of death across all age groups among people of color compared to White people and an older White population. . . . While disparities in cases and deaths have narrowed and widened during different periods over time, the underlying structural inequities in health and health care and social and economic factors that placed people of color at increased risk at the outset of the pandemic remain.[13]

A series of complex interrelated factors contributed to the high mortality rate in the U.S. compared to the rest of the industrialized world, and to the disparate impact on minority populations within the country. Without attempting to address those factors, the following assessment focuses on availability and access to medical care through a lean lens.

An Unlean Non-System

U.S. health care is delivered by a multitude of disparate parts, among public, private, and non-profit institutions and individual providers. In contrast, a health care system, as Dr. Michael Fine, Rhode Island's former Director of Public Health Services, defines it, "is an organized set of services and products made available to the entire population and designed to achieve a predetermined set of outcomes."

Economist Jeffrey Sachs testified to the Congressional House Oversight and Reform Committee, explaining that U.S. health care is not a system; it's "a hodgepodge of overpriced monopolies whether for profit or not for profit." Dr. Sachs priced the waste at $1 trillion per year[14].

The U.S. spends a far greater percentage of GDP on health care than any other country. In a study of 11 high-income countries, The Commonwealth Fund reported that the United States ranked last in access to care, administrative efficiency, equity, and health-care outcomes such as life expectancy and infant mortality. Ten of the countries spent 9 to 12% of GDP, while the United States spent 16.8%. Why this inverse relationship between cost and quality?[15]

The Commonwealth Fund's report ranked the United States last in "how well health systems reduce documentation (paperwork) and other bureaucratic tasks that patients and clinicians frequently face during care." Such administrative obstacles lead to higher costs and lesser quality. From a lean perspective, it is useful to apply Deming's observation that uncontrolled variation is the enemy of quality. Complexity and waste go hand in hand.

Hundreds of insurance companies market a myriad of policies. Employers and individuals shop for policies, attempting to balance price and coverage.

Health coverage was out of reach for more than 46 million Americans prior to the passage of the Affordable Care Act (ACA). The combination of Medicaid expansion and subsidies for insurance purchases expanded coverage for nearly 20 million people.[16] However, access to care remains out of reach for millions, as wasteful complexity and variation persist in the private insurance market. A range of policies are available on the exchange, Healthcare.gov, color-coded as bronze, silver, gold, or platinum to indicate the levels of deductibles. Plans may be in an HMO, PPO, POS, or EPO with specific in-network providers.

Lean practitioners would find layers of waste in the variation of policies. In addition to the administrative complexity, insurance company profits, executive salaries, lobbying, and advertising further add to the costs unrelated to medical care.

Dealing with insurance companies as intermediaries requires time on the part of both patients and medical providers. For providers, it requires considerable effort unrelated to medical care. Significant resources are devoted to reconciling patients' medical needs with their available coverage.

Wasted Expertise and Effort

The waste includes the time and effort expended by medical personnel for non-medical purposes:[17]

- Physicians were spending 3.4 hours per week interacting with multiple payers, including to obtain prior authorizations.
- Nurses and medical assistants were spending 20.6 hours per physician per week interacting with health plans.
- Administrative costs per physician per year are estimated to be $82,975.

In an attempt to deal with these challenges, medical professionals and staff have adopted CI tools to reduce waste as much as possible. For example, many hospitals use the "5S" technique (Sort, Straighten, Shine, Standardize, and Sustain) to standardize the layout of all supply closets, so that medical staff can readily find what they need when they work on different units.

In addition to using lean to streamline processes, hospitals and medical practices have adopted the CI tool of visual management to improve quality and efficiency. One of the most effective is a huddle, a brief gathering in front of a white board. The Center for Excellence in Primary Care calls them "healthy huddles" and explains that "all-staff huddles are used at some clinics to alert everyone to staffing issues, upcoming events, or important policy updates. They are usually no more than five minutes per day. Sometimes, all-staff huddles are followed by care-team huddles."[18] A sample video shows a team reviewing the day's roster of providers, expected patient flow, and statistics on incoming calls. They compare daily statistics for variation from expected standards and goals. Other sample videos are available on YouTube, including a lighthearted one by nurses at the Maine Medical Center, "Hustle to the Huddle."[19]

Regardless of these and other improvements in efficient, quality care delivery by providers, the patchwork maze of insurance plans continues to have negative consequences for many patients:

■ One in ten adults owed significant medical debt, estimated at $195 billion in 2019. High deductibles and other forms of cost sharing resulted in bills people were unable to pay, even if insured. A Kaiser Family Foundation study noted that "people with unaffordable medical bills are more likely to delay or skip needed care in order to avoid incurring more medical debt, cut back on other basic household expenses, take money out of retirement or college savings, or increase credit card debt."[20]

■ A survey conducted by Stanford Professor Jeffrey Pfeffer and Gallup found that Americans were spending about 12 million hours per week on the phone with insurance companies.[21]

■ The cost of time spent by employees dealing with health insurance administration on and off the clock approached $33 billion. The consequent productivity impact on employee job satisfaction was estimated at $95.6 billion.[22]

Lean practitioners seek to add customer value by reducing waste. In lean production, processes are designed to make optimal use of the resources necessary to produce a quality product. Lean management can make products better, faster, and cheaper. Better always comes first. While cost reduction is not the primary goal, it is often a by-product of waste reduction. Other nations have shown that better outcomes can be obtained using fewer resources. Consider how waste might be reduced in U.S. health care. Could those resources be reallocated to improve quality?

Universality Applied to Health Care

Medicare, like Social Security, applies without regard to income. The principle of universality allows an overhead of less than 2%.[23] However, the U.S. health care market is a hodgepodge of public programs and private insurance plans that generate massive overhead.[24]

FDR and his successor Harry Truman both proposed universal access to health care. Yet even incremental gains faced strong political opposition. It was not until 1965 that Medicare passed, and then, only for people 65 and older.

Using Medicare's lean design of universality, all Americans could have access to health care. As the Yale Public Health Study on pandemic mortality reported, such a policy change would save lives and money. The study characterized "Medicare for All" as pandemic preparedness, concluding:

> The COVID-19 outbreak has underscored the societal vulnerabilities that arise from the fragmented healthcare system in the United States. Universal healthcare coverage decoupled from employment and disconnected from profit motivations would have stood the country in better stead against a pandemic. . . . Universal single-payer healthcare is fundamental to pandemic preparedness. We determined that such a system could have saved 211,897 lives in 2020 alone. Strikingly, it would have done so at lower cost than the current healthcare system, saving the US $459 billion in 2020 at a time of economic tumult. To facilitate recovery from the ongoing crisis and bolster pandemic preparedness, as well as safeguard well-being and prosperity more broadly, now is the time to transition to a healthcare system that can better serve the American people.[25]

Access to medical care is only one part of a series of the complex factors that contribute to well-being. When life expectancy in the U.S. declined to its lowest level since 1996, Dr. Steven Woolf explained, "We are unique from other countries also in the massive amount of money we spend on health care, much higher than other countries and much higher than countries in which people live longer lives and are healthier. So, this is a lesson that health care is only a partial answer. Studies suggest it only accounts for about ten to 20 percent of health outcomes. Our health is really shaped by our living conditions, jobs, the wages we earn, our wealth accumulation, the education that enables us to get those jobs. And we're struggling in those areas".[26]

What Would a Cohesive Health Care System Look Like?

A functioning system is not just about funding streams. Seeking to design an integrated system, Dr. Michael Fine, Rhode Island's former Director of Public Health Services, studied models in other countries. Drawing on a model used in Finland, he recommended a system of municipal health centers, each serving 10,000 people.[27]

The centers would provide 90% of the area's health care needs, including medical, dental, behavioral, and preventive care. Staff would include social workers, counselors, nutritionists, and physical therapists. It would be open evenings and weekends. It would be responsible for ensuring that all immunizations and screenings for the entire population of that community were up to date. Services would include recovery and wellness programs.

The integrated model meets the lean criteria: more efficient, better customer value. It could be at the core of a functional, cost-effective, and humane health care system.

In his final State of the Union address, FDR proposed a "Second Bill of Rights" that included "the right to adequate medical care and the opportunity to achieve and enjoy good health." On the third anniversary of Social Security, in 1938, FDR declared, "We must face the fact that in this country we have a rich man's security and a poor man's security and that the Government owes equal obligations to both. National security is not a half and half matter: it is all or none."[28]

The possibility of realizing such noble aspirations will be explored in upcoming chapters. We will explore how the scientific thinking of Toyota Kata may offer a path forward to solve our most intractable problems while bringing people together.

Notes

1 Curtis Tate, "COVID-19 Travel Restrictions by State: What You Need to Know Before You Travel." *USA Today*, November 16, 2020.
2 Fareed Zakaria, *The Global Public Square. Commentary on CNN Broadcast*, March 29, 2000. https://transcripts.cnn.com
3 Matt Sedensky and Mike Stobbe, " 'So frustrating': Grave missteps seen in US virus response." *Associated Press*, October 29, 2020.
4 Resolve to Save Lives, *Tracking COVID-19 in the United States From Information Catastrophe to Empowered Communities*, July 21, 2020. https://preventepidemics.org
5 Michael Lewis, *The Premonition: A Pandemic Story* (W.W. Norton & Company, New York, NY, 2021), p. 206.
6 Ed Yong, "We're Already Barreling Toward the Next Pandemic." *The Atlantic*, September 29, 2021.
7 Lynn Arditi, "Departing Interim Health Director: R.I. Public Health Needs a Booster." *The Public's Radio*, June 3, 2022. https://thepublicsradio.org/article/departing-interim-health-director-r-i-public-health-needs-a-booster
8 David Himmelstein, "The Nation's Public Health Agencies are Ailing When They're Needed Most." *The Washington Post*, August 31, 2020.

9 As of December 2022, the U.S. had the 16th highest mortality rate in the world. Peru had the highest rate with 660.03, followed by Bulgaria at 547.76, and Hungary at 500.36. If New York City was reported separately, it would have been listed between Bulgaria and Hungary with 516 fatalities per 100,000. With 438, 437, and 426, respectively, Mississippi, Arizona, and West Virginia would be between Montenegro (444.22) and Croatia (422.75). Data from Johns Hopkins University Center for Systems Science and Engineering https://www.arcgis.com/apps/dashboards/bda7594740fd40299423467b48e9ecf6 and Centers for Disease Control and Prevention (CDC) https://covid.cdc.gov/covid-data-tracker/

10 Johns Hopkins Coronavirus Resource Center, *Mortality Analysis*, December 11, 2022. https://coronavirus.jhu.edu/data/mortality

11 A.P. Galvani, A.S. Parpia, A. Pandey, P. Sah, K. Colón, G. Friedman, T. Campbell, J.G. Kahn, B.H. Singer, and M.C. Fitzpatrick, "Universal Healthcare as Pandemic Preparedness: The Lives and Costs that Could Have Been Saved during the COVID-19 Pandemic." *Proceedings of the National Academy of Sciences of the United States of America* 119(25) (2022): e2200536119. DOI: 10.1073/pnas.2200536119 (Epub 2022 Jun 13. PMID: 35696578; PMCID: PMC9231482).

12 AIAN stands for "American Indian/Alaska Native."

13 Latoya Hill and Samantha Artiga, "COVID-19 Cases and Deaths by Race/Ethnicity: Current Data and Changes Over Time." *Kaiser Family Foundation*, August 22, 2022. www.kff.org/coronavirus-covid-19/issue-brief/covid-19-cases-and-deaths-by-race-ethnicity-current-data-and-changes-over-time/

14 Jeffrey Sachs, *Testimony to the House Oversight and Reform Committee on Examining Pathways to Universal Health Coverage*, March 29, 2022. Please cite source for this testimony

15 The Commonwealth Fund. *Mirror, Mirror 2021: Reflecting Poorly: Health Care in the U.S., Compared to Other High-Income Countries*, August 4, 2021. www.commonwealthfund.org/publications

16 Jennifer Tolbert, Patrick Drake, and Anthony Damico, "Key Facts about the Uninsured Population." *The Kaiser Family Foundation*, December 19, 2022. www.kff.org/uninsured/issue-brief/key-facts-about-the-uninsured-population/

17 Dante Morra, Sean Nicholson, Wendy Levinson, David N. Gans, Terry Hammons, and Lawrence P. Casalino, "US Physician Practices Versus Canadians: Spending Nearly Four Times As Much Money Interacting with Payers." *Health Affairs*, August 2021. DOI: 10.1377/hlthaff.2010.0893

18 University of California-San Francisco Center for Excellence in Primary Care, *Healthy Huddles*, January 6, 2023. https://cepc.ucsf.edu/healthy-huddles

19 DebBachand. Maine Medical Center, *Hustle to the Huddle* YouTube video, 2015. www.youtube.com/watch?v=Lu1StlOMVnE

20 Matthew Rae, Gary Claxton, Krutika Amin, Emma Wager, Jared Ortaliza, and Cynthia Cox, "The Burden of Medical Debt in the United States." *Peterson-KFF*, March 10, 2022. www.healthsystemtracker.org/brief/the-burden-of-medical-debt-in-the-united-states/

21 Dan Weissmann, "'An Arm and a Leg': Hello? We Spend 12 Million Hours a Week on the Phone With Insurers." *Kaiser Health Network. Podcast*, October 18, 2021. https://khn.org/news/article/an-arm-and-a-leg-hello-we-spend-12-million-hours-a-week-on-the-phone-with-insurers/

22 Jeffrey Pfeffer, Dan Witters, Sangeeta Agrawal, and James K. Harter, "Magnitude and Effects of 'Sludge' in Benefits Administration: How Health Insurance Hassles Burden Workers and Cost Employers." *Academy of Management Discoveries* 6(3) (2020): pp. 1–16.

23 CMS.gov, *2022 Annual Report of the Boards of Trustees of the Federal Hospital Insurance and Federal Supplementary Medical Insurance Trust Fund*. www.cms.gov/files/document/2022-medicare-trustees-report.pdf.

24 The Commonwealth Fund. *Mirror, Mirror 2021: Reflecting Poorly*, December 8, 2022. https://commonwealthfund.org/publications/fund-reports/2021/aug/mirror-mirror-2021-reflecting-poorly

25 A.P. Galvani, A.S. Parpia, A. Pandey, P. Sah, K. Colón, G. Friedman, T. Campbell, J.G. Kahn, B.H. Singer, and M.C. Fitzpatrick, "Universal health-care as pandemic preparedness: The lives and costs that could have been saved during the COVID-19 pandemic." *Proceedings of the National Academy of Sciences of the United States of America* 119(25) (2022): e2200536119. DOI: 10.1073/pnas.2200536119 (Epub 2022 Jun 13. PMID: 35696578; PMCID: PMC9231482).

26 PBS Newshour, *U.S. Life Expectancy Falls to Lowest Level Since Mid-1990s due to COVID and Drug Overdoses*, December 22, 2022. www.pbs.org/newshour/show/u-s-life-expectancy-falls-to-lowest-level-since-mid-1990s-due-to-covid-and-drug-overdoses

27 Michael Fine, *Health Care Revolt* (PM Press, New York, NY, 2018).

28 Social Security.gov, *FDR's Statements on Social Security*. www.ssa.gov/history/fdrstmts/html

Chapter 12

Applying CI to Public Administration

In seeking to lean government functions to achieve social policy goals, it is useful to begin with the same methodology used in private-sector organizations. Lean practitioners assess organizational function by focusing on the production of value. It starts with identifying the value streams of effort that are required to produce each of the products and services. Of the three streams of work by governments, Jim Womack noted that policy making is more difficult to lean than the design and delivery or operational functions.[1]

As discussed in Chapter 3, launching a lean initiative can get a real boost by going after the low-hanging fruit of process waste typically found in the operational functions. At New Hampshire's second Lean Summit in 2013, Womack provided guidance on applying lean to the value streams of government.[2] Explaining that government's value-creating activities include providing services and preventing harm, he suggested:

- Select your most important processes (value streams).
- Make the current state of these processes visible to everyone. (Yes, even the legislators and the voters!)
- Define the gap in performance.
- Determine the root cause of the gap.
- Identify the logical countermeasures.
- Conduct experiments (PDCA) with the most promising countermeasures.
- Decide if the results are good enough.
- Stabilize the successful countermeasures.

DOI: 10.4324/9781003372691-16

Co-facilitators support the creation of a swim-lane map.

The process-mapping tool is a visual method to create a common understanding of the workflow. As discussed in Chapter 3, process mapping is a great introduction to identifying and removing waste. Of the eight wastes waiting is most commonly identified by maps, but examples of the other seven may also be found.

The Eight Wastes

Lean in manufacturing initially targeted seven wastes: defects, overproduction, waiting, transportation, inventory, motion, and excess processing. The cost of producing unsold items (overproduction) or unusable items (defects) clearly impacts the bottom line.

In applying lean to the service sector (including government and nonprofits), the first seven wastes remain applicable, with an additional waste: underutilized people. In combination with excess processing and waiting, inefficient use of human talent is prevalent in bureaucracies. Administrators review work that has already been checked several times. They might make inconsequential edits and return it for rework, adding time and effort without increasing the value of the product. Each handoff increases the waste of waiting, and each new level of review involves excess processing.

© John M. Bernard, www.johnmbernard.com

As employees work in these processes, they may become jaded and demoralized. It's both disheartening and exhausting. Conversely, joining a lean team charged with redesigning the process can be a liberating experience. The underutilized human potential is unleashed.

CI Tools and Principles

The following summary of techniques is not exclusive to CI; many are commonly used in business management. The tools adopted for CI are typically team-based, using skilled facilitators to stimulate creativity and the development of a common understanding through a visual depiction.

There are many excellent resources to help public administrators that provide guidance on the use of CI tools, including the EPA's *Lean in Government Starter Kit*. This section offers a basic overview of some commonly used terms, techniques, and principles.[3]

Standard work: The optimum sequence of activities needed to perform a given operation. As John Shook of LEI explained, "Our aim with standardized work is to establish a baseline of operation from which improvement is possible."[4]

5S: An improvement process involving five steps (Sort, Set in order, Shine, Standardize, and Sustain) to create and maintain a clean, neat, and orderly workplace. 5S is often used to ready the workplace for future continual improvement efforts. Some organizations add a sixth "S" for Safety.

Visual controls: Used to reinforce standardized procedures and display the status of an activity so every employee can see it and take appropriate action.

Process walk: A team of employees walks through a work area to look for waste and then implements actions to immediately improve the process. By learning to identify inefficiencies and solve problems in their working environment, employees gain skills and habits necessary to incorporate lean thinking into their everyday work.

The Five Whys

One of the most interesting accounts in Martin O'Malley's *Smarter Government* serves as a lesson about the use of the "5 Whys," a technique of persistent inquiry. When he was Mayor of Baltimore, O'Malley noticed excessive overtime costs due to high absenteeism in one of the departments. When he inquired, the supervisors initially implied that the union contract prevented them from sanctioning employees for unexcused absences. However, it turned out that nothing in the contract prohibited managers from disciplining for cause. With continued inquiries, it was revealed that managers were reluctant to fire anyone because they believed they would not be permitted to hire any new full-time employees, so it was better to keep the ones they had. Further inquiry revealed these managers had never been informed that those hiring restrictions instituted years earlier were no longer in effect. The supervisors began managing appropriately, absenteeism fell, and more work was accomplished, which reduced both the overtime budget and citizen complaints.[5]

Fishbone Diagram

The fishbone cause-and-effect diagram was created by Kaoru Ishikawa, a Japanese professor of engineering, so it is also known as the Ishikawa diagram. Basic instructions: Write the problem in the head of the fish. Label the primary bones with headings in various categories such as equipment, rules/policy, and people/staff factors. Brainstorm contributing causes under each category and list them on the smaller fish bones.

Affinity Diagram

Affinity diagrams can be used by team members to organize their ideas by grouping them into categories. Team members write their ideas on sticky notes and place them on a wall. Next, the team rearranges them to group similar ideas together. Then, each of the sections is labeled by category.

Suppliers-Inputs-Process-Outputs-Customer (SIPOC)

A SIPOC is a high-level diagram that can be used as a first step in understanding a process, prior to process mapping. Its structured format shows the sequence of transactions and dependencies. According to *The Lean Handbook*, the SIPOC shows that "nothing in the organization is done in isolation. In one way or another, everyone serves either the customer or someone else who does."[6]

- ◾ Suppliers: The people or organizations that provide information, material, and resources to be worked on in the process.
- ◾ Inputs: The information/materials provided by suppliers that are transformed by the process.
- ◾ Process: The series of steps that transform the inputs.
- ◾ Outputs: The product or service used by the customer.
- ◾ Customer: The people, organization, or other process that receives the output from the process.

Some practitioners recommend starting with the Process (1), moving to Outputs (2), then Customer (3), back to Inputs (4) and then Suppliers (5). Others use a traditional left to right approach to complete the SIPOC.

Systems and Strategy

The same methodologies used to improve inefficient programs (the operations function of government) can be used for the other two functions of government: program design and policy development.

Lean tools should be linked to organizational strategy. If Lean is used only to do projects, interest will wane once the most painful processes have been improved. As a White Paper published by the Government Finance Officers Association (GFOA) notes, "While Lean is powerful for making significant improvements in business process performance, it is a tactical tool. If it is not linked to broader organizational strategy, Lean can lose relevance to the organization members and be discontinued. . . . Lean works best when it is treated as a discipline that is instilled into the fundamental way in which the organization thinks about service provision, rather than being treated as a one-off project. As such, public managers should carefully study Lean and consider how it might contribute to wider organization strategic objectives."[7]

As organizations seek to correlate inputs to outcomes, the identification of meaningful measurements comes first. For example, what if hundreds of employees took a Lean White Belt class, but never applied those skills to conduct improvement projects? Should we measure the percentage of employees trained in the workforce, compared with the number of *kaizens*? Those are outputs. As Mike Rother noted, "projects and workshops ≠ continuous improvement."[8]

It would be more meaningful to compare the percentage of employees who are trained in Lean to documented improvements. Would there be a positive correlation between the density of lean training and outcomes such as time saved and increased customer satisfaction?

It requires expertise to develop appropriate metrics that can distinguish causality from correlation, establishing links between inputs and outcomes. After deciding what to measure, data must be collected and analyzed.

In order to take on those more complex functions, lean practitioners and/or government managers should consider using a powerful tool with a short name: A3.

The A3

The name, A3, refers to a standard international paper size, roughly 11"x17", but the A3 format can be any size, including storyboards. It can be used for planning and problem-solving by individuals or teams. The A3 provides a problem-solving structure based on the principle of Plan-Do-Check-Act/Adjust (PDCA). The seven fields on a single sheet walk the user though a systematic approach that can be used to identify and implement best practices.[9] The outcomes are measured, creating a feedback loop of continuous improvement.

Background	Countermeasures
Current Condition	Plan
Management Goals	
Root Cause(s)	Follow-up/Sustainment

A3 format for problem-solving.

Experienced practitioners in the Lean Enterprise Institute provide guidance for the use of A3s in many aspects of lean management. John Shook stressed that its core value derives not from completing a form but from encouraging thinking. He noted, "The A3 problem-solving process encourages root cause analysis, documents processes, and represents goals and action plans in a format that triggers conversation and learning."[10]

Lean coach David Verble recommended using "slow thinking" with the A3 as a guide. He explained, "at each stage, you must first think about and investigate the problem situation and only then record your thinking. However, do not expect to complete the process sequentially. As you work through the A3 methodology and complete the storyboard, you will continue learning about your problem situation. So, be prepared to go back and revise what you wrote earlier as you get deeper into the problem."[11]

An A3 format can be used to illustrate each of the PDCA steps in a project. The format enables a complete and concise record of the *kaizen* project in a single page, easily shared by the team and sponsor. The inclusion of the implementation plan and dates for follow-up helps to foster accountability.

Applying CI Tools to Operational Challenges

The transition from reaction-driven government to results-driven requires consistent use of CI tools for operational quality and efficiency.

With persistent leadership, the techniques take hold and become common practice. This allows the organization to achieve a culture of continuous improvement and the operational competence indicative of Level Two maturity. For example, perhaps the wait at the DMV has been reduced from 90 minutes to ten minutes. Maybe the number of permit applications returned for rework went from 20% to zero. Perhaps the number of signatures required to approve out-of-state travel was reduced from six to one. Such results-oriented operational gains create a platform of competence from which to transition to Level Three.

Reaching Level Three maturity would enable governments to make quantifiable progress on problems such as child abuse, poverty, homelessness, and incarceration by addressing the root causes. As Bernard explains, "The foundation of Level Three is applying what has been learned in Level Two to social challenges."[12] Single tools will not get you there. Such a fundamental shift will require the use of scientific thinking, as in Toyota Kata.

Toyota Kata

Within the continuous improvement wheelhouse is Toyota Kata (TK), which was developed by researcher Mike Rother based on his studies of Toyota's employee-management routines. TK combines a scientific way of striving for goals with routines of deliberate practice. Lean and TK are not mutually exclusive or contraindicated; rather they can be considered symbiotic. As Rother explained in *Toyota Kata*, "Toyota's visible tools and techniques are built upon invisible management thinking and routines."[13]

Mike Rother.

As Rother explained at KataCon5, "Kata is not the solution to a problem—it's learning how to go about solving problems."[14] The TK practice routines, called "Starter Kata," help develop the meta skill of scientific thinking, well-suited to counter our natural bias for jumping to conclusions. Understanding that knowledge is not static, the scientific way of thinking and acting developed by practicing TK enables practitioners to incorporate new learning and to adjust accordingly. Centered in the principle of PDCA, Starter Kata is an essential component in the practice of Lean management.

The *Improvement Kata* (IK) is a four-step model of scientific thinking, with structured Starter Kata for each step of the model. The Starter Kata have the user apply (practice) scientific thinking patterns. The four steps of the IK model are:

1. Set a challenge or direction—a longer-term, overarching goal.
2. Grasp the current condition.
3. Set a next target condition (often about two weeks out).
4. Conduct experiments toward the target condition. Then go back to Step 2 and repeat until the big goal is reached.

Rother's graphics show the non-linear sequence of the steps to illustrate the dynamics of the experimentation stage between the current condition and the next target condition.

The Improvement Kata model comes from research into how Toyota manages people, which is summarized in *Toyota Kata* by Mike Rother.

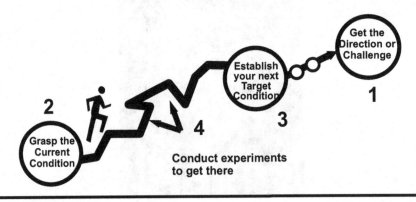

Improvement Kata by Mike Rother.

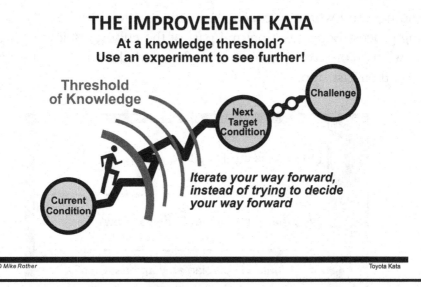

THE IMPROVEMENT KATA
At a knowledge threshold?
Use an experiment to see further!

Threshold of Knowledge by Mike Rother.

The combination of scientific thinking and deliberate practice is a functional, powerful combination. Scientific thinking addresses bias and knowledge thresholds. Deliberate practice is about developing new skills and habits to make change possible.

Repeated practice is self-reinforcing, allowing people to internalize skills and develop "muscle memory" for certain tasks. In the case of TK, the idea is to make some key scientific-thinking patterns more habitual while the practitioner consciously focuses on the situational aspects in pursuing their goal. Less conscious effort is required once habits have been formed. Attention and focus are available for other tasks. For example, initial driving lessons require full attention on the use of the brakes and gas pedal. These tasks later become intuitive, allowing the driver to focus on traffic and road conditions. Practice enables performance, which is best developed by learning from an experienced instructor, such as a driving teacher, a dance instructor, a swim coach, or a Kata coach.

Starter Kata and Coaching Kata

Proficiency is developed by practice under the guidance of a coach. In an organization practicing Kata, the learner's line manager typically serves as coach. The coach guides the learning through the process while providing corrective inputs. The Coaching Kata builds on five questions. The questions are headings, and what the coach asks between them will evolve as the thinking process becomes a natural part of the culture. Below is a card that shows the core five questions with the shaded area to ask the leaner to reflect on their last step.

The Coaching Kata card by Mike Rother.

Application of Toyota Kata for Lean Practitioners

While everyone can benefit by learning to practice scientific thinking, it is particularly valuable for rookie CI practitioners. The Improvement Kata pattern is an antidote to the natural tendency to jump to conclusions. This tendency is particularly tempting for change agents new to lean. In early kaizen projects, teams create process maps that peel back the curtain on bureaucratic waste. Unintended negative consequences can arise from the eagerness to be free of non-valued-added steps. Questions by cautious project sponsors may be viewed as resistance, and they may be pressured into approving untested changes. While mistakes are part of any CI initiative, a rush to implement poorly redesigned workflows can undermine confidence, lead to backsliding, and risk discrediting the CI initiative.

As Rother explains, The widespread definition of Lean as "eliminating waste" gains meaning and power when scientific thinking is brought into it. *Implementing* Lean would be the equivalent of a "push" approach. Lean is too big, complicated, and situation-dependent for that. It is more effective to start with a key "metaskill" like scientific thinking/PDCA/problem solving plus some context-appropriate Lean basics, and then keep growing your own Lean system from there based on what is happening and what's being learned. This is the symbiotic relationship between Lean and Toyota Kata that I mentioned earlier.[15]

Teams and sponsors who practice the Improvement Kata routines understand each target condition as a prediction and each step as an experiment, reinforcing the PDCA cycle. Enthusiastic change agents learn that the new workflow, now the current state, is also subject to improvement. Kata preserves the morale boost and sense of liberation experienced by these early adopters while teaching them to ask critical, scientific-thinking questions. Using the Kata routines, they learn to test ideas and compare what they think will happen with what actually happens, and to adjust based on what they discover from the difference. What is learned in each stage informs the next steps. It is a routine of intentionally coordinating between what is expected to happen and what actually happens, and adjusting based on what is learned from the difference.

As practitioners advance in CI learning, they can apply these Kata routines in increasingly complex and dynamic challenges. As Rother explains, "You can establish challenging goals for an organization *if* its people have

Learning by Mike Rother.

practiced and learned an effective way of meeting them."[16] Each improvement results in a new current condition, enabling users to set new target conditions in line with the organization's goals and conduct experiments to reach them.

With these habits ingrained in the organizational culture, practitioners can continually reset target conditions in the direction of their "true north," in pursuit of the organization's strategic and philosophical vision or purpose.[17] An essential skill for advancing CI initiatives, this broadly applicable model and practice method could also be useful in partnership with academic researchers and policy makers working to identify best practices for addressing social problems. For example:

- What was learned from the first experiment? Was it effective and sustainable?
- Grasp the new current condition: What needs remain unmet by the warming station? How many remained unsheltered?

Applying Toyota Kata to Community

Speaking at KataCon, the annual gathering of Kata practitioners, in 2019, Jason Schulist presented "Improving Your Community *as a Community*."[18] Applying the work of Mike Rother's Toyota Kata (TK),[19] Schulist demonstrated how TK can be used for community change, using the example of his work in Appleton, Wisconsin.

TK Step 1: In Schulist's example, two challenges were established. The team identified an ideal future state and a near-term challenge to be achieved within a year. Such an approach is useful for community work because of the complex factors involved in solving social problems. It is also helpful to those who are dedicated to solving them. Committed social reformers need to look at the big picture, but in order to maintain their dedication

Consider how TK might be used for dealing with the crisis of homelessness.

Kata steps in sequence			
Step 1	Step 2	Step 3	Step 4
The vision: Set the challenge	Grasp the current condition	Establish the next target condition	Conduct experiment to achieve target condition
No one is unhoused	An estimated 800 people are unhoused	100 unhoused persons have shelter	First experiment: Use the National Guard partnering with a social service agency to open an emergency warming station at the Armory

for the long term, they also need to tackle the problems in manageable steps. In that respect, TK is well suited to help idealists avoid burnout.

- The true north: Every household has financial stability, and jobs in the region are filled.
- A challenge intended to be achieved within a year: A 25% reduction in poverty for female heads of household (renter/owner) by July 2019.

TK Step 2: The discipline of scientific thinking enables the team to grasp the current condition with as much objectivity and specificity as possible. Using data, rather than assumptions and anecdotes, prepares the team to set the next target condition.

TK Step 3: The next target condition, to be achieved in upcoming weeks. The team set manageable goals such as developing an understanding of the cliff effect[20] among key influencers.

TK Step 4: Acknowledging the tendency of community advocates to engage in public policy debates, Schulist pointed out that the TK model had a place for such dialog. In the case presented, the team used the PDSA cycle to track the use of countermeasures, compare what they expected to happen with what actually happened, and study the learning that resulted. Studying the learning enabled them to establish the next target condition.

Jason Schulist.

Result: The project reported decreases in the rate of poverty in the targeted communities. In 2017, the metropolitan area of Appleton had a poverty rate of 5.21%, the fifth lowest in the country.

Summary. Using the Toyota Kata method, they developed a community vision, set each target condition, and used PDCA to experiment on various countermeasures. Tangible progress and learning occurred simultaneously as community members used scientific thinking for collaborative problem-solving. Given the complexity of intertwined social problems such as homelessness, joblessness, and drug addiction, the team was conducting as many as 20 to 30 PDCA cycles at a time.

At each stage, the team worked to overcome identified obstacles and track the results. Scientific thinking is particularly valuable in this type of work. "Because of 'unknown unknowns' there is a need to keep sensing the current state, learn, gage against a desired direction, and adjust," Schulist explained. Since the cause and effect are not simple, and there are many competing ideas, there is a need for creative approaches. This case demonstrates that using TK and adopting the discipline of

A way to approach a community issue

This is a scientific-thinking approach

1 Define Excellence or True North

Get the Challenge or AIM for the year

3 Establish the Next Qtr Target Condition

2 Grasp the Current Condition

4 Conduct Experiments – Make a change and test it

Community Alignment Work

What community issues must we address; not what *can* we address?

Community Improvement Work

Adapted from the *Toyota Kata Practice Guide*

Improving your community as a community.

Source: **Courtesy of the Generative Local Community Institute (GLCI)**

scientific thinking does not impede creativity. Rather, it facilitates innovation.

This case demonstrates the efficacy of a locally based community effort. This is a potentially replicable model for concerned community members coming together to address complex social problems. Schulist summarized five elements for building scientific-thinking skills and mindset in a group of people:

1. True north
2. Challenge
3. Method
4. Practice
5. Coaching

The benefit of TK is that it can be applied to deal with any number of scenarios because it is a core skill. Used in conjunction with standard CI methodology, governmental organizations could go from the results-driven to social-good-driven. The use of TK for community will be discussed further in Chapter 15. But first, it is useful to consider the challenge of developing lean public policy.

Notes

1 James P. Womack, *Lean Government*, June 26, 2014. www.lean.org/the-lean-post/articles/lean-government/

2 Jim Womack, "Lean Thinking for Government." Presented at the NH Lean Summit, September, 2013. https://lean.nh.gov/documents/Jim%20Womack%20-%20New%20Hampshire%20Lean%20Day,%20September%2024,%202013.pdf

3 Many of the descriptions and definitions in this section are based on the EPA's Lean Starter Kit.

4 John Shook, "How Standardized Work Integrates People with Process." *Lean Enterprise Institute. E-book*, 2019.

5 Martin O'Malley, *Smarter Government: How to Govern for Results in the Information Age* (Esri Press, Redlands, CA, 2019), pp. 17–18.

6 Anthony Manos and Chad Vincent, editors, *The Lean Handbook* (ASQ Quality Press, Milwaukee, WI, 2012), p. 155.

7 Shayne Kavanagh, "Less Time, Lower Cost, and Greater Quality: Making Government Work Better with Lean Process Improvement." White Paper. *Government Finance Officers Association*, pp. 25–26. www.gfoa.org/sites/default/files/GFOALeanWhitePaper.pdf

8 Mike Rother, *Toyota Kata* (McGraw-Hill Education, New York, NY, 2010), p. 11.

9 Some users prefer to work with eight or nine fields.

10 John Shook, Discovering the True Value of the A3 Process." *Lean Enterprise Institute. Lean Post Articles*, July 13, 2022. www.lean.org/the-lean-post/articles/the-a3-process-discovery-at-toyota-and-what-it-can-do-for-you/

11 David Verble, "How to start the A3 Problem Solving Process." *Lean Enterprise Institute. Lean Post Articles*, July 19, 2022. www.lean.org/the-lean-post/articles/how-do-i-start-my-a3/

12 John M. Bernard, "Level Three Government: Evolving State Operations from Reaction Driven to Results Driven to Social Good Driven." White Paper, 2021, p. 19. Level-Three-Government-WP-V2-FINAL.pdf (johnmbernard.com)

13 Mike Rother, *Toyota Kata* (McGraw-Hill Education, New York, NY, 2010), p. 5.

14 Mike Rother, "Developing and Utilizing Human Capabilities by Practicing Scientific Thinking." Conference presentation at KataCon5 (video and slides), February, 2019. www.youtube.com/watch?v=1l68cFskC7Y

15 Mike Rother, email communication to author, January 11, 2023.

16 Mike Rother, "Developing & Utilizing Human Capabilities by Practicing Scientific Thinking." Conference presentation at KataCon5 (video and slides), February, 2019. www.youtube.com/watch?v=1l68cFskC7Y

17 Chet Marchwinski, *Lean Lexicon* (Lean Enterprise Institute, Cambridge, MA, 2014), p. 113.

18 Jason Schulist and Mike Rother, "Improving Your Community as a Community." Presentation at KataCon9 https://leanfrontiers.com/katacon9/agenda/

19 Mike Rother, *Toyota Kata* (McGraw-Hill Education, New York, NY, 2010), p. 15.

20 Benefits "cliffs" refers to the sudden drop in public benefits that may result from a small wage increase.

Chapter 13

Lean Policy Development

Policy making is the most difficult of the governmental functions to lean.[1] Laws and programs are often enacted at the reaction-driven level of maturity. Political leaders concerned with image and reelection opt for the appearance of action over genuine solutions. Risk-averse administrators are likely to do the same. New programs are started with new names and overlapping purposes that require new layers of coordination.

In contrast to the ad-hoc and reactive approach, lean public policy differs both in purpose and function. Lean practitioners are systems thinkers. Viewing disparate processes as components of a whole, lean thinkers seek to integrate functions across silos to maximize value, quality, and efficiency.

Interestingly, one of the most important examples of lean program design began in the last century. With overhead costs at less than 1%, Social Security has had remarkable results. A report by the National Academy of Social Insurance explained the impact:

> Before Social Security, in 1934, roughly one half of seniors were estimated to be poor. Most had to rely on family or friends, or go to the poor house. As ever more seniors paid into Social Security and then received retirement benefits, the poverty rate among seniors steadily declined from circa 50 percent in the Great Depression to 35 percent in 1959, 25 percent in 1970, 15 percent in 1975, and around 10 percent in 2000, where it has hovered ever since. Today, were it not for Social Security, the senior poverty rate would be 43.5 percent, and just over half of elderly African Americans (51 percent) and Latinos (52 percent) would be poor.[2]

DOI: 10.4324/9781003372691-17

SOCIAL SECURITY'S LEAN DESIGN OF UNIVERSALITY

President Franklin Roosevelt's vision for social insurance: simplicity of design for social equity. Rather than establishing a bureaucracy that required seniors to apply for assistance, Roosevelt proposed contributory social insurance. Those who worked and paid into the system would be eligible, regardless of their personal financial status. As he signed it into law on August 14, 1935, Roosevelt proclaimed:

> "We can never insure one hundred percent of the population against one hundred percent of the hazards and vicissitudes of life, but we have tried to frame a law which will give some measure of protection to the average citizen and to his family against the loss of a job and against poverty-ridden old age."[3]

As Jacob Hacker explained in The Great Risk Shift, "social insurance transformed individual misfortunes into common problems. . . . [S]ocial insurance pools risks on terms that enable the poor as well as the rich, the aged as well as the young."[4]

The Benefits of Universality

Social Security differs from typical social programs in form and substance. Eligibility based on work records allows for an overhead of less than 1%,[5] in contrast to the complex regulations of traditional social services. In addition to administrative ease, there are social and political advantages to universality. Programs viewed as "welfare" carry a stigma and are frequent targets for budget cuts. Conversely, if everyone is eligible, everyone has a stake in it.

Constructing Lean Public Policy

Be skeptical of means testing. Avoid enacting redundant programs. Apply lean process design when enacting any new programs to avoid administrative complexity and rework-loops.

In the reaction-driven level of maturity in government, elected officials tend to enact new programs based on events in the news, or in response to a constituent request. The adage, "if the only tool you have is a hammer, everything looks like a nail," applies to legislators. They're elected to be lawmakers, so they tend to make laws.

As Jim Womack noted, policy making requires a "clear statement of the actual problem, followed by a structured process to identify and test countermeasures."[6] Lean legislators would research the root cause of the problem and collaborate with colleagues to find the best way to address it. However, pride of authorship and the desire to claim political credit work against such collaborative efforts.

Collaborative efforts may also be stymied if legislative research services have limited access to data about existing programs. The task of grasping the current condition is not a simple one for lawmakers. If states and federal agencies continue to develop results-driven operations, performance metrics will be more readily available. However, the proactive task of policy development will require the integration of CI tools with the TK discipline of scientific thinking.

TK can take on the complexity of developing effective public policy in several respects. Once proficiency is developed at the basic level, it is possible to apply these skills to address seemingly intractable problems. With a true north vision established, the discipline of grasping the current condition prior to setting the next target condition would shift the focus from the common reaction-driven approach. As experimentation brings learning, each subsequent target condition would be set based on an understanding of what has occurred to alter the current condition. Requiring attention to an ever-evolving current condition enables continuous course corrections on the path to the true north. This dynamic aspect is incredibly important, particularly given the speed of technological advances. The skill of scientific thinking enables the users to integrate new technological developments and changes in circumstances. Consider how this might be applied to leaning the "complexes."

Layers of Complexity

The complexity is not limited to the layers in the administrative bureaucracy. Significant sectors of the economy interact with government in various capacities. The interrelationship has been characterized as a "complex."

The Military-Industrial Complex

President Dwight D. Eisenhower issued his famous warning in his farewell address, on January 17, 1961, excerpted here:

> A vital element in keeping the peace is our military establishment. Our arms must be mighty, ready for instant action, so

that no potential aggressor may be tempted to risk his own destruction. . . .

Until the latest of our world conflicts, the United States had no armaments industry. American makers of plowshares could, with time and as required, make swords as well. But now we can no longer risk emergency improvisation of national defense; we have been compelled to create a permanent armaments industry of vast proportions. Added to this, three and a half million men and women are directly engaged in the defense establishment. We annually spend on military security more than the net income of all United State corporations.

This conjunction of an immense military establishment and a large arms industry is new in the American experience. The total influence—economic, political, even spiritual—is felt in every city, every state house, every office of the Federal government. We recognize the imperative need for this development. Yet we must not fail to comprehend its grave implications. Our toil, resources, and livelihood are all involved; so is the very structure of our society.

In the councils of government, we must guard against the acquisition of unwarranted influence, whether sought or unsought, by the military-industrial complex. The potential for the disastrous rise of misplaced power exists and will persist.[7]

The Medical-Industrial Complex

Decades later, Dr. Arnold Redmond harkened back to the speech, writing in the *New England Journal of Medicine*:

In his farewell address as President on January 17, 1961, Eisenhower warned his countrymen of what he called "the military-industrial complex," a huge and permanent armaments industry that, together with an immense military establishment, had acquired great political and economic power. He was concerned about the possible conflict between public and private interests in the crucial area of national defense.

The past decade has seen the rise of another kind of private "industrial complex" with an equally great potential for influence on public policy—this time in health care. What I will call the "new medical-industrial complex" is a large and growing network of private corporations engaged in the business of supplying

health-care services to patients for a profit—services heretofore
provided by nonprofit institutions or individual practitioners.[8]

Others have since used the term "medical-industrial complex" more broadly,
to describe the insurance companies and other intermediaries dealing with
coding, billing, and collections that interact with for-profit and nonprofit
providers of a wide range of medical specialties, treatment centers, and lab
services.

The majority of state governments have added a layer of insurance companies to manage the publicly funded Medicaid program. The increased
administrative complexity is counter-intuitive to a lean operation, which
seeks to minimize hand-offs.

A lean evaluation of a privatized Medicaid program would consider the
time, effort, and cost of contracting out services, and the capacity to assure
contractual compliance by multiple managed care organizations (MCOs), as
well as the fees charged by those entities. This would be compared to the
cost of administration by the state. A lean review would assess the cost-ben-
efit of failing to build internal capacity.

The extent of the gap between payment for medical care and total
program spending varies widely. Based on data from 2016-2017, *Health
Affairs* reported, "A five-fold variation in the amount of administrative overhead among states' managed care plans, and a 37-percentage-point spread
in the percentage of MCO revenues that are spent on actual care."[9] In 2021,
the Office of Inspector General reported that many of the 39 states using
MCOs had "[i]ncomplete or inaccurate information for the amounts paid,
allowed, and billed."[10]

The State of Connecticut conducted an audit in 2009, which found that
Connecticut overpaid MCOs by nearly $50 million. In 2012, the state discon-
tinued using MCOs for its Medicaid program, saving in excess of $40 million.
The gains were not solely financial. Moving from three MCOs to a common administrative entity consolidated patient data, allowing primary-care
doctors access to information about their patients' prescriptions, hospital
admissions, and treatment by specialists. That knowledge would "[h]elp
doctors reduce duplication, avoid errors, and ensure patients follow through
with their treatment plans," according to then-Commissioner of Social
Services Roderick Bremby.[11]

The same year as the audit in Connecticut, Rhode Island's Auditor
General recommended that the Department of Human Services "consider implementing independent audit requirements into managed care

agreements to validate the total cost of services provided to Medicaid eligible individuals." Subsequent annual reports repeated the recommendation, including a notation in 2015 that "[a]pproximately $208 million was estimated as overpayments to MCOs of which $133 million remained due to the State at June 30, 2015." In 2018, *Health Affairs* reported that Rhode Island's MCO contracting overhead was the second highest of the 32 states and D.C. using MCOs.[12] Legislation to require an audit has repeatedly stalled in the General Assembly. Consider applying lean principles to Medicaid management:

- The core tenet of Lean integrates efficiency with quality for the purpose of delivering value. Does contracting out drive cost without adding value to Medicaid recipients or medical providers? Does the privatization unnecessarily divert program funds to MCOs? Could states achieve savings similar to those in Connecticut and reallocate funds to enhance quality?
- Hand-offs are unlean. As Rhode Island physician Mark Ryan explained, *"MCOs are not actually health care providers.* Rather, they are inadequately monitored middlemen 'payers' who take money from patients and tax payers and pay **some** of that money to actual healthcare providers (hospitals, physicians, etc.)."[13]
- Administrative complexity is unlean. Is the state's administrative burden of issuing and managing contracts factored into the cost of the Medicaid program? What additional resources would be required for the state to properly oversee these private entities, as recommended by the Auditor General's report? How would that compare to building appropriate internal capacity?

The Nonprofit-Industrial Complex

In 2007, INCITE!, a network of radical feminists of color, published a series of essays, *The Revolution Will Not Be Funded: Beyond the Non-Profit Industrial Complex.*[14] Drawing from Gil Scott Heron's song, *The revolution will not be televised*, and Eisenhower's warning about the military industrial complex, INCITE! warned that social-justice organizations could be coopted by the need to survive by grant-seeking. The title creates a vivid and lasting image of a growing tangle of nonprofit organizations having their energy sapped and their purpose blurred as they compete for resources to survive.

Leaning the Complexes

The apt use of the term "complex" to describe each of these systems indicates the necessity of leaning each one. CI tools and TK are built to address complexity. In each case, improvements in efficiency would free up resources for other societal purposes. Yet grasping the current condition is not simple in any of these examples. Consider the questions a researcher might pose in pursuit of a bold vision for each:

Consider a vision for a robust, ever-ready national defense capacity, without undue influence or price-gouging. What is the current condition? How are weapons systems evaluated and selected by tactical value, and by whom? How are technological advances factored in? How are defense appropriations decided by Congress? What is the status of cost-overruns, and how are contracts monitored? How much is given in campaign contributions from the defense industry, by district, during each election cycle? Are outmoded systems continued as jobs programs in certain Congressional districts? Are there valuable components or innovations that are neglected?

Consider a vision for universal access to health care that minimizes or eliminates the role of non-value-added intermediaries without sacrificing medical advances or creating waiting lines. What is the current condition? What data can be collected on current health outcomes? Are there demographic or geographic patterns? What correlations have been established? What are the current costs for administrative functions, research and development, and direct care? What proposals exist to move toward the vision, and what might be the next target condition?

Consider a vision for a vibrant nonprofit sector that contributes to the advancement of society, with lean management providing good stewardship of funds and minimal redundancy. What is the current condition? How many non-profits exist, by category? What are their primary functions? Where are they located? Consider lean tools such as value stream maps or affinity diagrams to understand the current condition by community. What are the primary funding streams? Which provide services that are redundant to existing governmental agencies? Are there government-agency functions that are contracted to nonprofits? How many different IT systems are in use among agencies? How are opportunities for technological advancement identified and implemented?

The questions listed above are just a few of the many that could be asked while seeking to grasp the current condition in these complex systems. The iterative methodology of TK helps to structure the inquiry while still being mindful of a vision. Such scientific thinking necessitates adjusting for changes in circumstances. Consistently applied, it has the potential to keep a universal health care system innovative, with an appropriate transition for employees from the health insurance industry. An iterative process of policy experimentation could facilitate the economic transition for communities reliant on the construction of outmoded weapons systems.

Such a process might lead to discovering how to install technological upgrades to determine eligibility for human-service programs and provide timely access for those in need. Discussion of the potential for leaning the nonprofit-industrial complex will continue in Chapter 15.

Lean Lens on Public Policy

Given the vast challenges of using TK/CI on the "complexes," it is important to return to more immediate and practical applications. As the core principles become second nature, it is easy to add processes that need to be leaned. Organizational principles of quality, efficiency, and standard work are universally applicable to public administration.

Existing laws and regulations need to be examined prior to the chartering of a project. Ideally, lawmakers would join agency staff and customers on *kaizen* teams to review processes, identify value to the public, and recommend ways to reduce *muda*. A useful trigger for these *kaizens* could be a performance audit, which may be conducted by a legislative research office or comparable unit. If every performance audit triggered a *kaizen*, it could establish behaviors and set expectations, which would create habits, building toward a culture of continuous improvement.

Integrating technical capacity with structured routines and consistent leadership was at the heart of former Governor O'Malley's four tenets of performance management:[15]

- Timely, accurate information shared by all
- Rapid deployment of resources
- Effective tactics and strategies
- Relentless follow-up and assessment

Diligence and consistency are essential in continuous improvement initiatives. Initially, it may seem paradoxical to propose consistent experimentation along with standard work. Yet it is completely compatible. Each model of standard work is the new current condition from which a new target condition can be set, in the cycle of continuous improvement.

As Patricia Panchak of the James P. Womack Scholarship and Philanthropy Fund explained, "Among the many outcomes of continuous improvement practices is one that happens so frequently that it's become a lean truism. Nevertheless, the result continues to surprise even the most advanced lean practitioners. That truism is that nearly every time you address an issue with lean thinking and practices, you not only make progress toward resolving it. You also uncover more issues to address—and sometimes unexpected ones. This consistent outcome reminds us that lean is about learning as much as it is about removing waste, resolving problems, and improving the work environment."[16]

Notes

1 James P. Womack, *Lean Government*. June 26, 2014. www.lean.org/the-lean-post/articles/lean-government/
2 Benjamin Veghte, "Social Security's Past, Present and Future." *National Academy of Social Insurance*, August 13, 2015. www.nasi.org/discussion/social-securitys-past-present-and-future/
3 Social Security.gov, *Historical Background and Development of Social Security* December 8, 2022. www.ssa.gov/history/brief history3.html
4 Jacob Hacker, *The Great Risk Shift* (Oxford University Press, Oxford, UK, 2008).
5 Social Security.gov, *Social Security Administrative Expenses*. www.ssa.gov/oact/stats/admin.html
6 James P. Womack, *Lean Government*, June 26, 2014. www.lean.org/the-lean-post/articles/lean-government/
7 Farewell Address by President Dwight D. Eisenhower, January 17, 1961; Final TV Talk 1/17/61 (1), Box 38, Speech Series, Papers of Dwight D. Eisenhower as President, 1953–61, Eisenhower Library; National Archives and Records Administration www.archives.gov/milestone-documents/president-dwight-d-eisenhowers-farewell-address
8 Arnold S. Relman, "The New Medical-Industrial Complex." *The New England Journal of Medicine* 303 (1980): 963–970. DOI: 10.1056/NEJM198010233031703
9 Jeff C. Goldsmith, David Mosley, and Anne Jacobs, "Medicaid Managed Care: Lots Of Unanswered Questions (Part 2)," *Health Affairs*, May 14, 2018. www.healthaffairs.org/do/10.1377/forefront.20180430.510086/full/
10 U.S. Department of Health & Human Services. Office of Inspector General. Data Brief. Data on Medicaid, *Managed Care Payments to Providers Are Incomplete and Inaccurate*. https://oig.hhs.gov/oei/reports/OEI-02-19-00180.pdf

11 Christine Vestal, "Connecticut Revisits Old-School Medicaid Financing." *Pew Stateline Article*, April 8, 2012. www.pewtrusts.org/en/research-and-analysis/blogs/stateline/2012/04/08/connecticut-revisits-oldschool-medicaid-financing

12 Jeff C. Goldsmith, David Mosley, and Anne Jacobs, *Medicaid Managed Care: Lots of Unanswered Questions (Part 2)*, May 14, 2018. www.healthaffairs.org/do/10.1377/forefront.20180430.510086/full/

13 J. Mark Ryan, and Linda Ujifusa, *Want to Cut Rhode Island Medicaid Costs? Stop Ignoring the Elephant in the Room: MCOs.* https://upriseri.com/want-to-cut-rhode-island-medicaid-costs-stop-ignoring-the-elephant-in-the-room-mcos/ (emphasis as original).

14 INCITE! Women of Color Against Violence, *The Revolution Will Not Be Funded: Beyond the Non-Profit Industrial Complex* (The Duke University Press, Durham, 2017).

15 Martin O'Malley, *Smarter Government: How to Govern for Results in the Information Age* (Esri Press, Redlands, CA, 2019), p. 12.

16 Patricia Panchak, "Assessing a New Way to Develop More Lean Thinkers." *The James P. Womack Scholarship & Philanthropy Fund. Lean Enterprise Institute: E-book*, 2022, p. 16. www.lean.org/the-lean-post/articles/assessing-a-new-way-to-develop-more-lean-thinkers/

A LEAN FUTURE STATE IV

Excellence in operations and public policy. Part IV links the promise of CI to make government more effective to its potential to solve complex problems.

Chapter 14: Leaning Government Operations. How to achieve results-driven government and overcome threats and barriers to a sustainable culture of continuous improvement.

Chapter 15: Continuous Improvement for Thriving Communities. Exploring how results-driven government can become a platform from which social good-driven government can be built. It includes scenarios for applying CI and Toyota Kata in a range of possibilities, from building local communities to tackling social problems.

Chapter 16: Diffusion of Lean Culture and Level III Government. Wrapping in a broad summary of recommendations, this chapter poses a series of challenges and closes with a reflection on the purpose of government.

DOI: 10.4324/9781003372691-18

Chapter 14

Leaning Government Operations

Is Federalism Unlean? or a PCDA Opportunity?

Justice Brandeis famously championed the notion of states as laboratories for social and economic experiments:

> Denial of the right to experiment may be fraught with serious consequences to the nation. It is one of the happy incidents of the federal system that a single courageous state may, if its citizens choose, serve as a laboratory; and try novel social and economic experiments without risk to the rest of the country.
>
> Louis Brandeis, 1932

On the other hand, if such experiments are not guided by reason, the lack of cohesion can have tragic results. In May 2021, as pandemic deaths neared 600,000, Donald F. Kettl's column "How American-Style Federalism Is Hazardous to Our Health" explored possible structural causes for the U.S. COVID-19 fatality rate exceeding that of other comparable nations.[1]

Kettl posited that federalism might be to blame for the country's excessive losses, with different states adopting different policies. But he noted that other countries with federal systems, such as Germany and Canada, performed comparatively well. Then, suggesting that the governmental structure was not to blame, Kettl suggested, "Americans suffered more from COVID-19 because its decentralized system of federalism simply failed to rise to the

DOI: 10.4324/9781003372691-19

challenge." Quoting a Swiss colleague, Danny Buerkli, Kettl concluded there was "lots of experimentation" but "very little learning." He explained:

> In the U.S., there simply wasn't any mechanism for collecting nationally what the states and their cities were learning, and that handicapped the American response. In fact, one of the most profound American breakdowns was the failure even to recognize that this was an essential question in desperate need of a solid answer. And that, in turn, weakened the national hand on the COVID-19 steering wheel and the ability of the states to act as true laboratories.

Arguably, PDCA could be applied to the 50 states to do exactly what Kettl suggested: ask essential questions and seek solid answers. Imagine 50 laboratories, each testing pilot programs to accomplish broad social purposes. It would be extremely creative, but not necessarily lean, unless the experimentation resulted in learning. There must also be a system to share that learning, so that common problems do not need to be solved 50 different times.

To maximize the value of creativity without redundancy, John M. Bernard proposed using a national clearinghouse to share and replicate innovative solutions. The purpose, he explains, is the "end of the need to 'invent it here.'"[2]

Potential Gain from Standardization across State and Local Government Operations

The concept of standardization can be considered for the states—both within states and among states. Despite variation in agency configurations, the 50 states have a core set of common responsibilities. Should each state, and each agency within the state, design and acquire its own software system for functions conducted in all 50 jurisdictions?

Rework Is Unlean

Designing thousands of separate systems wastes a great deal of human effort and financial resources that could be redeployed to other urgent priorities. Cross-jurisdictional replication could avoid the rework of each municipality leaning each of its processes. For example, standard processes could enable the purchase of standard IT systems, avoiding costly customizations.

Lean techniques are in use in dozens of states and municipalities, and several states with robust CI programs encourage staff from municipalities to enroll in lean training programs. There have also been joint projects to improve processes between state and local governments, particularly related to transfer of funds. In addition to the efficiency gains, such projects build skills and lean thinking.

Town clerks, law enforcement, first responders, city planners, tax collectors, and other municipal officials in thousands of jurisdictions conduct similar public responsibilities with slight variations. They have all developed their own way of doing the same things. Why? There are two classic answers: "Because that's the way it's always been done," and "we're unique." Thousands of municipalities determine specifications, issue RFPs, evaluate bids, and work with vendors on customizations to automate common business processes such as permitting, tax collection, payroll, asset management, and purchasing.

NON-STANDARD FIRE TRUCKS

An example of the ripple effect of unlean municipal services emerged in a case study by the Lean Enterprise Institute (LEI). Ironically, the study was not about public-sector lean work. It was about how a private company, United Plastic Fabricating (UPF), which manufactures water tanks for fire trucks, adapted to extreme variation among its municipal customers.

As LEI's Matthew Savas reported, each local fire chief determines the design of that municipality's fire trucks, and there are nearly 30,000 fire departments in the United States. This amount of variation presented both engineering and production challenges for UPF. Savas explained that "the water tank's design is based on the void that remains following the installation of everything else, so UPF's engineers and factory workers must design, cut, and weld some gnarly shapes that are rarely identical."[3]

UPF met the challenge by using shopfloor *kaizens* and applying lean thinking to engineering. Among the changes was a transition from craft manufacturing, in which operators built tanks from start to finish in fixed stations, to flow manufacturing. UPF continued to apply lean techniques and principles, and within two years, the company had increased productivity by 60%. They successfully adapted to the needs of their customers.

UPF's success story embodies the core value of lean: value is defined by the customer. However, a public sector lean practitioner could start asking the Five Whys to understand why the fire chiefs order different trucks. Asking a series of "whys" might identify the optimal specifications of fire trucks based on a range of factors such as community size, density, street width, building height, the number of fire stations, and the size of each jurisdiction. Would there be benefits of economies of scale if similarly situated communities used standard designs that were optimal for their circumstances? Perhaps a *kaizen* could be convened with fire chiefs and partners such as UPF.

Local jurisdictions could save the cost of customizing everything from software to equipment. Standard permitting criteria and procedures could also facilitate economic development. Deming recalled his colleague Walter Shewhart's observation that building codes that differ ever so slightly from city to city "were more effective than tariff walls at throttling mass production and raising costs."[4]

Changes of that scope would need a Toyota Kata approach to test the effectiveness of each target condition. Since an effort to establish a standard regulatory system for building codes would be subject to pressure by developers favoring lenient standards, there is a risk for unintended negative consequences. As with any lean project, the voice of the customer—in this case, the permit applicant—is essential. Equally important is the establishment of a mission-driven true north, against which each target condition can be evaluated. The goldilocks level of regulation protects the public without unlean bureaucracy.

Consider how TK might be used to establish standard building codes.

Kata steps in sequence			
Step 1	*Step 2*	*Step 3*	*Step 4*
The vision: Set the challenge	Grasp the current condition	Establish the next target condition	Conduct experiment to achieve target condition
The state's building code protects public health and safety and prevents harm to the environment.	Every community has its own building code.	The majority of communities adopt the same standard for one aspect.	First experiment: Ask communities to adopt a standard aspect that is recommended by the State Fire Marshall. (If already in place, select another aspect.)

- ▪ What was learned from the first experiment? Was it effective?
- ▪ Grasp the new current condition: How many communities have adopted the recommended standard?

Challenges in Managing a CI Initiative

Many processes have never been documented and therefore lack performance metrics. Many programs have never established performance measures. Annual reports may contain outputs such as the number of clients served, rather than the number of people remaining below the poverty level. Not all of the available measurements provide meaningful information for the purpose of problem-solving. For example, should the unemployment rate be measured based on the number of people eligible to collect unemployment compensation or the number of people unable to find work?

Complexity in State Government Structures

Each state has dozens of agencies, many with overlapping jurisdictions. Although primary functions are the same, there is an array of configurations in each state, county, and municipality. Structural differences also complicate collection of data for meaningful cross-jurisdictional comparisons.

The thickening of government has extended into the for-profit sector, as some managerial and service-delivery functions have been contracted out. Hand-offs are generally unlean, increasing time, cost, and complexity. Government contracting requires the staffing of a matrix of regulatory functions to guard against impropriety and confirm deliverables. In order to bid for government contracts, organizations must meet a series of standards and reporting requirements. So there is plenty of non-value added work being performed by both parties just to authorize a contract, even before the profit margin is built in. How should the decision be made to contract out a function vs. conducting it in-house? If contracting is determined to be appropriate, the process should be as lean as possible. A *kaizen* team of administrators, customers, and stakeholders could design a streamlined process to minimize wait times and hand-offs while maintaining appropriate accountabilities.

A related project would be leaning the purchasing process, in which well-intentioned policies established to fight corruption and cronyism can result in significant waste. Consider addressing the problem statement: "How can the government procure timely, cost-effective, quality products with appropriate controls?"

Turning Managers into Change Agents

In *The Lean Toolbox*, the authors stress the significance of managers' involvement, noting that, "It is difficult to think of a successful Lean transformation that has not had real commitment and involvement from the top."[5] However, top managers' commitment may not permeate the organization, and they may not be able to differentiate a lack of understanding from a lack of agreement. The two may be interwoven if middle managers feel threatened by lean. As one administrator observed, "the life of a petty bureaucrat is hoard, hold, and hide." Many of them have learned to wait for new directives to go away, with the attitude of, "they're going to have to come find me, and there are too many of us." Another warned, "We must not underestimate the power of an experienced bureaucrat to passively resist."

It may not be resistance. Middle managers may avoid CI projects because their employees are responsible for critical tasks and are unable to participate in a week-long event. There are always pressing, competing priorities. If projects do take place, implementation may be postponed indefinitely. All managers are responsible for operations, but few are held responsible for improving systems. If upper management never articulated system improvement as an organizational priority, or assigned it as part of the job, are mid-level managers being resistant or realistic?

While acknowledging the most frequently cited cause for stalled CI initiatives is middle-management resistance, Jim Womack explains that "the root cause of regression . . . is confusion about priorities at different levels of the organization, compounded by the failure to make anyone responsible for the continuing performance of important value streams as they flow horizontally across the enterprise."[6] The alignment of authority and responsibility at appropriate levels requires clear expectations for operational excellence.

Those unfamiliar with the core principles may view lean practitioners as elite efficiency experts. Womack and co-authors John Shook, Peter Ward, and Josh Howell stressed the distinction: "Lean thinking and practice is not a linear descendent of scientific management where an expert designs the work and the worker executes. Standardized work in a Lean organization is developed and revised with participation of the people who do the work, unlike earlier practices described by Taylor (1911)[7] and others. Standardized work designed with worker involvement facilitates continuous, incremental process-level improvement by the people who do the work."[8]

It is difficult for those with decades of experience in traditional management to suddenly become lean managers. Perhaps they've heard good things about *kaizen* projects, and they're willing to try it out. If they are open to learning more, a workshop such as Nebraska's Certified Lean Leader program for supervisors, managers, and administrators could help them integrate process-improvement techniques within the overarching frame of lean management. Consider insights from CI and Toyota Production System (TPS) leader, Shigeo Shingo:

> The primary role of a leader is to drive the principles of operational excellence into the culture.
>
> The primary role of managers must shift from firefighting to designing, aligning, and improving systems.
>
> The more deeply leaders, managers, and associates understand the principles of operational excellence and the more perfectly systems are aligned to reinforce ideal behavior, the greater the probability of creating a sustainable culture of excellence where achieving ideal results is the norm rather than the aspiration.[9]

Threats to Lean Government

- Pressure to use CI to reduce spending. There is a risk that top leadership will focus on hard dollar savings rather than taking the opportunity to reallocate staff to other priorities. When early savings are realized by leaning the low hanging fruit, it can create the false impression that lean is about cost reduction rather than quality enhancement.
- Misunderstanding of the role of lean facilitators. Leaders with a superficial view of CI tools may try to deploy CI practitioners as efficiency experts, expecting them to tell employees how to do their work.

- Pressure to deregulate. When streamlining regulatory processes, it is important to guard against undue influence by those seeking to erode the purpose of the regulations.
- Restrictions on redeployment of staff. Narrow job classifications, contracts, or personnel rules may limit managers' flexibility to reallocate positions and assure that people do not lose their jobs or their level of compensation.
- Use it or lose it budgets. If managers don't spend their entire budgets during the fiscal year, the elected officials might give them less the following year, regardless of programmatic or equipment needs. The typical process of "last year plus" (or minus) is a lose-lose method. Needs go unmet, while baked-in waste continues.
- Belief that lean = *kaizen* events. While *kaizen* projects are a great way to get introduced to lean, there's a risk that people will think improvement occurs only through those events. The initiative will falter if the impression is that lean = process maps, and that CI work is specialized and intermittent, rather than an ongoing responsibility of all employees.

COUNTERMEASURES TO THREATS

- Educate legislators about CI. Administrators can preview the transformational potential during public hearings and invite legislators to tour worksites to hear directly from *kaizen* teams. Local private-sector leaders can provide testimony on how lean helped their businesses.
- PDCA for the training program. Once in place, maintain a dynamic PDCA in the Center of Operational Excellence and its network of agency coordinators. CI practitioners should be continuous learners. Course content for the training program should be refreshed regularly, including a robust continuing education component for the CI network. For example, NH BET Instructor Michael Moranti initially covered Toyota Kata in the Black Belt program; by 2022, he was introducing it in the Green Belt program.
- Training for managers and supervisors. All state programs would benefit from a requirement for supervisors to have CI training. Initial training will prepare them to sponsor projects. Advanced training with a mentor will help them become coaches.
- Lean tools accessible to all. Managers, supervisors, and agency lean liaisons should be demonstrating a broadly accessible range of tools,

such as 5S, to debunk the impression that CI = *kaizen* events. As they gain experience in coaching employees, they model the idea that CI is an ongoing responsibility of all staff.

- Ongoing mentoring and practice for supervisors. Preparing line managers for the coaching role is critical to the transition from disparate projects to internalizing CI as a way of doing business.

The initiative will never reach its full potential without broad transmission of skills and learned behaviors. Too much reliance on CI practitioners, even those internal to the organization, will limit the gains. Although a cadre of change agents fuels the launch, the methodology can't be hoarded by a club of nerds, geeks, and cool kids. If they function like external experts, they fail to transmit skills and lean thinking to the workforce. Dan Jones, co-author of *The Machine that Changed the World*, explained the consequence of failing to transform supervisors into CI coaches. In such cases, "the frontline teams did not sustain the initial successes" and the organizations may "end up using lean teams as cost-cutters or firefighters."[10]

Jones urged organizations to "build a daily management system in which line management learns to help teams to define their standard work as a baseline for improvement, make plan-versus-actual visible, and engage everyone in problem-solving to respond to deviations and to make improvements." Then, frontline managers and their teams will learn by doing, as they use PDCA in an A3 process of mentored dialog. These repeated learning cycles enhance the capacity "to formulate insightful hypotheses and possible countermeasures rather than jumping to solutions when tackling problems."

The Shingo Institute outlines a multidimensional model, explaining that "[o]perational excellence cannot be a program, another new set of tools, or a new management fad. Operational excellence is the consequence of an enterprise-wide practice of ideal behaviors based on correct principles. As long as improvement is seen as something outside the core work of the business, as long as it is viewed as 'something else to do,' operational excellence will remain elusive."[11]

With turnover of elected and administrative leadership always a threat to a COE's continuity, consider this advice from LEI:

> Time is of the essence for improvement efforts in many agencies since political winds and political appointees change regularly. . . .

[G]overnment leaders can quickly realize progress on small problems while also building a foundation for progress on tougher problems. . . . As more people are exposed to lean, even in small ways, they become more likely to influence new leaders to champion and sustain group efforts. Finally, lean management practices can be used to help leaders achieve a wide variety of policy or operational goals. Even when leaders and their goals change, *the management practices themselves are durable.* Those are likely to last in some form. Leaders who are serious about making a difference can use lean thinking to make sure their hard work and vision continues when they're gone.[12]

Continuous improvement requires an enduring commitment based on understanding the core principles. The potential is great. As Larry Terry asserted, public administrators have a duty to take on an active and legitimate role in governance. He described an empowered, invested leader intent on keeping the organization on mission. To that end, the administrative conservator "must be a good diagnostician as well as an adept strategist."[13] Deming issued a bold challenge: "It will not suffice to achieve brilliant successes here and there. Disjointed efforts will have no national impact."[14]

Notes

1 Donald F. Kettl, *How American-Style Federalism Is Hazardous to Our Health*, May 21, 2022. www.governing.com/now/how-american-style-federalism-is-dangerous-to-our-healthle Federalism Is Hazardous to Our Health (governing. com)

2 John M. Bernard, "Level Three Government: Evolving State Operations from Reaction Driven to Results Driven to Social Good Driven." *White Paper*, 2021, p. 28. Level-Three-Government-WP-V2-FINAL.pdf (johnmbernard.com)

3 Matthew Savas, "Overcoming Challenges with Lean Thinking Leads to Record-breaking Performance." *The Lean Post*, August 23, 2022. www.lean. org/the-lean-post/articles/overcoming-challenges-with-lean-thinking-leads-to-record-breaking-performance/

4 W. Edwards Deming, *Out of Crisis* (MIT Center for Advanced Educational Services, Cambridge, MA, 1982–1986), p. 301.

5 John Bicheno, and Matthias Holweg, *The Lean Toolbox*, 5th edition (Picsie Books, Buckingham, England, 2016), p. 90.

6 Jim Womack, *Gemba Walks* (The Lean Enterprise Institute, Cambridge, 2011), p. 92.

7 F.W. Taylor, *The Principles of Scientific Management* (Harper, New York, NY, 1911).
8 Michael A. Cusumano, Matthias Holweg, Josh Howell, Torbjørn Netland, Rachna Shah, John Shook, Peter Ward, and James Womack, "Commentaries on "The Lenses of Lean." *Journal of Operations Management* (2021): 6. DOI: 10.1002/joom.1138
9 The Shingo Institute https://shingo.org/
10 Dan Jones, *Why Lean Remains a Superior Business Model and Way of Thinking*, January 12, 2023. www.lean.org/the-lean-post/articles/why-lean-remains-a-superior-business-model-and-way-of-thinking/
11 The Shingo Institute, *The Shingo Model for Operational Excellence*, p. 11.
12 Lean Enterprise Institute, *5 Barriers to Lean in Government.* www.lean.org/the-lean-post/articles/5-barriers-to-lean-in-government/ (emphasis as original).
13 Larry D. Terry, *Leadership of Public Bureaucracies: The Administrator as Conservator* (M.E. Sharpe, New York, NY, 2003), p. 89.
14 W. Edwards Deming, *Out of the Crisis* (MIT Center for Advanced Educational Services, Cambridge, MA, 1982–1986), p. 488.

Chapter 15

Continuous Improvement for Thriving Communities

The path to social-good-driven government is built upon the foundation of efficient and effective government. Applying CI methodology, practitioners are finding potential far beyond the operational achievements.

In the introduction to *The Machine that Changed the World*, the authors echoed their title, predicting: "In this process we've become convinced that the principles of lean production can be applied equally in every industry across the globe and that the conversion to lean production will have a profound effect on human society—it will truly change the world."[1]

In his study of Toyota, Mike Rother found that the practices "had a potential beyond the business world. It shows us a scientifically systematic and constructive way of dealing with problems, uncertainty, and change . . . [and] how we can work together and achieve beyond what we can see."[2]

John Bernard sees a progression in the development of skills and the capacity to tackle problems deeply enmeshed in the social and economic systems of society that prevent people from thriving. He explains the trajectory of moving from the results-driven to the social-good-driven levels of government maturity:

> The skills, tools, thinking, and discipline developed in Level Two provide the foundation for Level Three. In fact, Level Three is Level Two that has matured to the extent it can best be described as "systemic" in addition to advancing several new capabilities. While Level Two is all about learning how to drive results, how to use

DOI: 10.4324/9781003372691-20

facts to identify root causes, the disciplines of process thinking and improvement inside the organization, and to function effectively as teams and as an organization, Level Three moves those same skills out of the building and into society, with the focus being the most complex challenges we face as a society: homelessness, opioid deaths, substance abuse, recidivism, poverty, dropping out of school or the workforce, suicide, obesity, mental health, veterans concerns, racism, child abuse and neglect, and mass violence.[3]

The Parable of the Babies in the River

There are many versions of a parable that is illustrative of core issues facing social reformers. One such version: You and two friends are hiking by a stream and notice a baby floating downstream. You rush in and rescue the baby. Then you see that there are two more to rescue, then two more, followed by a steadily increasing number. You are struggling to keep up to save as many babies as possible. Someone is needed to go for reinforcements to continue the rescues. Someone is needed to run up the hill and stop whoever is throwing them in.

For social reformers, the parable stimulates discussion about how to divide their efforts between direct services and social justice organizing. It is about symptoms and root causes. In either case, the lesson is the same: Society needs people who are going to save the babies *and* those who will run up the hill.

As Dr. James McDonald noted, ". . . people are sick and [we need] to help them right then and there, we're spending a lot of money doing that. . . . [W]hat can we do to prevent the problem in the first place? . . . Some of it is how you spend things to improve your social determinants of health . . . neighborhoods that are safe . . . schools that are effective . . . so people have jobs with health benefits—these [fundamentals] improve peoples' long term health outcomes. Housing that's stable. And this is where money should be invested."[4]

Leaning to Expand Capacity

While governments and nonprofits struggle to mitigate human suffering, CI methodologies can enable them to tackle root causes, too. Lean organizations can expend their resources more effectively, enabling them to meet the challenge of saving the babies *and* running up the hill.

Bernard is confident that the workforce is more than capable of delivering on mission. He wrote a series of open letters to state employees, under the headline, "We are in Trouble, We Need Your Help," on the networking site LinkedIn.[5]

Making the case that there was ample excess capacity, he used the example of process waste due to variation. One scenario involved work groups in different regional offices, where the employees were trained by different people at different times, with changes made along the way. In his experience with 14 teams that worked in regional offices around a state, all providing the same service, Bernard reported:

> Overall, the on-time completion of the work ran below 40 percent and the performance had been bad for years. Interestingly enough, one of the 14 teams was on time nearly 90 percent of the time and had the same level of volume-to-staff ratio as the others. Showing the 13 teams the one high-performing team's process was all it took to inspire process changes. Within six months all 14 teams were hitting on-time completion marks in the 90 percent range.

Rework and redundancy are also common, as Bernard recounted:

> A state learned it had 21 different departments running background checks. While the need for information varied based on the role the applicant was to play, many of the pieces of needed data were common between the processes. You won't be surprised to hear the state still has 21 departments running background checks because making the change would take a lot of effort across a lot of departments. And it's never easy to get a department to give up control over an important process.

In his experience, "If no one can recall that a long-standing process has completed a structured process improvement cycle, you can pretty well bet the process has at least 60 percent waste." He noted that 26 million people work for government, with the majority, 14.2 million, working for counties, cities, townships, and special districts, including schools.

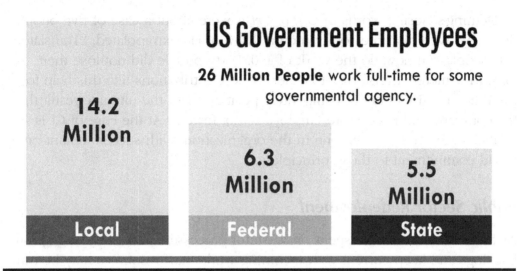

Employees at the federal, state, and local levels.
Source: Courtesy of John M. Bernard (2022).

Fueling the Effort with Redeployed Capacity

The idea is that once a robust CI initiative has transitioned into a culture of continuous improvement, the cost of government tackling the most serious problems would be virtually revenue-neutral. With the wasted time and effort removed, the current level of human and financial resources can be mobilized to accomplish great things. Before that transition can occur, though, states must be solidly into the results-driven phase, and must honor the commitment not to lay off staff.

Such a win-win strategy is critical for several reasons. First, lean principles insist that employees be insulated from any negative financial impact due to efficiency gains. Beyond the ethics, there are pragmatic considerations. Improvements are generated by collective efforts, and are particularly reliant on front-line workers who can best identify the waste. People will not willingly engage in "efficiency" campaigns intended to cut their jobs. Layoffs defeat lean efforts.

As Deming's first point of management declares: "Create constancy of purpose toward improvement of product and service, with the aim to become competitive and to stay in business, and to provide jobs." The practical coincides with the socially responsible. From a macro perspective, a lean culture within both the public and private sectors would have a positive impact on the nation's economy.

Deming's closing words in *Out of Crisis* were about a case of five people doing the work that previously required seven. He extrapolated, "Translated 100 people can now do the work of 140. Forty people did not lose their jobs: they merely transferred to other work. Contributions like this help to put the company in better competitive position, with the ultimate result that the company will need more employees, not fewer."[6] At the core of CI is quality, embraced by everyone in the organization, with success reliant on a broad commitment to those principles.

Public Sector Redeployment

As fewer labor-hours are spent on wasteful processes, staff can catch up on backlogs and keep current with incoming work. Staff resources may be transitioned to mission critical tasks, appropriately aligning skill sets. However, transferring employees among departments and new job descriptions can be challenging for administrators. Public-sector jobs tend to be segmented by role and pay grade. They may be linked by specific funding streams to particular duties. Supplemental training may be necessary to prepare employees for reassigned tasks. Given these considerations, preparing for the necessary flexibility may require adjustment in budgetary allocations, personnel rules, and consultation with labor bargaining units. It is critical for public administrators to complete these adjustments in order to prepare for the challenges of Level Three.

Tackling Complex Problems

According to Bernard, level three work is complex because it requires answering the "why" questions at ever deeper levels. It includes using Level Two tools and methods to address increasingly complex issues and applying process thinking to the development of human beings.

It is useful, from a lean perspective, to sort out symptoms from root causes and identify where efforts can have impact. The point of impact varies because some organizations seek to mitigate symptoms *and* to address root causes. As the parable of the babies in the river suggests, it is important to do both. A chain of reasoning can be facilitated using the 5 Whys to brainstorm possible interventions in response to symptoms and causes. Consider an example of addressing the problem of medical debt.

Medical Debt

As of June 2022, 100 million Americans; including 41% of adults, had medical debt.[7] Nearly 60% of all debt held by collection agencies is medical debt, owed by as many as 43 million households.[8] To address this problem, nonprofits have been raising money to help pay people's medical debts. One organization, RIP Medical Debt, helped more than four million families retire more than $7 billion of debt since its founding in 2014. Among RIP Medical Debt's donors, billionaire MacKenzie Scott gave the organization $50 million in 2020 and $30 million in 2022. Several municipalities have allocated American Rescue Plan Act (ARPA) funds to the organization. A report in *Governing* explained that medical debt is relatively cheap to buy. Roughly 20–30% of hospitals sell their debt, many for pennies on the dollar, to the secondary market. Others will sell directly to RIP Medical Debt.[9]

Targeted debt relief provides economic and social benefits to communities, preventing evictions and allowing families to put food on the table. In Lucas County, Ohio, $1.6 million in funding will be available to cancel up to $240 million in medical debt owed by households that earn up to 400% of the federal poverty line. Michele Grim of the Toledo City Council said that "It could be more than a one-to-100 return on investment of government dollars."[10]

In addition to making direct payments, several of the nonprofits also try to mitigate the problem. RIP Medical Debt supported a successful ballot initiative in Arizona to limit interest rates on medical debt. The organization Dollar For helped relieve more than $20 million of debt since 2012. It also helps people access charity care from not-for-profit hospitals. The Tennessee Justice Center, which helped eliminate more than $400,000 in medical debt, also trains providers and advocates on Medicaid enrollment.[11]

Examine the Problem from a Lean Lens

Current state: Millions of Americans have accumulated medical debt. Use the 5 Whys to define the symptoms and seek root causes; then brainstorm potential countermeasures. Generally, the first several "whys" reveal the symptoms. The possible countermeasures suggested to address the symptoms would need to be tested, measured for impact, and adjusted accordingly. Each inquiry and answer could go in any number of directions on an issue as complex as access to health care. Consider an example:

Problem: Americans have medical debt		Possible countermeasures
1. Why did they have medical debt?	They had medical bills that they could not afford to pay.	Actions to address this symptom: • Non-profits help people pay medical bills and/or help people negotiate payment terms. • Nonprofits advocate capping interest rates on medical debt.
2. Why did they have medical bills that they couldn't afford to pay?	Either they had no insurance, or their insurance did not cover the full cost of their care.	Actions to address this symptom: • Nonprofits advocate for expansion of relief programs and charity care. • Nonprofits assist individuals and train health care providers to facilitate enrollment into Medicaid or other programs.
3. Why didn't they have insurance coverage?	They might be unemployed or a part-time employee ineligible for an employer-sponsored or public plan.	Actions to address this symptom: • Nonprofits advocate for the expansion of Medicaid in states that have not done so under the ACA. • Nonprofits and federal and state governments promote the use of the Exchange to find subsidized insurance.
4. Why don't unemployed and part-time workers have access to health insurance?	There are gaps in eligibility for employer-sponsored plans and public plans.	Actions to address this symptom: (same as above) • Nonprofits advocate for the expansion of Medicaid in states that have not done so under the ACA. • Nonprofits and federal and state governments promote the use of the Exchange to find subsidized insurance.
5. Why are there gaps in eligibility?	The U.S. does not have a universal care system.	Actions to address the cause: • Nonprofits advocate for the expansion of Medicaid/Medicare into a single plan that includes everyone. • People organize political support for universal health care. • Elected officials enact universal health care.

Government and Community Partnership

In Level Three maturity a state becomes effective at partnering with the community to deal with complex social issues. Bernard asserts that if governments address the root causes that prevent people from thriving, people will be healthier and fewer resources will be expended dealing with the negative consequences, such as crime and addiction.

Bernard cited research on how Adverse Childhood Experiences (ACEs) are linked to a range of societal problems.[12] ACEs occur in the first 18 years of life and include physical, sexual, and emotional abuse; physical and emotional neglect; and challenges in the household such as substance misuse, mental illness, violence, or incarceration. Each of these factors can be addressed separately or in combination to mitigate children's suffering.

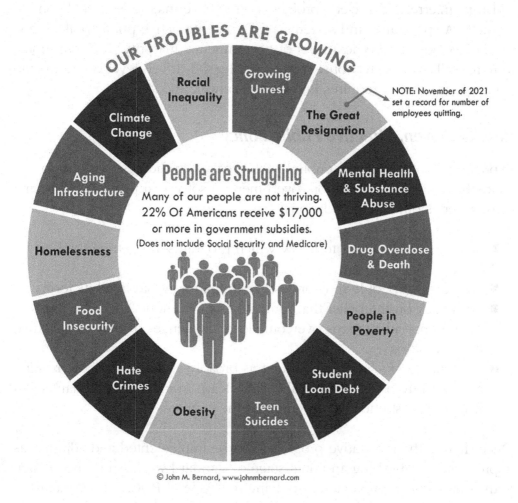

© John M. Bernard, www.johnmbernard.com

The nonprofit and governmental programs dealing with these problems can be leaned. The lean efforts should take place both in each organization's individual processes and at the system level for the myriad of interrelated services.

Leaning at both the programmatic level and the system level are crucial. For example, Lean practitioner Alyssa Elliott found that as many as nine agencies had some role in supervising and/or assisting people released from prison in Washington State. She referenced a simulation, *Picking up the Pieces*, where agency staff were put through the confounding matrix of regulatory obligations and elusive potential services.[13] Grasping the current condition and seeing it as a value stream is the first step, creating the capacity for change. Elliott believes in the transformational potential of the intersection of process improvement, systems, and social change to improve lives and communities.

Large, interrelated societal problems often have intergenerational consequences. As programs and systems are leaned, proactive public policies are needed to move to the next level of governmental maturity. The transition from a results-driven response to the social-good-driven level is not an automatic progression. It requires knowledge, power, and skill.

Results-Driven, Effective Public Policy

Expressing confidence that public employees are in the best position to make the changes required for government to solve real problems, Bernard made a series of recommendations. Among them:

■ Measure performance to know which programs are getting the best results.
■ Engage your people in relentlessly eliminating waste in all its forms.
■ Push back on the belief that "our situation is unique," because most often minor adaptations overcome local challenges. Fight "not invented here" thinking.
■ See what works, and then scale it as broadly as possible. Share results and learn from peers nationally. Find, learn from, and steal shamelessly from the most effective programs in the country.

Once shared, the innovative programs can be implemented and adjusted as appropriate. Establishing an initial stage of standard work is not inconsistent with continuous improvement. Applying the cycle of PDCA, the standard model is planned, launched, checked, and adjusted to the next standard. It may seem paradoxical to propose consistent experimentation with standard work. It is a methodical, not random, evolution that builds on the preceding work, a concept that will be familiar to academics. Working under the umbrella of lean management, this approach takes maximum advantage of the laboratories of democracy.

Lean and Toyota Kata for Social Good

In the application of Lean and Toyota Kata to government, finance, and health care, the principle of "respect for people" is often overlooked. A broad interpretation was articulated by Sakichi Toyoda, the founder of Toyota Automatic Loom Works: "The purpose of the company has always been twofold: to benefit society as well as the team members who make up the fabric of the company."[14]

Arguably the most important application is being conducted by teams of visionary social-community builders. As discussed in Chapter 12, CI principles are being applied in Appleton, Wisconsin, with significant successes and replicable potential.

Another example can be found in the work of the nonprofit Riverview Gardens, which Jason Schulist and team members Ben Hoseus and Kelly Nutty describe as "leveraging lean thinking to build community prosperity." The Riverview Gardens program is rooted "in the teachings of lean, which starts from the assumption that everyone, given the chance, wants to do a good job. . . . When people solve problems, value is created not only for the customer, but also for the employee through their learning and growth."[15]

The program has a three-fold impact: making an immediate difference in people's lives through job training and placement, addressing the root causes of social problems, and changing the community's perception of people in need. The latter goal is based on a lean idea: putting the blame on not the person, but the process. "If members of society are 'failing' we should consider whether we have developed systems in which they can thrive."[16]

Characterizing the adaptation of TK as a "rather neglected aspect of what this revolutionary methodology can achieve," they apply the lean concept of value-stream mapping to envision a value stream of humanity. Just as Toyota develops people throughout their employment, the Riverview community is developed, as are those within it. And they propose to extend the scope of human development to society in its entirety.

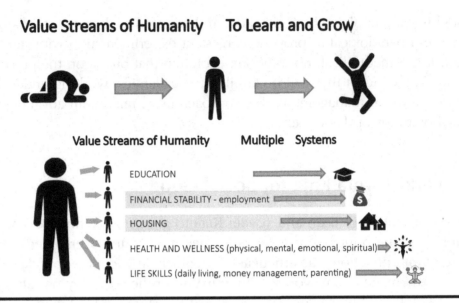

The value stream concept applied to human development.

Source: **Courtesy of the Generative Local Community Institute (GLCI).**

A Holistic, Transformative Model

Northeast Wisconsin is home to CI Squared: Continuous Improvement * Community Impact = Accelerated Community Outcomes.[17] With more than 50 volunteers, it is the largest CI community volunteer network in the world. CI Squared provides coaching, mentoring, and continuous-improvement support to northeast Wisconsin non-profits to achieve community impact objectives. The network draws on the work of the Generative Local Community Institute (GLCI), through Jason Schulist, who is President of GLCI and founder of Skillsfest, a yearly gathering of national leaders in community problem-solving.[18] Nonprofits with existing issues are paired with CI coaches to help match problem-solving tools to a wide range of issues facing the community.

GLCI took a methodical approach to find the elusive apples-to-apples comparisons in a world of data overload. To create a hub infrastructure usable for the community and scalable for the future, the team:

- Met with 45 different stakeholders about their community data needs and issues to identify duplication of efforts, and streams of data in integrating local community surveys with the 2020 Census update.

▪ Benchmarked 34 existing Community Data hubs across the country. Developed a team to create an A3 proposal worksheet to understand the problems and opportunities involved in creating a data hub. Developed a common data dictionary.

In pursuit of the vision "to help our communities thrive by providing data that shines a light on opportunities and engages people's hearts," they identified an ideal state for the data hub: "Establish the capability to verbally ask questions of the data and receive instant results AND advice including additional information to enhance the inquiry."[19] The Fox Valley Data Exchange (DEX), launched in early 2023, enables effective use of data to address community well-being issues.

The groundbreaking work in Appleton County demonstrates bridge-building between community organizing, public policy, and social services. GLCI created a collective vision and used data to select effective programs and direct resources, all while holding true to the core value of community building: working "with people," not "for people."

Connecting Kata in Community to Level Three Government

The goal of helping people flourish in community aligns with John Bernard's vision for social-good-driven government. The next step is to consider how the nonprofit work by Schulist fits with Bernard's model.

Leaning the Nonprofit-Industrial Complex

While the nonprofit sector provides many essential and often transformative services, there is a tangle of nonprofits in many communities. Well-intentioned organizations with overlapping missions compete for funding from an array of foundations and donors. Consider the waste generated by the redundancy.

Nonprofit organizations employ 10% of the U.S. workforce and are responsible for 5.7% of the GDP.[20] Cause IQ, which provides web-based tools to support nonprofits, reported that the majority of the country's 1.7 million nonprofits are religious or educational institutions, with roughly 7% characterized as focusing on human services and fewer organizations in other categories linked to human needs.[21] A study by *Governing* found a prevalence of service organizations in "older communities, especially those that are economically depressed," noting that, in those places, "strong non-profit sectors are helping beleaguered governments."[22]

A lean assessment of nonprofits in a community might start with an affinity diagram, grouping all of the like services by category. If there is significant redundancy, one may look to Appleton County where Jason Schulist and his team are working to maximize the efficiency of the nonprofit sector, while boosting its creativity and commitment to mission. They have made three important gains in efficiency: organizational, funding, and functionality.

- Organizational efficiency: Nonprofits with overlapping missions and jurisdictions are encouraged to join together to become greater than the sum of their parts.
- Funding efficiency: Local foundations provide a standard grant application, facilitating grant seeking. Funds are targeted for effective programs aligned with community priorities.
- Functional efficiency: Collective resources are available on a per-user basis, avoiding the need for each nonprofit to set up its own infrastructure for backend functions such as finance, HR, and software. This maximizes the resources available for mission.

Results-Driven Government as a Platform to Reach the Value Stream of Humanity

The results-driven phase provides outcome measurements, which inform the choices for next steps. Going forward, the skills and knowledge gained by achieving Level Two will form the base for reaching Level Three. Then, as John Bernard explained, "moving toward a systematic cycle of social change becomes viable." He envisioned, "the capability to model new behaviors and skills to those the state serves. Imagine a department of corrections involving its inmates on teams to solve problems and improve processes, often necessitating development of the very behaviors and skills they need to thrive in society."[23]

CI and TK for Level Three Maturity

As previously discussed, leaning the current tangle of overlapping and redundant bureaucratic programs is not simply an administrative task. While administrators have a certain amount of discretion, many of the changes will require legislative action. There is a wild card in the realm of elected officials and political power.

Politicians are generally risk-averse, and they often prefer to postpone responsible appropriations. At the reaction-driven level of maturity, for example, infrastructure repairs would be delayed until a bridge collapses. As folks from the Department of Transportations started telling us after the turn of the century, the federal highway system was built to last 50 years . . . 60 years ago. It is unlean to wait until roads crumble and bridges fall down. It's like buying a new car because you didn't want to change the oil in the one you had. Mature governments are guided by due diligence. Government at maturity Level Three will fund infrastructure maintenance, whether through user fees like tolls and gas taxes or other sources. In this example, however, operational maturity can be thwarted by a lack of political and fiscal responsibility.

A related political constraint results from elected officials' concern for image. There is a strong incentive to be seen as "doing something" for which personal credit can be claimed. This can result in solutions that are more form than substance, and in the creation of redundant or overlapping programs with trendy new names. The public may oppose consolidating programs that sound good, even in the face of evidence that greater impact can be gained by doing so.

Consider how TK in community might advance political maturity by involving all stakeholders in setting a vision. Together, they would develop a common understanding of the current condition and participate in experiments to identify evidence-based solutions to overcome obstacles and achieve successive target conditions. Elected officials, community members, and advocates with a common agenda could diminish the customary political pandering.

Applying Toyota Kata for Incremental Change

Optimal lean approaches may not be politically feasible. For example, there is ample evidence that a single-payer system is the leanest way to deliver universal health care. However, it would mean ending the current tangle of public and private insurance coverage.

A universal basic income may be the leanest way to end child poverty and hunger. However, it would mean closing a myriad of benefit programs widely dispersed among federal, state, and local governments, and nonprofit organizations.

Proposing either a single-payer health care system or a universal basic income would generate significant opposition from stakeholders in the current systems, and from those with ideological objections. However, with TK methodology using scientific thinking, the human-service bureaucracy, the nonprofit-industrial complex, and the medical-industrial complex could be leaned incrementally.

Although an incremental approach would delay the availability of currently wasted resources, a more measured pace could be more politically palatable and could provide the opportunity to design a transition plan for those currently working in human-service agencies, insurance companies, and other interrelated administrative jobs.

The difficult work of leaning public policy will also require change in management skills. Consider how the Kata improvement cycle could be applied. For example, in the case of health care, universal access to care, not the manner of funding, would be the true north. Each target condition could bring incremental changes. The experiments toward each target condition could confirm the improvements in well-being and financial savings. Continuous gains would be needed to reach vulnerable populations, find new cures for chronic diseases, assure prompt emergency care, conduct research, and respond to emerging threats.

Transitional proposals include expanding Medicare to adults aged 55–64 and children 0–18. Gradually, those 19–54 could be included, and 1% of the budget could be allocated for five years to assist displaced insurance workers.[24] Given the complexity of public-policy questions of this magnitude, using TK is essential because the methodology requires treating each of the proposed countermeasures as an experiment.

The following example starts with the year 2010 as the current condition:

Toyota Kata steps in sequence			
Step 1	*Step 2*	*Step 3*	*Step 4*
The vision: Set the challenge.	Grasp the current condition.	Establish the next target condition.	Conduct experiment to achieve target condition.
Universal health care.	More than 40 million are uninsured.	Expand coverage to 20 million people.	First experiment: Provide federal subsidies to state Medicaid programs to incentivize the expansion of eligibility for the working poor.

- What was learned from the first experiment? Was it effective? Sustainable?
- Grasp the new current condition: How many states expanded Medicaid? How many of the working poor remain uninsured?
- What is the next target condition?

With a true north of ending child poverty, target conditions could include experiments such as expansion of the child tax credit. Some data is already available, due to the temporary expansion in 2021. A report by Columbia University's Center on Poverty and Social Policy[25] found that child poverty fell by more than 46% when the credit was increased from July to December 2021. When the credit ended in January 2022, more than 3.7 million children fell below the poverty line.[26]

Toyota Kata steps in sequence			
Step 1	*Step 2*	*Step 3*	*Step 4*
The vision: Set the challenge.	Grasp the current condition.	Establish the next target condition.	Conduct experiment to achieve target condition.
End child poverty.	Nearly four million children are in poverty.	Reduce the number of children in poverty by half.	First experiment: Expand the child tax credit.

- What was learned from the first experiment? Was it effective?
- Grasp the new current condition: How many children remain in poverty?
- What is the next target condition?

Looking to the Laboratories of Democracy

The preceding examples were focused on policies at the national level. Using states as laboratories, experiments with innovative policies may be more readily conducted there. A successful program in one state could become a model for others.

The states can also customize federal programs to increase their effectiveness, as has been the case with the Medicaid program. Federal emergency provisions in response to the COVID-19 pandemic provided continuous enrollment in Medicaid until March 2023. Resuming annual re-enrollment resulted in administrative costs and interrupted access to care, forms of waste known as "churn" (or *muda* in lean lingo). Prior to the emergency continuous enrollment, 4.2% of recipients who were disenrolled were re-enrolled within three months and 6.9% within six months.[27] The majority of states applied for waivers to avoid the costs and consequences of resuming churn. Some of the waivers were intended to reduce bureaucratic waste by allowing Medicaid to be renewed based on the enrollees' eligibility for another means-tested program, such as the Supplemental Nutrition Assistance Program (SNAP) and/or Temporary Assistance to Needy Families (TANF). Others are intended to address the human costs, such as Oregon's policy to provide continuous enrollment for children through age six.[28]

TK, CI, and the Value Stream of Humanity

In many ways, Toyota Kata is the missing link. Policy makers typically get information concerning best practices from academic studies, various think tanks, and legislative research services. TK in the community can be a more nimble source, conducting experiments to find the path to a series of near-term target conditions.

The community building that goes on as a result of using this methodology goes beyond the specific projects. As Jason Schulist explains, "it's about developing holistic systems, like the shared vision project, the data exchange, the CI volunteers, common grant application, etc. all working in synergy within a community." In developing the vision, Schulist references "The Seven Vital Conditions for Health and Wellbeing":[29]

- Humane Housing: stable, safe places to live, and living in diverse, vibrant communities.
- Belonging and Civic Muscle: having fulfilling relationships and social support that people need to thrive.
- Lifelong Learning: a good education for all that ensures all people, regardless of age, background, or ability, are set up for success, to reach their full potential.
- Thriving Natural World: clean air, clean water, clean land, and well-functioning ecosystems.
- Meaningful work and wealth: Personal, family, and community wealth provides the means for healthy, secure lives. That includes good paying, fulfilling jobs and careers, and financial security across the life span.

- Health and safety: fresh air and water, nutritious food, and a stable home. Healthy relationships—with freedom to express gender and sexuality—and a life free from violence, injury, and toxic stress, with access to health care.
- Reliable Transportation: moving between home, work, school, and stores in daily life.

In pursuit of this holistic vision for the value stream of humanity, the use of TK and CI methodology facilitates a combination of purpose, technique, and persistence. It becomes a powerful formula for addressing complex social problems. Furthermore, it is the method of sustaining gains. No problems are solved permanently. The current condition is constantly evolving. As gains are made, new challenges will arise. Setbacks occur due to any number of causes—whether due to human frailty and foibles, natural disasters, or other calamities.

Dedicated CI practitioners have begun to chart a course to developing these capabilities. It begins by practicing the skills, saving time and resources, and then utilizing those resources to alleviate human suffering and ultimately to enable all people to thrive.

Moreover, the capability to accomplish bold social goals will be a morale boost for the population. Seemingly intractable problems are draining, and not just for the individuals who are unable to thrive. Bernard suggests, "If our states can use their current level of resources to dramatically improve, expand, and add programs that help improve the lives of those who have been marginalized, it will dramatically reduce the issues dividing our nation."

Notes

1 James P. Womack, Daniel T. Jones, and Daniel Roos, *The Machine That Changed the World* (Free Press, A Division of Simon & Schuster, New York, 1990–2007), p. 6.
2 Mike Rother, *Toyota Kata* (McGraw-Hill Education, New York, NY, 2010), p. xx.
3 John M. Bernard, "Level Three Government: Evolving State Operations from Reaction Driven to Results Driven to Social Good Driven." *White Paper*, 2021, p. 13. Level-Three-Government-WP-V2-FINAL.pdf (johnmbernard.com)
4 Lynn Arditi, "Departing Interim Health Director: R.I. Public Health Needs a Booster." *The Public's Radio*, June 3, 2022. https://thepublicsradio.org/article/departing-interim-health-director-r-i-public-health-needs-a-booster

5 John M. Bernard, *We are in Trouble, We Need Your Help*, January 20, 2022. www.linkedin.com/pulse/we-trouble-need-your-help-john-m-bernard/

6 W. Edwards Deming, *Out of the Crisis* (MIT Center for Advanced Educational Services, Cambridge, MA, 1982–1986), p. 492.

7 Noam N. Levey, "100 Million People in America Are Saddled With Health Care Debt." *Kaiser Health News and National Public Radio*, June 16, 2022. https://khn.org/news/article/diagnosis-debt-investigation-100-million-americans-hidden-medical-debt/

8 Consumer Finance Protection Bureau, *Medical Debt Burden in the United States*, February 2022. https://files.consumerfinance.gov/f/documents/cfpb_medical-debt-burden-in-the-united-states_report_2022–03.pdf

9 Oscar Perry Abello, "These Local Governments Are Using Federal Aid to Cancel Medical Debt." *Governing.com*, December 12, 2022. www.governing.com/finance/these-local-governments-are-using-federal-aid-to-cancel-medical-debt

10 Oscar Perry Abello, "These Local Governments Are Using Federal Aid to Cancel Medical Debt." *Governing.com*, December 12, 2022. www.governing.com/finance/these-local-governments-are-using-federal-aid-to-cancel-medical-debt

11 Kay Dervishi, "How Not-for-profits Help Millions Tackle Their Medical Debt." *The Chronicle of Philanthropy*, December 22, 2022. www.ibj.com/articles/how-not-for-profits-help-millions-tackle-their-medical-debt

12 Centers for Disease Control and Prevention (CDC), *Adverse Childhood Experiences (ACES)*. www.cdc.gov/violenceprevention/aces/index.html

13 State of Washington. Department of Social and Health Services. The U.S. Medical Center for Federal Prisoners, "Picking up the Pieces: A Reentry Simulation." *YouTube*, October 4, 2018. https://youtu.be/HhETuoXu8BU

14 Ben Hoseus, Kelly Nutty, and Jason Schulist, *Leveraging Lean Thinking to Build Community Prosperity*, October 18, 2017. https://planet-lean.com/lean-management-for-community-prosperity/

15 Ben Hoseus, Kelly Nutty, and Jason Schulist, *Leveraging Lean Thinking to Build Community Prosperity*, October 18, 2017. https://planet-lean.com/lean-management-for-community-prosperity/

16 Ben Hoseus, Kelly Nutty, and Jason Schulist, *Leveraging Lean Thinking to Build Community Prosperity*, October 18, 2017. https://planet-lean.com/lean-management-for-community-prosperity/

17 CI Squared. www.cisquared.org/

18 *Generative Local Community Institute (GLCI)*, January 30, 2023. https://genlocal.org/about/

19 Jason Schulist, "Your Life, Your Adventure: Choosing the Life you Want to Lead by Addressing Problems." *Powerpoint Program*, August 16, 2022.

20 Zippia, "25 Incredible Nonprofit Statistics [2022]: How Many Nonprofits are in the US?" *Zippia.com*, November 13, 2022. www.zippia.com/advice/nonprofit-statistics/

21 Cause IQ, *How Many Nonprofits Are in the US?* December 27, 2022. www.cau-seiq.com/insights/how-many-nonprofits-in-the-us/

22 Mike Maciag, "Where Nonprofits Are Most Prevalent in America." *Governing.com*, July 29, 2019. www.governing.com/archive/gov-nonprofits.html

23 John M. Bernard, *We are in Trouble, We Need Your Help*, January 20, 2022. www.linkedin.com/pulse/we-trouble-need-your-help-john-m-bernard/

24 U.S. Rep. Pramila Jayapal. H.R. 1976 Medicare for All Act of 2021. www.congress.gov/bill/117th-congress/house-bill/1976/text

25 Megan A. Curran, "Research Roundup of the Expanded Child Tax Credit: One Year On." *Center on Poverty and Social Policy at Columbia University*, November 15, 2022.

26 Kery Murakami, "A Last-ditch Effort to Revive the Expanded Child Tax Credit." *Route Fifty*, December 9, 2022. www.route-fifty.com/health-human-services/2022/12/last-ditch-effort-expand-child-tax-credit/380730/

27 Jennifer Tolbert, and Meghana Ammula, "10 Things to Know about the Unwinding of the Medicaid Continuous Enrollment Provision." *Kaiser Family Foundation*, January 11, 2023. www.kff.org/medicaid/issue-brief/10-things-to-know-about-the-unwinding-of-the-medicaid-continuous-enrollment-provision/

28 Phil Galewitz, "Stopping the Churn: Why Some States Want to Guarantee Medicaid Coverage From Birth to Age 6." *Kaiser Health News*, November 10, 2022. https://khn.org/news/article/churn-states-guarantee-medicaid-children/

29 Community Commons, *The Seven Vital Conditions for Health and Well-Being.* www.communitycommons.org/collections/Seven-Vital-Conditions-for-Health-and-Well-Being

Chapter 16

Diffusion of Lean Culture and Level Three Government

This is certainly not the final chapter in the journey to lean, operational excellence, or the true-north vision that all people can flourish in our value stream of humanity. It is, however, the last chapter in this exploration.

This book offered a snapshot of the current state of CI in the public sector. The recommendations in this chapter seek to build on what seems to be working and venture to look ahead to the next target condition. However, before moving to a summary of lessons and observations, it is valuable to consider how public sector officials and administrators learn about CI in the first place. It is not easy to change the way that we do business. What would cause public sector leaders to embark on this journey?

How Do We Learn about CI?

There are several elements in this critical area. The first is to reiterate that successful initiatives require comprehensive, ongoing CI training programs, as profiled throughout this book. The majority of public servants portrayed in this book became dedicated CI practitioners through such programs.

However, as we've seen, these initiatives rely on governors, other elected officials, and top agency administrators appreciating the transformative potential of these principles. As discussed, these leaders play a significant role in doing what it takes to launch and to sustain the effort. Urging them to do so presupposes that they know about Lean, Toyota Kata, and the field of CI in general.

 DOI: 10.4324/9781003372691-21

A cursory internet search in January 2023 found that the lessons of the Toyota Production System (TPS) are more commonly taught in business and engineering schools than in public administration or political science programs. Multiple institutions offer Lean Six Sigma Certificates, including the University of Massachusetts-Amherst's Isenberg School of Management, and Northeastern University's College of Engineering. Although these competencies are broadly applicable, the students in these programs are generally preparing for careers in the private sector.

"Decluttering Organizational Mess: The Art of Lean Process Improvement" is offered as an elective in the BA program in Organizational Leadership and Change at College Unbound. The introductory course covers the concepts and techniques that are particularly applicable to nonprofit and governmental organizations.

Among Master of Public Administration (MPA) programs, Roger Williams University has a course in Lean Thinking for Public Administration, which is geared toward managers working in healthcare, nonprofits, community organizations, and government agencies, and offers a hands-on component. While such courses are most likely available in other MPA programs, arguably they should be a standard part of the curriculum in all programs.

Lean and Toyota Kata occupy a space between businesses management, public administration, and human behavior. Studying these systems requires navigating where the academic world meets the pragmatic, and theory meets practice. The *Journal of Operations Management* (JOM) has published several articles exploring these topics.

In "The Lenses of Lean," James Womack, John Shook, Peter Ward, and Josh Howell explained that "research has lagged practice because Lean thinking and practice cross traditional academic disciplinary boundaries. Just as Lean practice crosses organizational silos by necessity, so there is a need for research that crosses the boundaries of academic disciplines."[1] Rachna Shah and Matthias Holweg observed that "the myopic view of equating Lean with efficiency prevails in both academia and practice." They noted, "Lean is not a singular concept. . . . I]ts under-representation in academic research does not mean it did not exist. In fact, the one characteristic of Lean that in our opinion is at the heart of the persistent interest in Lean is its ability to adapt. While the philosophy of Lean was developed at Toyota in a manufacturing context, its logic was inherently transferrable and could be adopted beyond repetitive manufacturing."[2]

In "A Lean view of Lean," Tyson R. Browning and Suzanne de Treville posed the question, "What is Lean? A phenomenon? An ideal? A philosophy?

A way of thinking? A collection of practices? A strategy? Widespread agreement is lacking."[3] Acknowledging that lean methodology relied upon "lean thinking," which enabled it to be adaptive beyond TPS, the article drew upon the work of scholars and practitioners to consider where Lean fits in a theoretical context. The authors recommended ongoing empirical study of Lean as "exploratory pre-theoretical work that aids in identifying, defining, measuring, and understanding formal concepts."[4]

Scholarly articles have also described the concepts and documented the impacts of Toyota Kata, building on the work of Mike Rother. Among them is a paper, "The Benefits of Deploying the Toyota Kata," that was presented at the International Conference on Advances in Production Management Systems.[5] Studies have also been published documenting TK applications beyond manufacturing, including "Optimizing value utilizing Toyota Kata methodology in a multidisciplinary clinic."[6]

While the link between academic study and CI remains somewhat fragmented, perhaps due to its multidisciplinary aspect, the body of work is growing. The brief references in this chapter are not intended to substitute for a comprehensive literature review, but rather to note that there are scholars on this path. In the meantime, we return to the question of how people learn about Lean and TK.

In efforts to close the gap between CI for business and CI for public administration, educators who understand the broad applicability of the principles are working to incorporate them into the curriculum.

Kata in the Classroom

Sylvain Landry, a Professor at HEC Montréal business school, encourages the use of *Kata in the Classroom: A simple pattern that helps you teach scientific thinking*. The Kata in the Classroom (KiC) program, created by Mike Rother, is broadly applicable for all subjects and grades to integrate the deliberate practice of scientific thinking.[7]

Rather than typical content memorization, KiC "teaches students how to mobilize their rational powers to become effective problem solvers, creative team members, and informed citizens. It is science as a creative human process." Students practice applying the 4-step Improvement Kata to a variety of assignments and projects.[8] Some of the program's anticipated outcomes include:

■ Acknowledging that our comprehension is always incomplete and possibly wrong.

- Assuming that answers will be found by test rather than just deliberation. (You make predictions and test them with experiments.)
- Appreciating that the differences between a prediction and what actually happens can be a useful source of learning and adjustment.

There is a downloadable lesson plan and a 50-minute exercise on katato-grow.com, which is freely available to educators under Creative Commons©. Landry uses a version of the program, which is applicable at all grade levels, in HEC's graduate school of management. In collaboration with Mike Rother, he is building a growing network of educators who are using Toyota Kata.

The JPW Fund

Jim Womack, co-author of *The Machine that Changed the World* and founder of the Lean Enterprise Institute (LEI), has founded the James P. Womack Scholarship and Philanthropy Fund (JPW Fund). The Fund advances LEI's mission is to "make things better by advancing lean thinking and practice" by addressing "the dearth of lean curricula at every level of academia and the resultant waste of rework—reeducating those steeped in traditional management."[9]

The JPW Fund supports creative learning experiences in partnership with schools teaching lean thinking and community-based service organizations willing to provide Gemba-based learning and improvement opportunities.[10] One such partnership is with Oakland University's Pawley Lean Institute, which offers a Graduate Certificate in Lean Leadership.

Through these partnerships with educational institutions, the Fund's internship program creates more lean thinkers by placing students in non-profit organizations. The program uses an interdisciplinary approach to lean thinking and practice for learners in universities, public- and private-sector institutions, and the community.

The benefits are multi-layered. Guided by an LEI coach, the student interns gain proficiency in using lean. The results enhance the host organization's capacity to serve the community, and its staff and volunteers learn to use lean tools and adopt lean thinking and practices. Together, they learn by doing.[11]

Case studies of several internships reported the significance of added lean thinking to nonprofits where mission-driven staff and volunteers were constantly firefighting, with little time to reflect and improve. Among the intern placements was Humble Design Detroit, an organization that provides furniture and home goods for previously unhoused individuals, families, and veterans. Along with the staff and volunteers, the JPW Fund interns applied a range of lean tools to reorganize the warehouse of donated goods.

The hands-on, learn-by-doing lean management experience is broadly applicable. The JPW Fund interns demonstrate lean tools and model lean thinking in their placements.

Professional Associations

For those in public service who attended college before the publication of *Toyota Kata* in 2010 (and *The Machine that Changed the World* in 1990), professional associations can help raise awareness and reinforce the principles of quality management. In conjunction with on-the-job (OJT) training programs, specialized conferences and peer-reviewed articles in professional journals can also help to advance the field. Among the examples:

■ The Government Finance Officers Association has published White Papers and journal articles, as well as offering workshops on Lean during conferences.
■ The National Governors Association has distributed copies of John M. Bernard's *Government That Works* to its members.
■ The American Society for Public Administration's online newsletter, the *PA Times*, carries a regular series of articles about Lean, with opportunities for presentations at national and regional conferences.
■ The National Conference of State Legislatures offers guidance and resources to enable results-driven operations and evidence-based programs.[12]

Continuing Education through Communities of Practice

Lean practitioners convene through networks, such as those organized by Gary Vansuch within state transportation departments and for statewide programs, and Heather Barto's Lean Learning Collaborative in New Hampshire's Department of Health and Human Services. These informal communities of practice are reinforced through statewide and regional summits such as the Continuous Improvement Lean Collaborative (CILC) in Maine, and online networks such as the Public Sector Change Practitioners on LinkedIn.[13]

Recommendations for Public Administrators

- Bring all public employees to a level of competency with the principles and techniques of lean management.
- Make continuous improvement principles and methodology a required part of the curriculum in all MPA programs, with a focus on lean management.
- Develop hybrid instructional modules for all Certified Public Manager (CPM) programs, with hands-on components and a required practicum.
- Make hands-on Lean training an essential part of in-service training for public employees and supervisors, including participation in a *kaizen* project.
- Use Lean at all levels of government and in nonprofit organizations to fix what we already do. This will improve services while reducing waste. Apply the theory of administrative conservatorship to make the changes that are within the purview of administrators and managers and redeploy the previously wasted time, effort, and resources toward effective solutions.
- Develop collaboration among researchers, practitioners, and policy makers using root cause analysis and scientific inquiry to determine evidence-based practices to address social problems.
- Deliver the findings to all stakeholders, including political leaders and the press. Conduct public forums to spread awareness and gain support for policy proposals.
- Hold an orientation for state legislators on connecting CI with policy evaluation. Include tours featuring *kaizen* projects at worksites and modeling of TK visual management.

Going forward, it would be valuable for those in the CI community to recommend methodologies to further these efforts. The innovative work of one can be the springboard for the next series of revelations. There are possibilities for models that are replicable, yet agile. There may be a template for a sustainable CI program that can replace the current state of fragmented and disparate programs. This may emerge as more practitioners conduct more experiments and share their learning throughout the community of practice.

In the spirit of PDCA, as conditions change in the current state, so must the next target condition—which brings us to operational recommendations.

Continuing Public Sector Journey to Lean

As the CI field continues to evolve, certain observations may be helpful to advance the journey and pave the way for future gains. The following checklist is by no means exhaustive and, as with all CI products, is subject to PDCA.

CHECKLIST FOR ROBUST PUBLIC SECTOR CI INITIATIVES

1. Mandate from the Governor
   - Executive Order
   - Resources
2. Support from the Legislature
   - Allocate resources.
   - Enact recommended regulatory reforms if legislative action is required.
   - Allow budget flexibility for agencies to retain and reallocate savings and transfer personnel.
   - Consolidate redundant programs as recommended and replace with evidence-based best practices.
3. An Office of Operational Excellence
   - A full-time state-wide coordinator with technical and administrative support.
   - Project management and reporting capacity with appropriate software.
   - A system for benchmarking meaningful performance metrics.
   - A completed survey of core value streams with identified process owners.
   - A team composed of coordinators from each agency and a representative from the Governor's office, and chaired by the state-wide coordinator.
   - Cross-agency projects in accordance with priorities set by the Executive Order.
   - A dynamic Hub within the state's website.
4. Agency Engagement
   - Top management commitment in accordance with the Executive Order.
   - Coordinators in each agency responsible for chartering projects within the agency and providing status/metrics reports to the Office of Operational Excellence.

- Participation in cross-agency initiatives chartered through the Office of Operational Excellence.
- A strong bench of employees trained and committed to continuous improvement.

5. Training
   - An internal program housed within the Center for Operational Excellence.
   - An online introduction to CI, required for all employees.
   - A Lean for Leaders workshop for all agency leadership teams, managers, and supervisors.
   - Training for managers and supervisors in Toyota Kata and Coaching Kata, with ongoing mentoring.
   - A minimum ratio of employees in each agency to be trained at the Yellow and Green Belt levels (example: two Green Belts per 100 employees)
   - Advanced training programs for CI practitioners and frontline supervisors with on-going mentoring, networking, and continuing education.

Advancing from Reaction-Driven to Results-Driven Maturity

As described throughout the book, the current state of CI programs across the country is uneven. Yet these initiatives are arguably the best path to move from reaction-driven to results-driven government. While considering the following, bear in mind the popular quote from George Box: "All models are wrong, but some models are useful."[14] Consider operationalizing the initiative in phases.

Phase One: The governor identifies the top priorities and the organizational processes needed to accomplish those priorities. Proceed to:

- Introduce the initiative and conduct a Lean for Leaders workshop for your management team.
- Arrange for basic CI training. Ask management team to identify motivated change agents to head up the effort in each agency, and send them to training.

- Conduct a survey of programmatic processes and backend processes that need to be improved to free up staff time to work on priorities.
- Send a message announcing the initiative to all employees, including expectations for their participation and a schedule for all employees to take the White Belt training. Supervisors and managers will also attend a Lean for Leaders workshop to prepare them to sponsor projects.
- Task agency heads with selecting initial projects within their agencies. Priority should be given to low-hanging fruit—archaic processes that will demonstrate proof of concept and energize early adopters.
- Encourage each agency's Lean coordinator, making it clear they are authorized to work with sponsors to prepare charters, schedule events, assign facilitators, document the redesigned workflow, track the implementation, and report progress to the management team.
- Send regular messages reporting and praising the gains and reinforcing the expectations. As noted in a GFOA White Paper, "A coordinator is not a substitute for consistent and conspicuous support from the organization's leadership, or for the engagement of the Lean event sponsor or the Lean team leader in both the Lean event and follow-up activities."[15]

Phase 2: Skill building, modeling behaviors, and ongoing practice.

- The Lean coordinators form a community of practice and a CI network, enabling them to share best practices, exchange facilitation resources, communicate about successes, and build Lean culture.
- Coordinators and facilitators attend advanced training, which includes an array of CI tools and an introduction to Toyota Kata (TK) and Coaching Kata (CK). They demonstrate the use of the tools to work teams in their agencies and mentor the frontline staff to develop and practice CI techniques. As Jim Womack explained, "We've learned that lean transformation must be led by line managers. So the job of the continuous improvement or Op-Ex department is to coach line managers on how to run experiments and provide technical assistance as necessary."[16]

- Managers and supervisors attend a series of hands-on workshops introducing TK and CK. They practice the skills with peers and begin using them in their work units.

Phase 3: Gearing up results-driven capacity using TK.

- Confirm and articulate the mission of the overall organization and that of each agency.
- Identify the core value streams in pursuit of each mission.
- Measures the outcomes of those value streams. Grasp the current condition in each one. What is the performance? What does it need to be? What is the gap?
- Set the next target condition—define a near-term goal that would advance toward the mission.
- Conduct experiments, try what might work, confirm results, and implement as appropriate.
- Grasp the new current condition and repeat . . . establishing each new target condition . . . and each new current condition.
- Continue measuring the outcomes of mission-critical value streams.

Every COE Needs a COOP

State CI initiatives all need a continuity-of-operations plan (COOP). According to the Federal Emergency Management Agency (FEMA), a COOP "is an effort within individual executive departments and agencies to ensure that Primary Mission Essential Functions (PMEFs) continue to be performed during a wide range of emergencies, including localized acts of nature, accidents, and technological or attack-related emergencies."[17] Perhaps it's a stretch to say that a change in gubernatorial leadership or the retirement of a key CI staff member is an act of nature. However, these occurrences potentially disrupt operations, necessitating a plan to ensure that the mission is not lost. Consider the following:

- Is the Center for Operational Excellence (COE) recognized as an integral part of the management of state government, as much as accounting or human-resources units are? Or is it dependent on the willingness of each governor to renew and rebrand it? The COOP would be different for each circumstance.

- Is the director's job a permanent position or a special appointment by the governor? What are the job description and qualifications? What happens when the director leaves or retires?
- Has the purpose been distorted or eroded? Is the COE staff functioning as an elite group of experts, or are they continuing to facilitate the expansion of lean culture? Do they send the message that CI=projects and lean=process mapping? Are they under pressure to prioritize financial savings over gains in quality? If the COE goes off course, how will its purpose be restored?
- Is there a mechanism for ongoing hands-on training, practice, and mentoring? How will learning continue to be introduced and diffused throughout the workforce, with all frontline managers prepared to be coaches? Are all employees engaged in learning and improving?
- Building the mission. Is the COE part of a results-driven government, with the capacity for program evaluation and outcome measurements? Are these linked to significant quality-of-life indicators? Is there a mechanism for the COE to report to elected officials with recommendations for regulatory reform and the enactment or expansion of effective policies?

Diffusion of Lean Thinking and Commitment

Persistent application can move government from the reaction level to the results level of maturity. The leap to the social-good level will require significantly more effort. The road map suggested here can move government in that direction, but significantly more research and experimentation will be required along the way. PDCA and TK methodology provide a framework to define the current condition and to conduct experiments to reach for each target condition while keeping the true north in sight.

The idea is that government can run well *and* accomplish important social goals. As Bernard asserted, "Lean is no longer optional. It is the most viable strategy to transform government." Connecting effective operations with impactful policy will require a purposeful, comprehensive, and multifaceted strategy using research, conducting experiments, and adjusting to achieve meaningful results.

Lean is non-ideological, but it is not value neutral. As the Lean Enterprise Institute explains, "Lean thinking has a moral compass: respect for the humanity of customers, employees, suppliers, investors, and our communities with the belief that all can and will be better off through lean practices."[18]

To Promote the General Welfare

As the preamble to the Constitution indicates, the duty to promote the general welfare is not a singular act. It is ongoing. Here, the achievement of operational excellence is not the end goal. It facilitates the action that will enable people to thrive in our society.

Partnerships between academic researchers and lean practitioners will be valuable since the scientific method of inquiry is familiar to both. The terms, such as *kaizen*, PDCA, Toyota Kata, and A3, may differ, but the concepts are the same. Together, academics and practitioners can collaborate to develop best practices, conduct pilot programs, evaluate findings, and recommend adjustments based on those findings.

Similarly, political scientists, public administrators, and CI practitioners are needed to study the dynamics of change that can facilitate governmental organizations moving from Level One to Level Three maturity. As former Maryland Governor Martin O'Malley noted, "Leadership is an art. Politics is a game of timing, character, and chance. But effective governance is a science."[19]

To Insure Domestic Tranquility

The preamble to the Constitution includes the goal of insuring domestic tranquility. Certainly, this goal is not easily accomplished, and Americans have fallen short of it throughout our history. Arguably, the field of CI can contribute to progress in several respects.

In *Bringing Scientific Thinking to Life*, Sylvain Landry includes a series of thought-provoking quotes. Among them is one by Alvin Toffler: "The illiterate of the 21st century will not be those who cannot read and write, but those who cannot learn, unlearn, and relearn."[20] As a meta skill, the kata routines of scientific reasoning could inoculate people against misinformation that sows discord. Learning problem-solving skills is both empowering and liberating.

John Bernard theorized that the social problems dividing our society could be addressed by making government more effective. As governments move to Level Three maturity, we will have the capacity to do great things, and CI can enable us to do so. Achieving demonstrable gains can erode cynicism and despair.

The Threshold of Knowledge

The speed of advancement in technology is an increasingly significant variable. As previously noted, public administrators and policy makers often lack the expertise to select new systems, or the funds to acquire, install, operate, and train users on them. The challenge of keeping up with IT results in waste, particularly the waste of rework if every jurisdiction grapples with it separately.

The ability to manage results-driven operations is significantly expanded by tools for data mapping and evaluation. Organizations that can keep up with new technologies will leap ahead in identifying best practices and tracking outcomes. Data hubs and knowledge-management tools discussed in this book may be reconfigured or obsolete by the time of publication.

Perhaps the most significant impact of technological change will be on the work itself. How can we better serve the public? And what do our customers expect? People who had complained about not being able to reach a live person on the phone are now asking why they can't just conduct their business online. Yet they will still need to reach someone if the Chatbot can't help them. And who programs the Chatbot?

Matthew Savas of LEI reflected on the potential impact of AI, opening with a quote from Eiji Toyoda: "Society has reached the point where one can push a button and be immediately deluged with technical and managerial information. This is all very convenient, of course, but if one is not careful, there is a danger of losing the ability to think. We must remember that, in the end, it is the individual human being who must solve the problems."[21]

While acknowledging the potential to increase productivity by automating routine tasks, Savas wondered if it "may unintentionally cause dependence, thereby obstructing its users' development. For example, why learn how to write or code when a machine can do it? . . . Alternatively, ChatGPT could accelerate development. By freeing people from mindless drudgery, people can pursue more fulfilling work."[22]

The discussion of the potential impact of such tools reminds us that the current state is constantly in flux. Step two in the TK methodology requires that we grasp the current condition. And from a technological perspective, the current state is increasingly fluid.

Each day there are new examples of innovations in the public sector, as well as additional cases of organizations, agencies, programs, and processes that should be leaned. Rather than looking at lean and TK as solutions to any particular problem, we learn *how* to solve problems as we practice scientific thinking.

As progress is made, we find ourselves at new thresholds of knowledge. Scholars and practitioners continue to experiment along this path, but it is impossible to know what is ahead. The crucial requirement is to develop the capability to figure things out. As Sylvain Landry explained:

> The fact that more organizations around the world are practicing Toyota Kata is heartening. As Mike Rother noted, we don't know what the future will be and we don't know the obstacles we will one day have to overcome. The success of an organization does not depend so much on the solutions put in place at any given moment, but on its ability to continually learn through action in a constantly changing environment. The best we can do is know how we'll deal with the unknown and the complexity.[23]

Leaning Forward. In many ways, we are in the "Stone Age" of lean development in the public sector. While some initiatives are sustained, others grow and recede, and still others persist and regrow. There are many differences among these initiatives, but one consistent core theme animates them all: dedicated public servants. In this book you have met just a few of the many individuals who are committed to being good stewards of public resources and doing their best to deliver excellent customer service in furtherance of their missions.

The path to social-good-driven government will be discovered along the way as we head toward the true north of enabling all people to thrive, in order to meet the preamble's bold charge of insuring domestic tranquility and promoting the general welfare.

Notes

1 M.A. Cusumano, M. Holweg, J. Howell, et al., Commentaries on "The Lenses of Lean." *Journal of Operations Management* (2021): 1–13. DOI: 10.1002/joom.1138

2 M.A. Cusumano, M. Holweg, J. Howell, et al., Commentaries on "The Lenses of Lean." *Journal of Operations Management* (2021): 1–13. DOI: 10.1002/joom.1138

3 Tyson R. Browning, and Suzanne de Treville, "A Lean View of Lean." *Journal of Operations Management* 67 (2021): 636. DOI: 10.1002/joom.1153

4 Tyson R. Browning, and Suzanne de Treville, "A Lean View of Lean." *Journal of Operations Management* 67 (2021): 659. DOI: 10.1002/joom.1153

5 G.V. Borges, A.B. Santos, L.F. Torres, M.B. Silva, G.N. Santos, and R.D. Calado, "The Benefits of Deploying the Toyota Kata." in A. Dolgui, A. Bernard, D. Lemoine, G. von Cieminski, and D. Romero (eds), *Advances in Production Management Systems. Artificial Intelligence for Sustainable and Resilient Production Systems. APMS 2021. IFIP Advances in Information and Communication Technology*, vol 631 (Springer, Cham, 2021). DOI: 10.1007/978-3-030-85902-2_35

6 Paul A. Merguerian, Richard Grady, John Waldhausen, Arlene Libby, Whitney Murphy, Lilah Melzer, and Jeffrey Avansino, "Optimizing Value Utilizing Toyota Kata Methodology in a Multidisciplinary Clinic." *Journal of Pediatric Urology* 11(4) (2015). DOI: 10.1016/j.jpurol.2015.05.010

7 Sylvain Landry, *Kata in the Classroom: A Simple Pattern That Helps You Teach Scientific Thinking.* www.katatogrow.com/

8 Mike Rother, "Kata in the Classroom: Concept Overview." *Katatogrow.com.* http://www-personal.umich.edu/~mrother/KATA_Files/KiC_Overview.pdf

9 Patricia Panchak, "Assessing a New Way to Develop More Lean Thinkers." *The James P. Womack Scholarship & Philanthropy Fund. Lean Enterprise Institute: E-book*, 2022. www.lean.org/the-lean-post/articles/assessing-a-new-way-to-develop-more-lean-thinkers/

10 James P. Womack, *Scholarship & Philanthropy Fund. Web Page about us*, December 23, 2022. www.jpwfund.org/about-us

11 Patricia Panchak, "Assessing a New Way to Develop More Lean Thinkers." *The James P. Womack Scholarship & Philanthropy Fund. Lean Enterprise Institute: E-book*, 2022, p. 9. www.lean.org/the-lean-post/articles/assessing-a-new-way-to-develop-more-lean-thinkers/

12 Darci Cherry, "Data-Driven Decision-Making: From Rhetoric to Results." *National Conference of State Legislatures*, August 23, 2022. www.ncsl.org/resources/details/data-driven-decision-making-from-rhetoric-to-results

13 This is far from an exhaustive list; the closer I got to completing this study, the more avenues I discovered.

14 Box in Landry. Sylvain Landry, *Bringing Scientific Thinking to Life: An Introduction to Toyota Kata for the Next Generation of Business Leaders (and those who would like to be)* (Les Éditions JFD Montréal, Montréal, 2022), p. 28.

15 Shayne Kavanagh, "Less Time, Lower Cost, and Greater Quality: Making Government Work Better with Lean Process Improvement." *White Paper. Government Finance Officers Association*, p. 25.

16 James (Jim) Womack, PhD, "Getting Started with Lean Thinking and Practice." *Lean Enterprise Institute*, January 26, 2023. www.lean.org/the-lean-post/articles/getting-started-with-lean/

17 Federal Emergency Management Agency (FEMA), *What is Continuity of Operations?* www.fema.gov/pdf/about/org/ncp/coop_brochure.pdf

18 Lean Enterprise Institute, *What is Lean?* www.lean.org/explore-lean/what-is-lean/

19 Martin O'Malley, *Smarter Government: How to Govern for Results in the Information Age* (Esri Press, Redlands, CA, 2019), p. 259.

20 Sylvain Landry, *Bringing Scientific Thinking to Life: An Introduction to Toyota Kata for the Next Generation of Business Leaders (and those who would like to be)* (Les Éditions JFD Montréal, Montréal, 2022), pp. 147–148.

21 Matthew Savas, *A New Era of Jidoka: How ChatGPT Could Alter the Relationship between Machines, Humans, and their Minds*, February 13, 2023. www.lean.org/the-lean-post/articles/a-new-era-of-jidoka-how-chatgpt-could-alter-the-relationship-between-machines-humans-and-their-minds/

22 Matthew Savas, *A New Era of Jidoka: How ChatGPT Could Alter the Relationship between Machines, Humans, and their Minds*, February 13, 2023. www.lean.org/the-lean-post/articles/a-new-era-of-jidoka-how-chatgpt-could-alter-the-relationship-between-machines-humans-and-their-minds/

23 Sylvain Landry, PhD, *Bringing Scientific Thinking to Life: An Introduction to Toyota Kata for the Next Generation of Business Leaders (and those who would like to be)* (Les Éditions JFD Montréal, Montréal, 2022), p. 135.

Appendix A

Deming's 14 Points for Management

1. Create constancy of purpose toward improvement of product and service, with the aim to become competitive and to stay in business, and to provide jobs.
2. Adopt the new philosophy. We are in a new economic age. Western management must awaken to the challenge, must learn their responsibilities, and take on leadership for change.
3. Cease dependence on inspection to achieve quality. Eliminate the need for inspection on a mass basis by building quality into the product in the first place.
4. End the practice of awarding business on the basis of price tag. Instead, minimize total cost. Move toward a single supplier for any one item, on a long-term relationship of loyalty and trust.
5. Improve constantly and forever the system of production and service, to improve quality and productivity, and thus constantly decrease costs.
6. Institute training on the job.
7. Institute leadership. The aim of supervision should be to help people and machines and gadgets to do a better job. Supervision of management is in need of overhaul, as well as supervision of production workers.
8. Drive out fear, so that everyone may work effectively for the company.
9. Break down barriers between departments. People in research, design, sales, and production must work as a team, to foresee problems of

production and in use that may be encountered with the product or service.

10. Eliminate slogans, exhortations, and targets for the work force asking for zero defects and new levels of productivity. Such exhortations only create adversarial relationships, as the bulk of the causes of low quality and low productivity belong to the system and thus lie beyond the power of the work force.

11a. Eliminate work standards (quotas) on the factory floor. Substitute leadership.

11b. Eliminate management by objective. Eliminate management by numbers, numerical goals. Substitute leadership.

12a. Remove barriers that rob the hourly worker of his right to pride of workmanship. The responsibility of supervisors must be changed from sheer numbers to quality.

12b. Remove barriers that rob people in management and in engineering of their right to pride of workmanship. This means, inter alia, abolishment of the annual or merit rating and of management by objective.

13. Institute a vigorous program of education and self-improvement.

14. Put everybody in the company to work to accomplish the transformation. The transformation is everybody's job.

W. Edwards Deming, *Out of Crisis,* p. 23–24

Appendix B

ASPA Code of Ethics

The American Society for Public Administration (ASPA) advances the science, art, and practice of public administration. The Society affirms its responsibility to develop the spirit of responsible professionalism within its membership and to increase awareness and commitment to ethical principles and standards among all those who work in public service in all sectors. To this end, we, the members of the Society, commit ourselves to uphold the following principles:

1. **Advance the Public Interest**. Promote the interests of the public and put service to the public above service to oneself.
2. **Uphold the Constitution and the Law.** Respect and support government constitutions and laws, while seeking to improve laws and policies to promote the public good.
3. **Promote democratic participation.** Inform the public and encourage active engagement in governance. Be open, transparent, and responsive, and respect and assist all persons in their dealings with public organizations.
4. **Strengthen social equity.** Treat all persons with fairness, justice, and equality and respect individual differences, rights, and freedoms. Promote affirmative action and other initiatives to reduce unfairness, injustice, and inequality in society.
5. **Fully Inform and Advise.** Provide accurate, honest, comprehensive, and timely information and advice to elected and appointed officials and governing board members, and to staff members in your organization.

6. **Demonstrate personal integrity.** Adhere to the highest standards of conduct to inspire public confidence and trust in public service.
7. **Promote Ethical Organizations:** Strive to attain the highest standards of ethics, stewardship, and public service in organizations that serve the public.
8. **Advance Professional Excellence:** Strengthen personal capabilities to act competently and ethically and encourage the professional development of others.

American Society for Public Administration, 2022

Appendix C

Applying the Lessons

What the Governor can do: Learn about lean management and Toyota Kata and require agency heads to be trained in the principles. Issue an Executive Order requiring all agencies to participate in a lean initiative focused on furthering the articulated goals and priorities for the state, and assure that there will be no layoffs due to the initiative. Establish a central office for Lean, with a coordinator reporting directly to the Governor. Work with the legislature to develop a budget that includes the Lean office, and appropriate resources so that agencies all have equal access to training. Hold agency heads accountable for participation and reporting progress to the statewide coordinator.

What legislators can do: Learn about Lean and Toyota Kata. Appropriate resources for a state office of Lean training, and guarantee no layoffs due to Lean initiatives. Allow agencies to keep 20% of documented savings for future budgets. Remove antiquated legal restrictions and consolidate redundant programs, as recommended by the Lean initiative. Reallocate savings as indicated by evidence-based findings.

What administrators can do: Learn about lean management, Toyota Kata, and scientific thinking. Align authority and responsibility at the lowest possible level. Understand the need to link *kaizen* events to broader organizational strategy, and focus the efforts accordingly. Assign coordinators, identify priority projects that align with the agency's mission, assign sponsors to the projects, provide resources, and require follow-through. Reiterate that there will be no layoffs due to CI projects. Do daily Gemba walks. Ask how you can help the employees succeed.

What managers and supervisors can do: Learn about lean management, Toyota Kata, and scientific thinking. Sponsor *kaizen* projects and assign project teams. Facilitate the participation of all appropriate team members by modifying schedules and job duties, if necessary. Practice lean management by aligning authority and responsibility at the lowest possible level. Use scientific thinking and become a Toyota Kata coach. Do daily Gemba walks. Ask how you can help the employees succeed.

What all staff can do: Learn about lean, Toyota Kata, and scientific thinking, and how to apply them. Understand how *kaizen* promotes organizational excellence and empowers employees to reduce waste and add value. Help to identify projects and participate on teams. Build lean culture through continuous-improvement activities and ongoing responsibility for excellent customer service.

What Lean activists can do: Continually learn more about Lean and Toyota Kata, and apply them in practice. Facilitate projects and document gains. Demonstrate scientific thinking and promote best practices. Mentor new practitioners, model behaviors of continuous improvement, and spread lean culture. Develop collaborative models, including cross-silo facilitator swaps and participation as guest faculty in training programs. Create a broad community of practice and a thriving community of excellence. Keep innovating.

Appendix D

Internal Training Programs

Training Programs Offered by Nebraska's Center for Operational Excellence

- **Lean Six Sigma White Belt for all state employees**. White Belt training is a one-hour session that introduces State of Nebraska team members to basic Lean Six Sigma concepts. The goal is to begin to help the recipient see waste in the process around them and have a basic level of understanding of how to combat that waste. Length: 1 Hour Prerequisites: None Availability: Online and In person

- **Lean Six Sigma Yellow Belt for all state administrators, managers, and supervisors**. Yellow Belt training is the next level for learning about process improvement for the State of Nebraska. It reviews how to make daily improvements in the workplace. The training will focus on establishing QDIP boards, KPI's, and use of problem-solving tools like: The Pareto Principle, 5 Why's, Fishbone Diagrams and Control charts. Length: 4 Hours Prerequisites: Certified Lean Six Sigma White Belt Availability: Classroom

- **Lean Six Sigma Green Belt for Process Improvement Coordinators (PICs)** Green Belt training is the foundation for professional process improvement in the State of Nebraska. It covers an in-depth understanding of: Leadership, team dynamics, motivational theories, and an intimate description of all DMAIC tools used in the State of Nebraska. Participants are required to apply the knowledge and skills back in their agencies for process improvement projects, and to collaborate and mentor with others in the COE network. Length: 2 Months + 2 Projects

Prerequisites: Completion of Lean Six Sigma White Belt and Lean Six Sigma Yellow Belt Availability: Classroom

Lean Six Sigma Executive Green Belt for executive level directors and officers at both the enterprise and agency level. Executive Green Belt training serves as the foundation for how to manage and mentor the same information in the normal Lean Six Sigma Green Belt Training, but also goes into depth describing the decision sciences and how to use lean techniques to make the "Executive Decision" focused on finding large scale improvements in their agencies. Participants are required to apply the knowledge and skills back in their agencies for process improvement projects, and to collaborate and mentor with others in the COE network. Length: 2 months + 3 Assignments Prerequisites: Completion of Lean Six Sigma White Belt and Lean Six Sigma Yellow Belt Availability: Online + Conversation with Master Black Belt

Lean Six Sigma Black Belt high functioning Process Improvement Coordinators. Black Belt training is an intense 24-week classroom-based training that reviews all aspects of project management, DMAIC method, Leadership, Team Development, Strategy, Crucial Conversations, among other important Lean Six Sigma tools. This training is focused on producing deliverable bottom line results resulting from data driven management techniques. It includes outside reading material and a proven track record of success within the State's Lean Six Sigma program. Length: 24 Weeks of training + 8 Projects Prerequisites: Completion of Lean Six Sigma White Belt, Lean Six Sigma Yellow Belt and Lean Six Sigma Green Belt (including 8 highly successful projects) Availability: In person—classroom and extensive mentorship.

Certified Lean Leader for supervisors, managers, and administrators: Certified Lean Leader is the next level of learning about process improvement for the State of Nebraska. It focuses on the use of basics of Lean in an applied setting such as transactional office spaces, administrative environments, truck yards, print shops, and all front-line functional work areas. The application of tools such as Just-In-Time (JIT), Kanban, Cellular Flow, and Fishbone Diagrams are some of the techniques that empower staff to make daily improvements to their work areas. Length: 2 Days Prerequisites: Completion of Lean Six Sigma White Belt, Lean Six Sigma Yellow Belt. Availability: In person—classroom and mentorship with Agency Process Improvement Coordinators.

Training Programs Offered by LeanOhio

White Belt Training. Online training introduces participants to core Lean Six Sigma concepts. It shifts mindsets from tolerating process problems to addressing those problems and seeking solutions— while pointing the way to improvement opportunities and building interest in furthering people's Lean learning. For: State employees. Length: 1.5 hours Prerequisites: None Available: Through Ohio Learn

Yellow Belt Training. Introductory course about using Lean thinking to make daily improvements in the workplace. The training provides tools for attaining and sustaining awareness around Lean Daily Management. For: State employees. 1 day. Prerequisites: None

LeanOhio Boot Camp is an intensive four-day-long training that gets people learning and using Lean methods and tools. The entire program is tailored to the public-sector workplace and public-sector processes. This is practical training aimed at generating results. Participants will be able to use their new knowledge and skills immediately—to make government simpler, faster, better, and less costly. Intended for: State and local government. Length: 4 days + Project. Prerequisites: White Belt via Ohio Learn. Project Expectations: Process improvement project and submission of A3 and serving as a fresh perspective during a *Kaizen* event and submission of A3. Belt earned: Camo (after completing project).

Lean Six Sigma Green Belt. Whether tasked with leading projects or looking to expand your knowledge, the Green Belt training will help you develop skills in process improvement tools, techniques, and applications. The training is available as in-class or online learning and provides content on Six Sigma, with added focus on data and data analysis in order to promote objective problem-solving and decision-making. Upon completion of this program, participants will be proficient in the basic analytical tools necessary to Define, Measure, Analyze, Improve, and Control Lean Six Sigma improvement projects. Length: 4 days in-class (or at your own pace online) + Project. Prerequisites: LeanOhio Boot Camp, Process improvement project and submission of A3 results. Project Expectations: Complete a project using the DMAIC methodology, Demonstrate use of Lean tools and collect and use data as part of the project, present the project to LeanOhio Network.

Introduction to Managing Change. Change Management (CM) is a structured discipline to address the people side of change. This training is a high-level overview of why and how state employees should integrate CM with continuous improvement methodologies to help sustain the changes we experience in state government. Length: 1.5 hours Prerequisites: None

Managing Change for Supervisors. Often, organizational initiatives are implemented from a top-down approach, leaving the bulk of the burden to communicate and effect change with middle managers. This training will review the multifaceted role of a manager in times of change and how to successfully guide your team towards success. For: State supervisors and managers. Length: 1.5 hours. Prerequisites: None

Appendix E

Annotated Bibliography of CI Literature on My Bookshelf

Books

Bringing Scientific Thinking to Life: An Introduction to Toyota Kata for the Next Generation of Business Leaders (and those who would like to be). Sylvain Landry. A wonderfully accessible guide to understanding and using TK. Connects the capacity for scientific thinking to learning and to the development of learning organizations. (Les Éditions JFD, Montréal, Quebec, 2022.)

Extreme Government Makeover: Increasing Our Capacity to Do More Good. Ken Miller. Miller sums it up: "The work of government is noble. The people of government are amazing. The systems of government are a mess." Also, check out "The Paradoxical Commandments of Government" on page 210. (Governing Books, a Division of Governing Magazine, Washington, DC, 2011.)

Gemba Kaizen. Masaaki Imai. An opportunity to connect the legacy of quality management to a path of practical and sustainable implementation. Allows readers to gain a deeper understanding of *muda*, *mura*, and *muri*. Includes practical guidance, case studies, and a comprehensive glossary. (McGraw-Hill, New York, 2012.)

Gemba Walks. Jim Womack. A collection of Womack's insights and observations in multiple settings and scenarios. The reader is given a path to go beyond the use of basic tools and to grasp the concept of lean management. And it is an important reminder to go to the *gemba*, the place value is made. (The Lean Enterprise Institute, Cambridge, MA, 2011.)

Government That Works: The Results Revolution in the States.
John M. Bernard. Using examples of states that have successfully linked
process improvement to measurable gains in outcomes, Bernard pre-
scribes the use of results-driven management. He explained, "We're not
just making things work better, we're accomplishing things. And, measuring them." (Results for America: Thomson-Shore, Dexter, MI, 2015.)

***The Kaizen Event Planner: Achieving Rapid Improvement in
Office, Service and Technical Environments***. Karen Martin and
Mike Osterling. A terrific resource full of practical templates and tools
with clear definitions and context for each. Bonus features: Glossary of
terms and support materials. (CRC Press, Taylor & Francis Group, Boca
Raton, FL, 2007.)

***The Leadership of Public Bureaucracies: The Administrator as
Conservator***. Larry D. Terry. Grounded in the theory of administrative
conservatorship and constitutional history, Terry provides a comprehensive academic response to the prerogative stereotypes of the public sector. Mission-driven readers will appreciate his vision as he argues, "public
bureaucracies are national treasurers." (M.E. Sharpe, New York, NY, 2003.)

***Lean for the Public Sector: The Pursuit of Perfection in Public
Service*** Bert Teeuween. A core resource that applies lean in a way that
resonates with those facing an entire range of bureaucratic challenges,
including inverse incentives in public budgeting. Teeuween's model of a
compliance pyramid demonstrates the value of visual control tools over
procedure manuals. (Taylor & Francis Group/Productivity Press, New
York, NY, 2011.)

Lean Lexicon: a graphical glossary for lean thinkers. 5th Edition.
Chet Marchwinski, editor. A graphical glossary for lean thinkers. An
excellent resource for novices and seasoned practitioners alike. A comprehensive guide including translations of Japanese terms, detailed
explanations, and diagrams to illustrate the concepts. (Lean Enterprise
Institute. Cambridge, MA, 2014.)

***The Lean Handbook: A Guide to the Bronze Certification Body of
Knowledge***. Anthony Manos and Chad Vincent, editors. Excellent detail
with clear explanations of an entire range of tools, firmly grounded in
the context of principles. Reminding readers, "It has also been proven
many times that even 100% inspection is only 80–90% effective. Quality
at the source involves a cultural change." A superb resource whether
you're prepping for a certification or not. (The ASQ Quality Press,
Milwaukee, WI, 2012.)

Lean Six Sigma Yellow Belt. Juran Global. A comprehensive, step-by-step guide to the principles and techniques underlying the synthesis of Lean and Six Sigma. Written in workbook style with graphics and templates. Juran Global was founded as the Juran Institute in 1979 by Dr. Joseph Juran, one of the pioneers in the field of quality management. (Juran Institute, Create Space Independent Publishing Platform, USA, 2015.)

The Lean Toolbox: A Handbook for Lean Transformation. 5th Edition. John Bicheno and Matthias Holweg. An excellent reference, not only for the nuts and bolts. It is a valuable guide for practitioners and policy makers on the path to a sustainable lean management system. It covers the multi-layered elements. There is both range and depth, so users can learn the tools and study change management. Bonus features: the historical chronology of lean, and an acronym decoder. (PICSIE Books, Buckingham, England, 2016.)

The Machine That Changed the World James P. Womack, Daniel T. Jones, and Daniel Roos. Researchers from MIT's International Motor Vehicle Program describe Toyota's successful use of lean. They contrast the principles and outcomes with American hierarchical management, enabling readers to extrapolate to all fields. "In this process we've become convinced that the principles of lean production can be applied equally in every industry across the globe and that the conversion to lean production will have a profound effect on human society—it will truly change the world." (Free Press, A Division of Simon & Schuster, New York, NY, 1990, 2007.)

A Public Sector Journey to Lean: Fighting Muda in Times of Muri. Kate McGovern. An introduction to lean principles and techniques as applied to state governments. The story of New Hampshire's program is woven throughout, along with examples of lean initiatives in other states. Outlines and content for training programs at the White, Yellow, and Green Belt levels are included. It closes with recommendations based on lessons learned. (Routledge, Taylor-Francis Group, New York, 2019.)

Smarter Government: How to Govern for Results in the Information Age. Martin O'Malley. An enlightening narrative of former Maryland Governor O'Malley's insights, lessons, and tips for public administrators, starting with his term as Mayor of Baltimore. Applies CI concepts throughout without jargon. (Esri Press. Redlands, CA, 2019.)

Toyota Kata: Managing People for Improvement, Adaptiveness, and Superior Results. Mike Rother. Many ah-ha moments for readers seeking to maintain the lessons they learned from Toyota. Rother introduces the discipline of kata and explains how managers can utilize improvement kata and coaching kata to build and sustain organizational cultures of continuous improvement. (McGraw-Hill Education, New York, 2010.)

The Toyota Kata Practice Guide: Practicing Scientific Thinking for Superior Results in 20 Minute a Day. Mike Rother. An important step by step guide to imbedding Toyota Kata (TK)—not just the how, but the why underlying each element. Be sure to read the introduction which includes the TK backstory with the two research questions that guided Rother's study of Toyota. (McGraw-Hill Education, New York, 2018.)

Journal Articles, Reports, and Resources Accessed Online

"Commentaries on the Lenses of Lean." Michael A. Cusumano, Matthias Holweg, Josh Howell, Torbjørn Netland, Rachna Shah, John Shook, Peter Ward, and James Womack. *Journal of Operations Management.* 2021;1–13. https://doi.org/10.1002/joom.1138

"The Eight Sources of Waste and How to Eliminate Them." Shayne Kavanagh and David Krings. *Government Finance Review.* 2011;19.

"Grading the States: A Management Report Card". Katherine Barrett and Richard Greene. Pew Charitable Trusts. *Governing Magazine*, March, 2008. www.pewtrusts.org/~/media/legacy/uploadedfiles/pcs_assets/2008/gradingthestates2008pdf.pdf

John Shook Explains the Lean Transformation Model. The Lean Enterprise Institute. *Published on You Tube*, January 21, 2014. www.youtube.com/watch?v=kEcdliWZH30

Lean in Government Starter Kit, Version 4.0. Environmental Protection Agency. www.epa.gov/sites/default/files/2017-11/documents/lean-starter-kit-version-4.pdf

Less Time, Lower Cost, and Greater Quality: Making Government Work Better with Lean Process Improvement. *White Paper. Shayne Kavanagh. Government Finance Officers Association.* www.gfoa.org

Meals Per Hour (video). Written by Jeff Gonic. Directed by Henry Joost and Ariel Shulman. *Supermarche*, June 19, 2013. www.youtube.com/watch?v=EedMmMedj3M

Program to Improve Vermont Outcomes Together (PIVOT). Executive Order by Philip Scott, Governor of Vermont, PIVOT E.O. 17–04. http://governor.vermont.gov/sites/scott/files/documents/EO4PIVOT%20EO%20Final.pdf

Report of the Governor's Commission on Innovation, Efficiency, and Transparency. Submitted to New Hampshire Governor Maggie Hassan on January 19, 2015. Commission composed of private-sector and governmental leaders recommended the redesign of 15% of executive branch processes annually, with the target of reducing time and resources required by 20% and applying at least 0.1% of operating expenses to innovation efforts.

The Shingo Model for Operational Excellence. Handbook. *The Shingo Institute*. https://shingo.org/

Index

Note: Page numbers in *italics* indicate a figure or photo on the corresponding page.

Printed in the United States
by Baker & Taylor Publisher Services